WAR AND MODERNITY

**To let them kill each other stone-cold
The Last Judgement has been put on hold.**

Johann Wolfgang von Goethe

WAR AND MODERNITY

HANS JOAS

Translated by Rodney Livingstone

polity

First published in Germany as *Kriege und Werte: Studien zur Gewaltgeschichte des 20. Jahrhunderts* (© Velbrüch Wissenschaft, Weilerswist, 2000). Chapter 7 first published in English as 'Between Power Politics and Pacifist Utopia: Peace and War in Sociological Theory', in *Current Sociology* 39 (1991), © International Sociological Association 1991.

The right of Hans Joas to be identified as author of this work has been asserted in accordance with the Copyright, Designs and Patents Act 1988.

First published in 2003 by Polity Press in association with Blackwell Publishing Ltd.

Published with the assistance of the Freie Universität Berlin.

Editorial office:
Polity Press
65 Bridge Street
Cambridge CB2 1UR, UK

Marketing and production:
Blackwell Publishing Ltd
108 Cowley Road
Oxford OX4 1JF, UK

Published in the USA by
Blackwell Publishing Inc.
350 Main Street
Malden, MA 02148, USA

A catalogue record for this book is available from the British Library.

Library of Congress Cataloging-in-Publication Data

Joas, Hans, 1948–
[Kriege und werte. English]
War and modernity / Hans Joas; translated by Rodney Livingstone.
        p.   cm.
Includes bibliographical references and index.
ISBN 0-7456-2644-0 – ISBN 0-7456-2645-9
1. War and society.   2. History, Modern – 20th century.   I. Title.
HM554 .J613 2002
303.6'6 – dc21

                                                            2002009838

Typeset in 10 on 12 pt Palatino
by SNP Best-set Typesetter Ltd., Hong Kong
Printed in Great Britain by MPG Books, Bodmin, Cornwall

This book is printed on acid-free paper.

Contents

PART III   WAR AND VIOLENCE IN SOCIAL THEORY 123

Preface

The Introduction provides a sufficient explanation of the origins of this book and the motives that led up to it. For this reason I should like merely to take the opportunity to express my thanks to all those who have helped me.

The majority of the chapters have been read and commented on by two scholars: my admired colleague and fatherly adviser, Shmuel Eisenstadt, and my highly talented younger colleague, Wolfgang Knöbl. My first thanks go to them.

In the autumn of 1999 I was provided with excellent working conditions at the Swedish Collegium for Advanced Study in the Social Sciences (SCASSS) in Uppsala, Sweden. This enabled me to give final shape to my manuscript. I should like to express my gratitude to the Director, Björn Wittrock, and his colleagues Barbro Klein and Göran Therborn, as well as to all their assistants for their generous and discreet hospitality.

My secretary, Regina Wenzel, has shown great charm and verve in overcoming all obstacles or eliminating them. I should like to express my warmest thanks to her. I am grateful to Heinrich Yberg and Susanne Rham for their valuable assistance in producing the notes, the index and in helping with the necessary corrections.

Dieter Senghaas was generous with his encouragement and advice at important stages of my work. I have benefited from his impressive writings more than is reflected in the notes.

I should like to thank my Berlin colleague Martin Kohli for his willingness to let me publish in this volume the text of one chapter written jointly with him.

I owe a debt to Rodney Livingstone, my translator.

And, lastly, though by no means least, my great thanks are due to the person who has accompanied all my work for a quarter of a century and who has made it possible: my wife Heidrun.

Erfurt, 2002

Introduction
Wars and Values

Whoever takes seriously the history of violence in the twentieth century will find it hard to believe in myths of progress. This book examines the hopes and expectations of peace that prevailed in the liberal and socialist traditions against the background of the reality of war and state-organized violence in the century that has just come to a close. Yet it is concerned neither with pacifist moralizing, nor with a de-moralizing of war in the spirit of *realpolitik*. In the studies collected here, questions are asked from a number of different vantage-points about the relation between wars and values in a variety of configurations. The double undefined plural in the subtitle to this introduction – 'wars' and 'values' – serves to underscore the fluctuating nature of these relations. Why have wars been the reason for the production of so many major interpretations and indeed whole interpretative systems? What are the fascinating features and what are the hidden difficulties of the dream of a modernity without violence? Are there parallels between the experience of binding values and of violence? Are there universalist justifications for military interventions?

The chapters of this book revolve round questions like these. The volume contains a considerable proportion of the essays on the sociology of war and violence that I wrote in the 1990s. Influenced in many ways by the events of the 1980s and 1990s, work on them has constantly accompanied and supplemented my more systematic efforts in such fields as the theory of action, the philosophy of values and social theory in general. The studies presented here share one feature with those systematic writings. This can be called a hermeneutic 'refraction', a perspective derived from the history of ideas, which is currently thought to be rather old-fashioned, for all the fashionable talk about hermeneutics, and which finds itself clearly on the defensive in both philosophy and the social sciences. What is meant by it is a method that approaches the subjects to be investigated via an intensive engagement with the history of earlier research, and does not accept the idea of unmediated access to the matters in hand or believe in the progress of knowledge through ignorance of what has previously been thought. The notion that previously existing ideas have rightly fallen into oblivion is itself the product of the myth of progress – a myth that has its most powerful bastion in the realm of science, and particularly in the way in which scholars conceive their own role. Notwithstanding all philosophical critiques and refutations based on the history of science, that conception of science and the scholar's role in it remains one of a cumulative and progressive development of the sciences towards the discovery of universal, empirically proven laws that form a coherent whole. From this perspective older knowledge is simply obsolete. However, my aim is not to deny the possibility of scientific or historical progress. Such a global denial would simply involve inverting the belief in progress and transforming it into a pessimistic myth of decline and fall. It would mean that all human strivings for an amelioration of human conditions would be doomed to failure and no insight into the mechanisms of that failure would ever be able to prevent it.

Thus a pessimistic myth of that kind is not our aim, if in what follows we maintain at least a methodological distance from the belief in progress. Instead, our concern is to bear in mind the insight that is doubtless suggested by every immersion in the history of science or in universal history, to say nothing of the history of violence in the twentieth century – the insight into how twisted and uncertain every road to progress really is and how frequently the retrospective construction of straight lines from the past into a benevolent present or an even better future is no more than an optical illusion on the part of the observer. Herbert Butterfield,[1] who has produced one of the most powerful attacks on this way of thinking, mainly had the complacency of a liberal Protestantism in mind when he spoke out against the 'whig interpretation of history'. His scepticism continues to be justified today, since such tacit assumptions are still at work even in contemporary historiography, to say nothing of many sociological theories of social change in which a straight line is drawn from the Reformation, passing through the Enlightenment, to peace, democracy and human rights in our own time. However, Butterfield himself was well aware[2] that the way of thinking he condemned was not just entrenched among Protestants and liberals, but is a constant danger in every reconstruction of the past – regardless of the values guiding it. Whoever wants to believe in the power of Providence in history, he wrote, must also have the humility to recognize how mysterious are its ways and how ultimately unknowable they are.[3]

Thus two motifs underlie my rejection of the seductive power of the myths of progress. As far as the past is concerned, we must not be allowed to forget the tragic dimension of the configuration of events from which improvements have sometimes emerged – I am thinking of the terrible losses that can never be justified in retrospect even by creative solutions to catastrophes. And as for the future, after the events of the twentieth century, there can be no reassurance that we have now discovered the key to lasting peace and social stability. Even the most plausible vision of peace must be scrutinized again and again to see whether it still does justice to reality and does not generate an unwarranted confidence in our ability to secure conditions of peace.

In tune with these considerations, questions about the relations between 'wars' and 'values' will not be treated abstractly in this book, but will instead take the form of individual studies, mainly of concrete historical constellations. However, attention will focus not on the historical events and processes themselves, but on the blind spots and perspectival distortions in the way they are perceived. This means that these studies will not result in a continuous history of the socio-philosophical and social-scientific preoccupation with war and other forms of state-organized violence; even less can they lay claim to presenting so much as an outline theory of the state from this point of view. For all that, the author hopes that, taken together, these studies will form a mosaic from which basic features of the social sciences' preoccupation with war in the twentieth century can be read off, and that they comprise a number of largely secure insights, as well as many open questions.

If these premises are accepted, it is only logical to begin with some reflections upon the origins of the studies presented here. I will do this both in terms of (1) time and (2) place, and follow these sections with an attempt to disentangle some of the connections between these studies and systematic questions of (3) social theory and (4) the philosophy of value. Finally (5), there will be a brief discussion of the question of the possible justification of wars under the conditions of universalist morality.

I

There are few topics where the impact of events causes such marked fluctuations of public interest as does war. The reason for the enormous range of these fluctuations lies in the 'interpretative intensity' of the nature of war, a concept with which we shall need to deal. My own scholarly interest in these questions dates unmistakably from the peace movement of the early and mid-1980s. I was greatly attracted to this movement. I attempted to make a modest, but active contribution to it, in part at least by exploring the question of the interest in war and peace that had been shown by the social sciences up to that time, and I presented the results of my researches both in academic teaching and in talks to peace groups and at peace congresses. The question I was concerned with had a double aspect. What insight did the social sciences have to offer into the origins of wars, and in what light do the social sciences themselves appear when they are scrutinized from this point of view? My initial intuition was that because of the long-standing neglect of this subject, a relative failure of the great traditions in the social sciences had to be assumed. Right from the start, I placed great hopes in the research of social psychologists into what would enable internationalist points of view to prevail, and in the consequences for peace of the spread of democracy. Both my initial intuition and my hopes sprang from my strong leaning towards American intellectual traditions, in particular pragmatism, whose representatives had provided active critical support for President Wilson's peace policy and in the establishment of the League of Nations.

Looking back on that period, it may seem as if the fear that gripped us at the time of a new Cold War, or even of a casually unleashed 'hot', that is, nuclear, war, was completely exaggerated and even hysterical. Even today we repeatedly find it insinuated that the peace movement failed to understand what President Reagan had perceived, namely that there was an opportunity to force the Soviet Union along the road of collapse by upgrading the weapons of the West and introducing other rearmament measures. And even worse than its failure to understand it – it is insinuated – was the peace movement's unwillingness to do so because of its overt or covert sympathy with 'actually existing socialism'. It is a fact that in June 1987 when Reagan publicly called on Gorbachev in Berlin to tear down the Wall, this failed to ignite a storm of enthusiasm either in the peace movement or in the population of Berlin. Instead, it produced incomprehension and even alarm. But the reason for this did not lie in the wish to perpetuate the division of Germany or to help stabilize the GDR regime or the Soviet Union. To be sure, it cannot be denied that in parts of the peace movement and reaching even into the SPD, there were tendencies naïvely to gloss over the foreign policy of the Warsaw Pact and the internal conditions in the socialist countries, to say nothing of agents of the East who had directly infiltrated the movement. But what characterized the peace movement and public opinion more generally in my view was something quite different. People simply could not believe that the Soviet Union would ever be willing to release the GDR peacefully from its sphere of influence, or that the Soviet empire would just collapse, and they feared that under sustained strategic pressure the Soviet Union would be more likely to risk a war than to accept its own demise without a fuss. For this reason, people were suspicious of Reagan's call to tear down the Wall as dangerously destabilizing a situation that could only be kept in a peaceful equilibrium by careful diplomacy. Thus the reason for the alarmed reaction to Reagan's statement lay not in people's reluctance to believe in the objective (the opening of the Wall), but in the fact that they did not dare hope that it might happen.

There were powerful reasons for this – at least, there had been in the past. I personally had been deeply impressed by Willy Brandt's and Egon Bahr's accounts of how the building of the Wall in 1961 had brought the definitive, painful realization that not everything that one wished to change, and that it seemed morally imperative to change, could be changed politically in actual fact. In a sense it is the basic insight of all responsible politics that we should be able to acknowledge existing realities independently of our own desires.[4] The acceptance of the division of Germany in this sense was, therefore, the premise for the emergence of a halfway acceptable *modus vivendi*, and also for the programme of what Egon Bahr termed 'change through rapprochement', that is to say, the attempt to influence regimes through the constant effort to establish contacts and set up collaborative projects at all levels. Even in retrospect I believe that this strategy really did make a significant contribution to the collapse of the GDR. Taking the development of historiography in the GDR as an example, Martin Sabrow has attempted to show that

> the decisive factor in the self-paralysis of power may have lain in the paradox that for an astonishingly long period erosion appeared in the guise of consolidation and the internal destabilization of the imposed order of reality was perceived as the stabilization of the socialist system through international integration. . . . Precisely because the external façade of the discursive legitimation of domination remained intact and was even reinforced by growing international recognition, the inner process of erosion could proceed undisturbed and culminate in a sudden implosion.[5]

But these were precisely the wildest hopes of the strategists of change through rapprochement! And every criticism of that strategy derived from the superior knowledge of hindsight must at least concede that the same moral dilemma of peaceful coexistence with other powers constantly reasserts itself and will continue to do so.

The concept of détente found its classical expression in the 1980s in the position paper that was produced jointly by the SED and SPD and was subsequently much disparaged. This paper, 'Ideological Disagreements and Collective Security', embodied a conception that had originally been fuelled by the experiences of the early 1960s in Berlin. In it, divergent views were captured in a joint document, cautious processes of change were initiated and everything was subordinated to the goal of a common wish to prevent another war. I mention this here for a further reason. This is that while my interest in the sociology of war had been awakened by the peace movement, it soon assumed an institutional shape that resembled this initiative in the politics of détente and did so partly as the result of conscious imitation. The opportunity for this presented itself in 1984 with a symposium on 'Sociology and Peace', organized by the GDR Academy of Sciences. In the conditions prevailing in the GDR, the subject of peace was a legitimate pretext for scholars there to communicate with academics from the West, and this was done in the spirit of the ambiguity just described. Dogmatic proclamations of Marxist-Leninist doctrine or academically worthless, barely disguised justifications of the foreign policy line of the socialist camp stood side by side with entirely serious, for the most part historical analyses that were perfectly open to dialogue. There was a huge gulf between the official business of the conference and the informal exchange of views that often took up more time than the official programme. It was during this conference that the plan was formed for a joint East–West project to provide a comprehensive historical examination of the treatment of war and peace in the social sciences. In the years that followed, this project was pursued under the umbrella of a research committee of the International Sociological Association. The Eastern scholar I co-operated with was Helmut Steiner, a convinced Marxist, but also a renowned GDR sociologist who was very open to dialogue. For political reasons, that is to say, because of the GDR leadership's fear of too close a German–German co-operation, the project had to be set up as an international collaboration of scholars of different countries from both Eastern and Western Europe.

In the course of this collaboration, a space for authentic debate soon opened up. However, the publication of its findings encountered countless obstacles. These ranged from trivial questions, such as the arrangements for the payments of fees between East and West, to unforeseen differences of opinion between authors from the GDR and those from Gorbachev's Soviet Union on such matters as the assessment of Lenin. The most important visible product was ultimately a volume of essays that included contributions from two Italians, one Briton, one Bulgarian and two Russians, in addition to the West German and East

German writers.[6] When the editors finally sent the volume to the printers in the spring of 1989, after overcoming a myriad of difficulties, they expected that the volume would be received not just as a substantial scholarly contribution, but also as one of the first, if not actually the very first, testimony to such East–West co-operation in the social sciences.

However, by the time the book appeared in the late autumn of 1989, the Wall had miraculously opened up; the GDR regime lay in its death-throes and any East–West co-operation across the frontiers between the two blocs was no longer worth talking about, since the frontier that had been so impassable could now be crossed by anyone in either direction at any time. The contributions of Eastern academics who in the past had to fight their supervising authorities for every formulation and whose authors were proud of every little concession suddenly appeared anachronistic, as voices from beyond the grave of a dictatorship that had perished.

Few could or wished to resist the euphoria that broke out everywhere. The fear of nuclear war that had cast a shadow over all other political issues for decades had now disappeared. The possibility of a lasting peace in Europe and beyond seemed within reach. From the perspective of dissidents, some of whom had become the political leaders and representatives of their countries with the collapse of communism, the theme of peace was now devalued because of the way it had constantly been used to legitimize the communist parties. As during the period of détente in the 1970s, public opinion quickly turned away from the problems of war and focused instead on dealing with the effects of the surprising collapse of the communist regimes. What was astonishing was, first, that practically no one in the social sciences – and not even in the secret services[7] – had foreseen this collapse. And second, no less astonishing was the fact that once the events had taken place, the most diverse sociological theories and research trends briskly produced their attempts to show how with hindsight their methods could provide the most convincing explanation of this collapse.[8] Butterfield had drawn attention to the way in which the historians' retrospective gaze tends to smooth out events and cover over great chasms. These tendencies have seldom been as much in evidence as in this case. Just as the outbreak of a war triggers a search for new interpretations of history, so too a sudden and surprising step towards peace seems to unleash 'normalizing activities': attempts to restore the broken continuity with the aid of swift reinterpretations.

But the euphoria did not last long. It is true that I personally still experience feelings of elation about the reunification that fell into the laps of the Germans, and that I have some slight feelings of contempt for people who tend to forget the magnitude of this good fortune because of the problems that have arisen in its wake. But the notion that a peaceful world had drawn nearer was soon dissipated by events inside and outside Germany. In Germany itself, both in the eastern and western parts of the reunited country, there was a wave of violence directed at foreigners. It may be possible to discern mitigating circumstances here and there; but the brutality of these actions and the contempt for humanity they displayed can only arouse a sense of outrage. This horror was reinforced by the applause of eyewitnesses to such acts of violence and by the often naïve and blindly provocative use of National Socialist symbols by the perpetrators. This wave of violence has since receded, but it has also left behind it a core of organizations with a more incorrigible ideology and given to outbursts of violent xenophobia. This has had at least two consequences for academics concerned with the study of violence. On the one hand, interest grew in the dynamics of spontaneous collective acts of violence and the meaning of so-called 'meaningless' violence. By this is meant violence that is not instrumental but that frequently gives the perpetrators powerful feelings of euphoria. Admittedly, recourse could be had to existing knowledge, in particular the results of American research on racial unrest, but sociologists whose own research was based on assumptions of rational action soon came to an impasse because for deviant phenomena they were left with the analytically worthless umbrella concept of the irrational.[9] On the other hand, many people experienced a shift in their standard assumptions about the role of the state as a peacemaker. For authors of left-wing peace studies before 1989, for example Ekkehart Krippendorff, the state had emerged above all as a threat, as the source of tensions with other states.[10] Suddenly, however, it was the left that issued urgent calls for the strengthening and rigorous enforcement of the state monopoly of the means of violence in order to ensure that everyone in Germany could have the necessary security. Of course, the one-sidedly negative view of the state and its monopoly of the means of violence had been criticized before.[11] But there was now a real sea-change in which values that had reigned supreme over sections of the intellectual community since the late sixties were swept away and replaced by others.

Externally, it was the wars in the Balkans and the Gulf that put an abrupt end to the dream of a peaceful, or at least a more peaceful, world. It is true that in the age of nuclear stand-off between the two power blocs the fear of the great disaster for the whole of humankind formed the background to everything. But for that very reason a sense of confidence had emerged that smaller conflicts could be contained.

One frequently heard the assurance that, thanks to nuclear armaments, waging war was no longer practicable. Suddenly, however, in this new situation the question of waging wars surfaced once again, and with it came the question of how to justify such new wars. These questions were put more urgently in Germany than in countries where the consensus against future wars was less deeply rooted, partly perhaps because outside Germany the history of the Second World War included the memory of a justified and victorious war. Here, however, the question of German involvement in a war – even if only in the form of lending indirect support, as in the Gulf War – struck at the deepest roots of national consciousness since 1945, and had a correspondingly polarizing impact on the public. In the view of the majority a war fought only from motives of national interest or loyalty to an alliance could never be justified; there would have to be at least the possibility of a universalist justification. But even where such a thing existed, the memory of the abominable acts committed by the Germans and a profound scepticism towards any justification of war stood in the way of an approval of the war.

In the case of the Gulf War, where a more prominent German role was not at issue, it proved particularly difficult to disentangle the relationship between universalist aims (expelling the aggressor Saddam Hussein from Kuwait; the defence of Israel) and particularist motives (protecting Western oil supplies). In the same way, questions about the chosen strategy, the victims of the war and the consequences of the way it was brought to a conclusion will remain the subject of controversy for a long time to come, even if it is rather muted at present. During the Gulf War itself, however, German social scientists largely remained silent. Then, a year after the Gulf War, appeared the ambitious attempt of Karl Otto Hondrich to situate the war in larger theoretical and political contexts.[12] This provoked my own consciously polemical response,[13] since Hondrich clearly did not undertake these difficult clarifications, or attempt to assess relative values. Instead, employing an astonishingly old-fashioned rhetoric of War as Teacher, he simply assumed that the war and the world dominance of the Western powers served the cause of strengthening and disseminating universalist values. Whereas these questions rapidly caught fire in the case of the Gulf War, they just smouldered in the case of the wars and civil wars in the Balkans during the nineties. In the latter instance, what probably stands out is the tendency to seek immunity from the irritating effects of events in interpretations that have been hurriedly cobbled together – a typical response is to talk of the 'relapse into primitive tribal conflicts'. Once the USA had put an end to the war in Bosnia in

1995, it was not until the Kosovo War of 1999 that questions surfaced about whether a military intervention could be justified in principle. I shall say more about these questions in what follows.

As in my own case, a significant proportion of the supporters of the war in Kosovo had come from the peace movement. It seems, therefore, that it is not a matter of a few individuals deciding to change their minds, but rather something that lies in a certain logic of events. On the other hand, those who subscribed more to the idea of *realpolitik* could understand neither the excited mood of the peace movement nor the moral enthusiasm of the supporters of humanitarian intervention. Yet others, clinging to their pacifist convictions on principle, refused to make a distinction between different historical situations and so rejected the use of military force under all circumstances. To that extent both 'pacifists' and proponents of power-political realism shared a refusal to admit how difficult and variable the relation between 'wars' and 'values' is. In this confused situation, an influential intellectual like Hans Magnus Enzensberger could assemble the most varied phenomena into a single horrific picture of a wave of violence rising throughout the world.[14] This led him to moral conclusions that were aimed at dampening down the excessive expectations placed on universalist moral norms. Of course, it can be valuable to work out the connections between different examples of violence that seem initially to be quite distinct. This applies to such questions as the long-term effects of violence in war on civilian life,[15] spontaneous violence (as in massacres) during a war or the relationship between the bureaucratized organization of killing and the spontaneous violence of the National Socialist persecution of the Jews.[16] But Enzensberger quite fails to produce any surprising links between seemingly unconnected phenomena, succeeding instead only in scrambling them all together in an amorphous mix. It follows that he was unable to answer the questions about moral evaluation in a way that was sensitive to the specific elements of particular configurations of events. It appears to me, however, that there is not just an analytical need, but also a moral one, to create or increase our sensitivity to the distinctions between different kinds of acts of violence, instead of applying a global formula that reduces them all to the same level.

II

All the discussions in this book are predicated on the conviction that contemporary events and processes profoundly influence academic work – even when scholars remain quite unaware of this influence or

consciously resist it. What is even harder to raise to the level of consciousness than these historical events is the impact upon scholarly
work of experiences in the spatial environment: for example, perceptions that do not stem from the time devoted to such work but that
enter into it as pre-conscious certainties. We might speculate about the
impact of different backgrounds on the thought of scientists – large
towns, small towns, heterogeneous and homogeneous milieus, or the
effect of shallow or deep local roots. This is worth mentioning in the
present context because it is my argument that in a place like Berlin
and its hinterland, where the marks of the history of twentieth-century
violence are evident to anyone who has eyes to see, myths of progress
lose all their credibility. This assertion holds good for the city of Berlin
itself, but even more so for its much mutilated surroundings. Berlin is
rich in buildings that bear witness to the designs of National Socialism
and communism for the future, and rich in the traces of the destruction wrought by these designs or by war and enforced division.[17] But
Berlin has also been shaped by the elimination of older buildings often
without a trace, in the age of industrialization, in the course of speedy
rebuilding after the destruction of the Second World War and also after
reunification. In addition, the large waves of migration to and from
Berlin have undoubtedly made it harder to form a collective memory
that spans the generations. It is likewise the case that the Brandenburg
hinterland has experienced a variety of gaps in tradition even in rural
districts, because of the population changes resulting from flight and
new settlement. However, the features of its landscape and its buildings that bear witness to the history of the twentieth century have not
been obscured to anything like the same extent as in Berlin by the
addition of superficially pleasing or commercially attractive façades.
Foucault's metaphorical talk of 'archaeology' teaches us to think of
history more as the accretion of the relics of lost civilizations than as a
linear progress that comes down to us today. This seems to me to be
literally true of Brandenburg and the German East in general. The pain
of collective learning processes appears before your very eyes, as does
the uncertainty about whether what you have learnt will turn out to
be no more than a new mistake that will again appear to posterity as
an incomprehensible wrong turning. I should like once again to take
the liberty of reflecting in an explicitly subjective, but for that reason
perhaps also vivid, manner on a particular place in Brandenburg in
which the majority of the texts collected here came into being and
which may explain, at least in part, the point of view I have adopted.

   The place I have in mind is a village to the north of Berlin, about one
hour's drive from the metropolis. The village has a hundred inhabitants and is surrounded by a huge forested area. It can only be reached

by a cul-de-sac that comes to a dead end on the bank of the old canal on which the village lies. At first glance, there is little about the village that seems inviting. The people are taciturn and distrustful, rather than friendly and approachable. Years after the end of the GDR, the houses are still plastered with the uniform grey sgraffito rendering that was typical of the GDR. The external appearance of the place is skewed by the presence of a significant number of 'dachas', the modest weekend cottages of the East Berliners. The inn looks off-putting and the fare it provides is monotonous. The only shop in the village had been a hut where goods had been delivered in the days of the communists; it has not survived the improvements in transport and the competition with more efficient suppliers in other places outside the village. However, the beauty of the natural surroundings, the variety of the woods and water-courses, a nearby lake and an idyllic forest pond, make up for its unapproachable appearance, even on a first impression. And on closer acquaintance, the rich and warm-hearted social life of both the villagers and the weekenders becomes visible and gradually opens up to the outsider.

So far, so trivial. We experienced the intrusion of history into our idyllic dream when our enthusiasm about the forest pond was cut short by the explanation that this pond had not always been there. It had been a clay quarry worked by the inmates of the concentration camp on the edge of the region's main town and this was how the pond came into being. There were also the overgrown railtracks that we had to cross on our way into the village. We had given no thought to why they were there, but they turned out to have been the railway used by the clinker works belonging to the concentration camp. In the woods leading from these works to the village and beyond, mass graves belonging to the victims of Soviet persecution in the postwar period were discovered in the early 1990s. The Soviet Union had simply taken over the Nazi concentration-camp buildings and filled them with new inmates who could not be mentioned during the lifetime of the GDR, and who really were mostly consigned to oblivion. The shocked gaze discovered everywhere, both in the immediate vicinity and further afield, the signs of National Socialism, war and communism. The raised ground in the garden that was used as a dance floor turned out to be the roof of a wartime bunker. The pretty houses along the road in a cosy, old-German style had been built to the taste of their first inhabitants – officers of the concentration camp SS guards. The cemetery at the entrance to the village was not the resting place of the villagers, who were buried in a rather more remote place, but a Soviet military cemetery. We were reminded of this by a monument with a pompous Russian inscription and brown-flecked photos on the tombstones of the young Soviet soldiers who fell in 1945. They died fighting for the canal crossing near our village against the last defensive rings of Hitler's armies, when the village changed hands several times. There is no cemetery for the fallen German soldiers. A number of cobblestone paths by the canal used to lead to bridges before the war; these bridges were never rebuilt afterwards, and some of them are still recognizable as rusting stumps.

Moreover, in the more distant surroundings of the village, the sense of the ambiguities of history is repeated at every step. If you came across an asphalted forest path, it mainly turned out to have had a military purpose. The woods concealed rocket silos and the nuclear bunker of the GDR leadership; today it is used as an underground shooting range. A transmitter mast was used by the GDR propaganda stations. When the country roads suddenly broaden out and their quality improves, you know that you are in the vicinity of the residential enclave of the GDR leadership that, as everybody knows, lay outside Berlin. The communist leaders who commuted daily along the 'protocol route' passed through surroundings that resembled one of Potemkin's villages, but were supposed to reflect the success of their policies. The forests themselves, which lie close to the former East–West frontier, were often used for troop manoeuvres and they display the scars of this use. In the villages, in addition to the farmers' houses and ordinary domestic dwellings, you are struck by two kinds of building, which have mainly been allowed to fall into decay. Many churches are in a miserable state; they were neglected for decades or went to rack and ruin during or after the war. Birch trees can be seen growing through the church towers and astonished visitors looking at a church can find themselves being approached by local inhabitants who ask them whether they would like to buy it. On the edge of the villages, you can see, often also in ruins, the long sheds of the co-operative farms that were built following the forced collectivization of agriculture in the GDR. The small towns bear the marks of de-industrialization, in the shape of factory ruins, that followed the collapse of the GDR. Most memorable for me, for many years, was the sight of a ruined factory with the name of 'Progress'; its name-plate had long outlasted the company. The aristocratic culture that had shaped the life of Brandenburg until the war, with its manor-houses, most of which were called 'Schloß' [Castle], has completely vanished. Even its buildings were destroyed in a blind fury during the postwar period, while those that survived were either neglected or altered beyond recognition. In the old towns, most houses have suffered from creeping decay. Damage resulting from fighting on land or in the air – and Brandenburg suffered greatly from both types of warfare – can still be recognized today and badly disfigures the towns. In these surroundings the buildings put up by the National Socialists look like object lessons in hollow monumentality. The regional, that is, Brandenburg, identity of the inhabitants has been radically devalued, as has their state, that is, Prussian, identity. The Jewish population has vanished and Christianity, too, has lost its ability to set its stamp on the culture of the region.

The devaluation of the past always went hand in hand with the promise of a new age, a utopian future. The ruins of these promises of a glorious future and the crimes committed in its name now lie one on top of the other, in layers. Even reunification and the Westernization of the East that has now finally begun have, tragically, been accompanied by new losses. Old forms of community that the observer may think had no more than compensatory functions under the dictatorships on German soil will, if they disappear, be mourned as genuine losses by those affected.[18] Economic collapse devalues professional qualifications, acquired experience at work and personal networks, and plunges those affected into profound crises of their sense of self-worth. In this situation everything tells us, from the point of view of both facts and values, that a better future is to be expected from democracy, the rule of law and the market economy. But it will not do to assume a triumphalist expression and proclaim this better future as a new political salvation. When it comes to questions of political salvation, German soil is tired or even exhausted. What is wanted is an attitude towards modernization that does not repress the losses it entails and that remains conscious of the contingent nature of its outcomes. This holds good in all fields, but particularly in the matter of guaranteeing peace.

III

As with all human activity, scholarly work is motivationally over-determined, at least when the scholar is an autonomous agent. The sustained attempt to reflect upon the temporal and spatial conditions governing the emergence of one's own attitudes should not be taken to imply that factors external to scholarship are the only ones at work. In my own case, my interest in the sociology of wars and in the different schools of thought about war was bound up with the hope that this was the way to move towards a theory of social change that would do justice to the course of events in the twentieth century. The most ambitious theory of social change, and the one that dominated international social science in the fifties and sixties, was the theory of modernization. For a variety of reasons, this theory did not, and still does not, appear to me to provide a satisfactory solution. The present volume contains my attempt to give a critical account of the difficulties modernization theory encounters in trying to understand war,[19] and also to take issue with the theory of the risk society, the 'second' or 'reflexive' modernity.[20] At first sight, 'reflexive' modernity seems to be fundamentally different from modernization theory as such, but on closer inspection it quickly becomes clear that it shares an astonishing number of premises with conventional modernization theory. However, its proclamation of a historical shift towards a fundamentally different modernity tends to conceal this rather than justify it.

In the book I wrote on action theory in 1992,[21] I presented my ideas about the wellsprings that nourish an emphasis on the creativity of human action that goes beyond models of rational and normatively oriented action. I also examined the consequences of a shift in action theory to a model of creative action for the theory of social order and social change. I contested the frequently defended view that classical sociological theory was based on a naïve theory of progress,[22] and attempted to show instead that all the classical thinkers shared the belief that 'only when the naïve belief in progress is lost can we move forward to understanding the openness of the historical future, the risk- and responsibility-laden nature of present action'.[23] The inferences drawn in individual cases about the conceptualization of human action were of course extremely varied, but one thing was common to all thinkers who had forsaken teleological philosophies of history and evolutionist notions of progress. They all believed that the only hope for the emergence of new and better things lay in human action. But what did such a concentration on the creativity of action mean for the analysis of social change? It is easy to fall into the trap of imagining that this general perspective implies a hopelessly exaggerated view of the opportunities available for the collective control of social change, or else a view of the relationship between individual and collective action that is excessively harmonious and eliminates possible paradoxes. But as far as I am concerned, the right inference to be drawn from a theory of action based on creativity is not to project creativity onto macro-subjects or to assume an unproblematic increase in both individual and collective liberty, but to devise a theory of social change that takes the *contingent* nature of socio-historical processes extremely seriously. At this point we are confronted by the threat of a second misunderstanding. This is the assumption that the emphasis on contingency means the end of all theory, that it would spell the bankruptcy of every sociological theory of social change and leave the field completely to narrative historiography. But it is perfectly possible to make theoretically significant statements about the consequences of increasing the contingent nature of actions by enlarging the number of individual options for decisions, or about the structural reasons for the declining ability to 'repress' historical contingency in the twentieth century. This can only be touched upon here,[24] but it forms the background assumption that explains why I think of modernization theory as a characteristic theory of the postwar period, but as an ultimately untenable new version of a type of thinking repressing contingency.

Despite this scepticism we need to bear in mind that – unless you believe in Marxism – the social sciences have so far failed to produce a rival theory of social change superior to modernization theory. Therefore, we are concerned here not with a global rejection but with modifications and historical qualifications.[25] A criticism that goes far beyond the demonstration of thematic neglect in modernization theory is one that focuses on the inadequacy of its deep-seated assumptions, for example on the defects of its treatment of differentiation theory, to whose abstract logic many a more concrete assumption of modernization theory can be traced.[26] Differentiation theory, too, will remain an important component of a more comprehensive whole. The skirmish with the question of a 'special German path' running through many chapters of this book is quite crucial and urgent in this context. This is because the idea that the 'German catastrophe' derives from a specific disharmony between several dimensions of modernization arises from the presumption of the normally given 'eurhythmia' (C.S. Whitaker) of these processes, which seems untenable to me. The thesis of Germany's special path seems to contain a false reassurance about the consequences of the processes of modernization. We must accustom ourselves to the idea that discrepancies between different social realms are normal and that the concept of 'modernization' may be no more than a collective name for a series of changes between which many variable relations are possible and actually exist.

This idea seems in fact to be gaining ground increasingly, the more all the talk of 'postmodernity' and of 'reflexive modernity' begins to fade – or at least the claim that its arrival signifies a historical shift into a new age.[27] This change in consciousness is in my view very much to be welcomed. An exemplary expression of it is the typology of fundamental answers to the question of the relation of 'modernity' to 'barbarism', as presented in a volume dedicated to this relationship. The editors rightly remind us that in the self-image of modernity, civilization is pre-eminently the 'principle of modern society, barbarism its anti-principle'.[28] However, they go on to say that, under the impact of National Socialism and Stalinism, thinkers like Horkheimer and Adorno regard the modern repression of pre-modern barbarism, in other words, the civilizing process itself, likewise as barbaric.

Thus barbarism can be understood either as the anti-principle or, in opposition to this, as the secret underlying principle of modern society. But this does not exhaust all the possibilities of interpretation. A third possible basic answer to the question of the relations of modernism and barbarism runs as follows: the project of modernity is fulfilled if modernity becomes conscious of its potential for barbarism and strives to overcome it through a civilizing process.[29]

However, this third possibility does not mark a new epoch of reflexivity, but attempts to learn from the history of violence in the twentieth century. What it amounts to is a multiply refracted consciousness of ourselves and our age – a consciousness that makes no attempt to proclaim optimistically the modern possibility of controlling the danger that arises from a new barbarism, but strives to remain constantly alert to the permanence of that danger. Shmuel Eisenstadt has attempted to show in greater detail how the danger of turning single points of view into absolutes is inherent in the political 'programme' of modernity, its ideas and institutions, from the primordial to the universalist. This danger, whether expressed in socialist, nationalist or fundamentalist religious movements, gave rise to 'strong principled exclusionist tendencies' and thus to a modern barbarism. Only a complex pluralism of the different strata of collective identity appears to him to offer an – always fragile – defence against barbarism. 'Thus the challenge of barbarism inherent in the programmes of modernity will be with us with the continual development of modernity and of its earned institutional forms.'[30] Therefore, if we wish to understand the 'complex pluralism' that Eisenstadt and others have proposed, and with that the preconditions for preventing a modern barbarism, the most useful conceptual tools are not such terms as 'equilibrium' and the 'discrepancy' between the various dimensions of the modernization process – these are the categories of a conventional modernization theory. We need instead to determine what equilibrium between the different forms of action orientation and the different institutions will fulfil these expectations before we can speak of it meaningfully. But one thing is certain: it will not be the equilibrium of a homogeneous modernization.[31]

IV

Wars are a challenge to existing interpretations and valuations, and stimulate us to produce new interpretations and valuations. In retrospect, it often appears that we have simply applied existing interpretations to new cases, and this impression is reinforced because the originators of new interpretations frequently have the very greatest interest in claiming that their interpretations are not new, but ancient and based on tradition. Thus everything points to the creation of a retrospective illusion of a linear historical process. Relating this to the First World War, for example, we should be cautious before we accept all too literally the self-portraits that emerge from the newspaper articles of chauvinistic professors. Thomas Nipperdey has cast doubt on whether the ideas they contain are 'merely the collective expression of academic ideas that prevailed before 1914 or whether they are one, very real, possibility that only became reality through the exceptional situation of the world war'.[32] Special studies of particular cases have provided a complex picture and interpret many an exaggerated justification of the war not as the expression of long-standing militaristic convictions, but as the feverish attempt to create or maintain popular enthusiasm for the war.[33] Such changes of views or such one-sided interpretations are not for the most part the product of strategic decisions, but belong to a situation in which many people were simply carried away by the events of the war itself. Sociologists showed very early on how, in wars that are fought with nationalist fervour, soldiers and civilians, the elites and the rank-and-file, frequently change their attitudes at a stroke and develop new motives for their actions. It was also noted that the way wars end usually has a dramatic effect on the values and loyalties of the population. Military victories strengthen people's bonds with a regime, regardless of its nature; military defeats weaken them and lead to the rapid devaluation of existing bonds. Beyond these observations, for example in the context of the First World War in the writings of Georg Simmel,[34] the war is idealized into the existential experience of an 'absolute situation', in other words, an emotive experience of the absolute validity of a value for participants, who perceive that their courage and readiness to make sacrifices surpass all rational considerations and discursive justifications. This brings the experience of war – in Simmel's thinking, but not only there[35] – close to the deepest religious and sexual experiences, those that constitute our values and personality.

It is tempting, and legitimate, to condemn these ideas as the extravagant fantasies of an intellectual far from the realities of war at the front.[36] Anyone who reacts to extraordinary experiences of a religious or sexual nature with rationalist scepticism is sure to reach the limits of his or her tolerance when confronted with this view of the experience of war or violence in general. But in so doing, he or she may miss the opportunity to gain an insight into the deeper motives of human action. For all the differences, there are in fact parallels or structural homologies between the experience underlying the constitution of values and the experience of violence – whether suffered or perpetrated. The experience of violence is the 'perverted twin' of the experience of value commitment.

Following the literary and philosophical assimilation of the experience of violence in the First World War, but partly also under the direct influence of elements of Nietzsche's philosophy, attempts were made after the war to take serious theoretical account of this affinity between the ecstatic experience of creativity and of destructiveness and to make this insight analytically productive. I am of course not thinking here of Mussolini's completely amoral view of violence in the fascist movement, or of Carl Schmitt's fascistoid political existentialism, in which decision and conflict as such become charged with value.[37] I have in mind rather the remarkable combination of ideas taken from Durkheim's sociology of religion and Ernst Jünger's book on 'struggle as inner experience' that is to be found in one strand of French sociology of the interwar period. The work of Roger Caillois,[38] in particular, interprets aspects of war as a modern form of collective release, in the spirit of Durkheim's study of archaic religiosity. Among these aspects are the wastefulness of war, the licence for violence and the ecstatic public gathering. In these circles, too, there was only a narrow dividing line separating the utilization of these insights that were rooted in a sociology of the sacred from the bizarre turn to a 'sacred sociology',[39] complete with the sectarian group experiments and fantasies of violence that were celebrated as escapes from the conflicts of modernity and as a liberation leading to true sovereignty. However, if we are prepared to make analytic use of such knowledge, we shall obtain an initial answer to the question of why wars are so 'interpretation-intensive'. Like all experiences out of the ordinary, those of war and violence quickly go by definition beyond the interpretative frameworks of ordinary life. However, these experiences need to be reintegrated into such frameworks, and this enhances the hunger for convincing interpretations and the prospects of charismatic renewal. The entire personality of those involved is at stake in these experiences and their interpretation.

In order to avoid a merely metaphorical paraphrasing of these processes, and also to prevent our crossing the frontier separating analysis from the conversion of experience into myth, it is necessary to expand our knowledge and the conception of identity in the social sciences so as to include these experiences. This expansion is necessary because, following the two classical exponents of this approach, George Herbert Mead and Erik Erikson, nothing like enough attention was paid to the way in which the communicative constitution of identity is intertwined with power and exclusion. In Mead's analysis of the exclusion of external enemies or of criminals, such phenomena do indeed put in an appearance, but without really shaping the character of the theory.[40] In my book *The Genesis of Values*,[41] I have tried to provide a phenomenological record of the experiences that constitute value commitments and to analyse them theoretically. The central claim I make is that value commitments arise from experiences of self-formation and self-transcendence. Self-transcendence means an opening of the symbolically drawn boundaries of identity. In order to understand how it resembles, and how it differs from, destructive and self-destructive forms of the abolition of the boundaries of the self, it must be clear that not every such opening occurs voluntarily, and not every opening of the boundaries of identity, whether voluntary or not, is followed by a successful reintegration into ordinary, everyday life. An involuntary opening represents a trauma from which the persons affected can no more free themselves than they can free themselves from the value commitments that constitute their identity. But in contrast to the latter, where there is such a trauma they have no story to tell that will establish values, and nor will they experience the paradoxical feeling of the greatest freedom in the greatest commitment. The experience of violence, too, transforms a person's self-image, and this may give rise to a feeling of self-betrayal. It contains the experience of the non-acceptable sides of our own person, or the 'guilt of survival', if we find that we have only survived for radically contingent reasons. In the present volume, the ideas we have just only outlined are investigated further with reference to American research on the soldiers who fought in Vietnam,[42] but there can be no doubt that to some extent this is territory that has still to be explored.

In his theory of the struggle for recognition, Axel Honneth has attempted in a subtle study to do justice to the way in which dialogue and exclusion become interwoven in the processes of identity formation.[43] This involved him in recourse to Hegel's philosophy and a critical debate with George Herbert Mead. While his theory takes experiences of wrongs and injustices into consideration, it takes no account of violence, whether inflicted or suffered. In the case of wrongs, it may be plausible to suggest that to experience them may generate a dynamic that will lead to ascending forms of justice, so that the logic of a struggle for recognition simultaneously becomes a teleology moving in the direction of a universalist morality.[44] However, this theory would falter if the phenomenon of violence were more strongly emphasized. The consequences of experiencing violence and the identity changes that follow from it frequently do not point the way to better things, but lead instead to traumatic attempts at evasive action and repetition compulsions, to renewed acts of violence, cyclically mounting spirals of violence and, in a general way, to the contingent nature of historical processes. Within these processes a laborious learning from disasters may take place; but, equally, they can lead to people being hopelessly trapped by the curse of evil deeds.

V

However, only through such an opening to the contingent – and this is what forms the leitmotif of these arguments – can a defence of universalist values be plausibly made. Only by renouncing the attempt to discover guarantees of these values in the philosophy of history will the last vestiges of the myths of progress be overcome. Only after that renunciation will they be replaced by the search for traces of values made actual in history and for the possibilities and risks inherent in the stabilization of achieved instances of 'progress' in the future. With this the tension between universalism and historicism reappears in all its harshness. This tension will disappear if power politics take over and all (foreign policy) actions are seen to derive from particular interests, thus falling outside the scope of a value-orientated view. But in my opinion, this tension will also disappear if pacifists fail to make a distinction between politics and morality and so maintain that the use of force is harmful in all circumstances.

In Germany in the nineteenth century, historicism had entered into a close alliance with power politics.[45] This alliance was anything but logically compelling. It led to the undermining not just of the foundation of moral universalism in natural law, but of that universalism itself. In Germany, at the time of the First World War, every moral argument in foreign policy, however mediated, was rejected as the hypocritical cloaking of particular interests, and at the same time it was claimed that there was a difference of principle between one's own values and those of everyone in the enemy camp. With the entry of the USA into the war in 1917, the founding of the League of Nations (1920) and subsequent efforts to outlaw war (the Kellogg Pact of 1928), the question of a moral dimension in foreign policy became unavoidable and this provoked Carl Schmitt to intensify the polemic from the point of view of power politics. 'With the declarations with which President Wilson brought his country into the World War against Germany on 2 April 1917, the problem of a discriminatory concept of war entered the history of the new international law.'[46] This 'turn to a discriminatory concept of war' was one that in his view would actually exacerbate wars. If he is to be believed, wars can best be held in check if they are fought simply for specific interests and without any illusions. However, if they are fought with feelings of moral superiority and with the conviction that one is fighting for a morally better cause, then all inhibitions are put to one side, since it is no longer a matter of a fight between equal opponents, but a struggle between good and evil, between the preservers of order and its destroyers. This argument has shown itself to be extraordinarily tenacious and recourse is still had to it today,[47] even though it has since been shown to be neither empirically nor ethically convincing. Admittedly, it is true that even where we feel we are morally in the right, we must not neglect to consider the appropriateness of our means and the foreseeable consequences that may follow from our actions. Nor should we overlook the ever-present danger of the hypocritical concealment of interests beneath the cloak of morality. But empirically, the history of violence in the twentieth century contains nothing to suggest that it was mainly the Western powers with their universalist moral arguments that tended to remove the barriers to the use of force – quite the reverse, in fact. And from an ethical point of view, this argument fails to recognize that the supporters of a universalist standpoint did not simply propose a moral view of international politics while neglecting the need to create institutions and procedures. On the contrary, what they wanted was to create legal norms and organizations with which to enforce them on an international plane.

> For the establishment of a cosmopolitan order means that violations of human rights are no longer judged and combated *immediately* from the moral point of view, but rather are prosecuted, *like* criminal actions, within the framework of a state-organized legal order, in accordance with institutionalized legal procedures. Precisely the juridification of the state of nature among states prevents a moral de-differentiation of law and guarantees the accused full legal protection, and hence protection against unmediated moral discrimination, even in the currently relevant cases of war crimes and crimes against humanity.[48]

Jürgen Habermas's objection to Carl Schmitt here misses the point slightly since Schmitt had focused on the dynamics of war itself and did not have the prosecution of war crimes in mind. But he is right to argue that the law can interpose itself between morality and politics, and in so doing it can overcome the dangers that a 'fundamentalist belief in human rights' can pose for peace.

In the major Western nations, thinking in terms of power politics never became as dominant as in Germany. It is significant that the word *'realpolitik'*, uttered in a triumphalist undertone, should have entered other languages from German. In contrast, from its foundation in the eighteenth century on, the American Republic had promised a new sort of diplomacy and foreign policy. Apart from all other aspects, it is certainly not to be understood without that sense of mission, and because of it American foreign policy has always been criticized.[49] But in Great Britain during the nineteenth century, too, particularly among liberals, there was much discussion about when military intervention was permissible or imperative, whether particular interests could ever make it legitimate to violate the sovereignty of other states, and whether there were situations in which non-intervention, too, stood in need of justification.[50] It is quite evident that there was no question here of an unrestricted moralization of foreign policy; but equally, the brisk elimination of morality from politics was not on the agenda either. The complex conflicts of values and the weighing-up of different moral goods that appear here inevitably continue to preoccupy us today, following the end of the dreadful balance of power of the East–West nuclear confrontation.

The central conflict of values in this sphere today is the conflict between national sovereignty and the universalist claims of human rights. Every statement about this conflict ought to begin by recognizing that national sovereignty, and hence, too, the assurance that one is safe from intervention in fact, is itself a value. Of fundamental importance for the preservation of peace is undoubtedly the willingness to trust other states, societies and cultures, and acknowledge their right to self-determination, to choose their own political order and to undergo their own learning processes. Any violation of this important value can only be justified if even higher values are at stake. In the liberal tradition it was conceded that there could be grounds for such decisions in the conflict of values. John Stuart Mill, for example,[51] believed that intervention was justifiable in principle if it was part of a nation's attempt to liberate itself from an enemy yoke or to overthrow a native tyranny supported by a foreign military power. Other grounds for intervention were the fight against slavery and colonialism, and, furthermore, existed also if a state massacred parts of its own population or treated them with systematic cruelty. Thus essential justifications of the principle have long since been discussed. In the same way, certain insights of pragmatic reason have long since been formulated. It has been held, for example, that before every military intervention the possibilities of influencing other states by peaceful means must have been exhausted and also that in every intervention there must be due proportionality in the relation of means to the desired ends. This shows, then, that adjudicating between values can indeed result in a morally grounded right to intervene.

However, such a moral *right* does not necessarily lead to a *duty* to intervene. The lead-up to a decision to intervene inevitably involves an assessment of one's own ability to intervene, and of one's own forces and interests. In concrete terms, even the USA, or the whole of NATO, would not have the power to intervene in a number of trouble spots at once in the way in which it intervened in Kosovo in 1999. Carl Friedrich von Weizsäcker's formula of 'internal world politics' [*Weltinnenpolitik*] does indeed describe a necessary change of consciousness, but not an actual given state of affairs. We do not live in a planetary community, but there is probably also no way back to a potentially warlike collection of coexisting states, as understood in classical international law. In this situation, there are two conceivable ways forward. The first way has been most explicitly advocated by Habermas in the context of the war in Kosovo.[52] It points towards completely subjecting international relations to the rule of law. It envisages a world in which the United Nations is able to exercise a monopoly of the means of violence, a situation that could only be legitimized on the basis of a fundamental reform of its organization. Whoever is unable to believe that any one of the permanent members of the Security Council might refuse to abandon its right of veto will find the second approach more realistic for a long time to come. This way has two aspects. On the one hand, it involves making every possible effort to strengthen the United Nations and reform it in the ways referred to above, and, in the event of great conflicts breaking out, to establish a consensus within the international community of nations. On the other hand, however, in rare cases, there must be a readiness to act without a consensus and without the desired backing. Therefore, this approach consists in doing everything possible to make sure that the belief in human rights establishes deeper roots in Europe and that it is able to influence political decisions. At the same time, attempts must be made to tie the USA firmly into a multilateral foreign policy, since such a policy increases the pressure to justify the grounds on which to intervene.

The case of Kosovo illustrates in exemplary fashion the difficulty and uncertainty, indeed the tragic nature, of the decisions involved in conflicts of values that are typical of all action, certainly of all political action, and most powerfully, no doubt, of all matters of war and peace where people's lives are literally at stake.[53] People always have to act in the present, and the burden of responsibility is no more removed by imagining future procedures than it is by reflecting upon missed opportunities in the past. Well thought-out plans for peace can act as a guide,[54] but they cannot relieve us of the need to make decisions. Peace can be made more stable by the rule of law, reliable expectations, economic equity, intercultural understanding and institutional integration between states. Nevertheless, conflicts like the war in Kosovo are sure to break out in the twenty-first century. Furthermore, our European point of view should not blind us to the probability that other kinds of war will continue to deface the new century: wars between nations (like India and Pakistan), wars arising in the process of nation-building (as in the wake of the disintegration of the Soviet Union), conflicts between warlords in states in dissolution (as in Africa), a war with terrorism on a completely new scale, and wars for scarce resources (like water). A glance at the history of violence in the twentieth century tells us that conflicts about 'wars' and 'values' are here to stay. But a pessimism of the intellect can go hand in hand with an optimism of the will.

PART I

THE MODERNITY OF WAR

1

The Dream of a Modernity without Violence

Violence has currently become a focal point of widespread public debate. The depressing reasons for this are obvious. Europe is experiencing the Balkan war and its cruelties as the return of a horror that we all imagined had long since been overcome. Hoyerswerda and Rostock, Mölln and Solingen,[1] are the symbols of an eruption of violence in the midst of a reunited Germany. The bewilderment of the politicians is matched by the confusion of the majority of social scientists, from peace researchers to sociologists of youth. The traditional strengths of the social sciences have never included a preoccupation with violence within societies and violence between states, and we are now paying the price for this. Admittedly, in their comments on the politics of the day and in historical flashbacks, the founders and classics of sociology expressed their views on the causes, the course and the effect of wars, class struggles and other conflicts fought out with violence. But for the most part the relation of these statements to the systematic core of their theories remains obscure. Similarly, peace research and the study of international relations by political scientists have had little impact on the development of theory in general. Social scientists have always paid far greater attention to economic, social and political inequality than to the manifestations of violence. Even the legitimate institutions of the state monopoly of the means of violence have attracted only marginal interest from the social sciences – an astonishing fact, given their size and importance. We are indebted to Hans Paul Bahrdt for the perceptive comment, one whose validity is by no means confined to Germany, that a scrutiny of school textbooks on social studies or introductions to sociology must give the impression that the societies we live in have neither armed forces nor police.

Studies of the police focus mainly on their treatment of individual offenders. And in general, more attention is paid to the violent behaviour of *individual* criminals than to the origins of *collective* and *state* violence. The 1993 report by the American panel on violence goes so far as to ignore the latter altogether and to revert to a biological interpretation of violent tendencies.[2] Analyses of collective violence frequently suffer from a misleading application of explanatory models designed to explore the origins of individual violence. They fluctuate for the most part between rationalist and irrationalist exaggerations. Some seek to present violence as the coolly selected and deployed tool of the interests of a nation or class, about which little can be said apart from its instrumentality. Others are unable to think of violence except in terms of the collapse of all social order, normative orientation and individual rationality. Admittedly, a passing increase in scholarly interest and in the number of respectable reports by committees of experts was triggered by certain spectacular public events, such as the racial disturbances of the 1960s in the USA or the radical left-wing terrorism in the German Federal Republic in the 1970s, as well as isolated outbreaks of unrest among the young. But for the most part the sociologists' interest waned as quickly as that of the general public. The deeply rooted ideas about what is relevant in the social sciences soon reasserted themselves, to the detriment of any concern with the subject of collective violence.

How can we explain this? I believe that the explanation for this curious distribution of scholarly attention lies in the close ties between Western social sciences and the world-view of liberalism. In the philosophy of liberalism, wars and violent domestic conflicts necessarily appeared as the relics of a dying age that had not yet been illuminated by the dawn of the Enlightenment. Early liberals regarded contemporary wars as the product of the aristocratic military spirit, or the uncontrolled whims of despots, and, more recently, even the First World War was perceived by American liberal intellectuals as evidence of European backwardness, in contrast to American modernity. Despotism and the aristocratic military spirit were themselves viewed as relics of primitive stages of humankind; *civilized* life ought also to be *civil*, with martial traits and needs not simply prohibited by religion and morality, but eased and sublimated into sporting or economic competition ('*le doux commerce*').[3] Even if this did not mean that the age of non-violence had been completely achieved, enlightened liberals might feel that they could see where the road was leading and what steps were needed to perfect a rational order. Just as torture and public punishments had to be banished from the realm of criminal justice, war and violence of every sort against persons and things had to be eliminated from modern, that is, civil, society. In the modernization theory of the postwar period the non-violent resolution of conflict even became a defining feature of modernity. However, this blunt rejection of violence was accompanied by a certain tendency to underestimate its importance in the present. It allowed an optimistic gaze firmly fixed on the future to view the bad old world in its death-throes with impatience and without genuine interest.

Even classical Marxism is a descendant of this liberal world-view where this faith in the future is concerned. Admittedly, its representatives emphasized the violence implicit in the way in which the capitalist mode of production established itself, as well as the inexorable material compulsion concealed behind the façade of freely negotiated contracts and the class rule disguised by the equality of individuals. For this reason, the idea that class rule could only be overthrown by force did not weigh too heavily on its conscience, no more than the idea that even after the victory of the revolution, the 'dictatorship of the proletariat' would continue to use force to restrain its opponents for a considerable period. But in a sense, classical Marxism only extended the liberal world-view for a further epoch: after the violence required for the worldwide revolution, what was envisaged was the emergence of a social order consisting of a universal, free association of producers in which violence would no longer feature. In the final analysis, for Marxism, the end of violent social conflict was the consequence of the disappearance of divergent interests in a completely just, spontaneously self-regulating order. Since all wars or ethnic conflicts were held to be the expression of class contradictions, they would disappear along with the disappearance of class conflicts.

The real resistance to this optimistic turning away from the role of force came from anti-liberals and from those defenders of bourgeois society who were prepared, more or less without reservation, to abandon their original hopes. We should begin by mentioning the old-fashioned militarism that saw in war the father of all things and was convinced that a peaceful civilization and the disappearance of warlike virtues would lead to a general decline in morals and a rise of softness and effeminacy. This strand of thought was combined, in the course of the nineteenth century, with a tendency, borrowed from Darwin and others, to biologize social and political issues in order to justify the uninhibited competition of individuals, as well as nations, races or ethnic groups. Exponents of this kind of thinking were undoubtedly to be found among the early representatives of sociology, from Gumplowicz and Ratzenhofer to Sumner. Significantly, however, instead of gaining inclusion in the living heritage of the discipline, they have in fact been forgotten.[4] This contrasts with a continuous tradition of power-political realism that without any great ideological superstructure simply treats it as an indisputable fact that states and collectives act in their own interest, and that in social conflicts they have force at their disposal and will inevitably use it. A further version of the anti-liberal attitude to the role of force occurs where old-fashioned militarism is dressed up with ideas taken from *Lebens-philosophie* or existentialism: violence as creativity, struggle as inner experience, the community of soldiers at the front as the inspiration for a new type of state order. Particularly in Germany, but by no means only there, this way of thinking plays a significant role, from Nietzsche via the so-called 'ideas of 1914' down to the National Socialist movement. Alien though this way of thinking may have become to us today, an element of actual experience is preserved here, too.

It appears, therefore, that we face the following dilemma. The Enlightenment, liberalism and also Marxism promise us a world without violence, but also lead us again and again into situations in which we are rudely awakened from our dream and are astounded by the persistence of this apparent lack of civilization. Militarism, Social Darwinism, power-political realism and the mythology of violence do indeed direct our attention to the pervasive nature of violence, but they also deprive us of all hope of a stable, peaceful world. *We can only escape from this dilemma with the aid of a process of reflection that begins (1) by undermining the self-confidence of a power-political realism, that goes on from there to a dispassionate study of the persuasive power of conceptions of peace, particularly those of liberalism (2/3), and finally (4) attempts to learn even from the mythologies of violence in order to avoid the limitations and reductionisms of traditional research into violence.*

I

Let us begin by inquiring into the empirical persuasiveness of power-political realism. Are the social sciences obliged to see the world without illusions as an eternal struggle of conflicting interests, or can sociology prove that *'realpolitik'* is itself an ideology? Are there indications of a peaceful order in the world that promise more than a temporary armistice in the midst of the eternal struggle? As an appropriate starting-point from which to answer this question, we may turn to Thomas Hobbes's thought experiment: given a state of nature in which everyone pursues only his own advantage, not shrinking from force and fraud, but also constantly aware that he may himself become the victim of fraud and violence, and can therefore never enjoy his life and his possessions in peace – how can this state of nature lead to a

peaceful and safe social order? As is well known, Hobbes's own solution was that, motivated by the fear of death, everyone would be
willing to submit to a strong state or the strong will of a universally
accepted ruler, and this solution became one of the basic models of
modern political thought. Now, what is interesting is that almost no
one noticed that in solving this problem, Hobbes only created another
one. Internal peace may indeed be guaranteed by the existence of
powerful, centralized states, but this merely provokes the risk of conflict between these states or leviathans! The effect of conflicts between
states is to undermine again the security of the individual citizen and
thus partly to demolish the attempt to justify the existence of a strong
state as a response to the dangers of civil wars – if we assume that there
may be a lesser risk of conflicts between weak states. Hobbes's own
reaction to this problem was not wholly consistent. On the one hand,
he by no means ignored the fact of wars between states; he made use
of it not just as a metaphor, but as empirical proof that the state of
nature he described was not just an assumed fiction, but a real, actually experienced problem. On the other hand, however, even though
he had recognized with an unprecedented clarity the explosive character of the problem for life within societies, he tended to play it down
at the level of relations between societies. The state of nature between
states, according to Hobbes, was less problematic and less inevitable
than between individuals. States, so he believed, were more capable of
self-restraint, so that it was not necessary for the entire population of
a state to become involved in a war. Moreover, states were stronger
than individuals and hence less concerned to expand their power still
further. This circumstance made the question of security between states
less acute and created the possibility of an equilibrium between them.
Whatever we may think of Hobbes's explanations, and whether or not
we believe that they are still valid in an age of total war, it is evident
that he does not propose the same solution for conflicts between states
as for internal conflicts. He neither expects a centralized superstate to
emerge in empirical fact, nor does he advocate it. He relies instead
much more strongly on the suppression of internal aspirations towards expansion and on 'restricting war to a pure war between states'
(Reinhart Koselleck). This internal contradiction in Hobbes was recognized in the peace discourse of the early Enlightenment, and for that
reason thinkers in a line from the Abbé de St Pierre through Rousseau
and on to Kant cast doubt on the possibility of a stable equilibrium
between the powers. According to Swift, Hobbes's system resembled a
building whose stability was threatened by a bird landing on the roof.
For this reason St Pierre proposed that international treaties should
be agreed; Rousseau was in favour of reducing the interdependence

of states and increasing their isolation and autarky, while Kant looked to links between republican constitutions and the establishing of bonds under international law as a way out of the instability that was a constant threat.[5] These non-Hobbesian ways of thinking have in common the fact that they have been forced by Hobbes's inconsistency to return to the question of whether relations between states actually possess the extra-legal or even extra-moral character that the Hobbesian tradition attributes to them. The fact that this tradition of thought continually resurfaces shows how unclear the Hobbesian power-political realism is with its view of states as unified actors, each with an unambiguous set of interests. As a rule, we do not know what the interests of a state or a large-scale collective really are, who defines them, how this definition is arrived at, what conceptions of the world enter into it, whether power and security are conceived in an expansionist or defensive manner and whether these are mutually compatible in each individual case. For all its demonstrable resilience in the real world, power-political realism is by no means a simple reflection of reality, but rather something that arises from a programmatic de-moralization and an empirically problematic abstraction from the normative and interpretative character of reality. If we inquire not just into the causes of war, but also into the causes of peace, of available solutions to the dilemmas of security, we may well discover not just that liberal conceptions are more optimistic and normatively more attractive, but also that they are more sustainable empirically than those of power-political realism.

II

For all classical liberals, whose political goals lay in limiting state power and enhancing the scope for individual action, and who advanced from those beliefs to a positive attitude towards domestic and foreign free trade, wars were always as immoral as they were harmful. The damage they caused in the economic sphere was plain for all to see. The depopulation of entire tracts of land, the destruction of capital, the increasing burden of taxes, the growth of government debt, the shrinking of international trade, general impoverishment – these are just a few of the headings that have been used to describe the economic consequences of war and warlike regimes. But morally, too, classical liberals condemned wars as the actions of warlike classes and rulers who mindlessly inflicted death and injustice for selfish reasons – and that means a misconceived notion of their own best interests. The two oldest sociological theories maintaining that states have the capacity for peace, theories that have been highly influential and are still worth taking seriously today, both come from the general ambit of *liberalism*. They are associated with the names of Immanuel Kant and Adam Smith. Kant had made a connection between a state's capacity for peace and its internal political structure, and arrived at the conclusion that republics are peaceable by nature. His conception of republics was concerned not with the overthrow of monarchs, but with making monarchical power constitutional and juridified. If only the well-understood interests of the citizens could be taken into account in making foreign policy decisions, this would lead to the avoidance of war and the establishment of mutually beneficial relations between states. According to Kant, it is the establishment of a legal relationship between states that fully creates the preconditions required to enable every individual to live in accordance with the imperatives of reason, even within a state, whereas a world-state would always contain the risk of a universal despotism. Adam Smith, in his turn, together with some of his predecessors (for instance, Montesquieu) and, above all, the emerging discipline of political economy, trusted in the pacifying effects of free trade. Instead of mutual threats, destruction and plundering between states, the peaceable exchange of needed goods would enhance the well-being of all participants and make war superfluous. A civilizing effect is attributed to trade between states that is greater even than in the case of domestic trade. These two conceptions could be described as the *republican* and the *utilitarian* versions of liberal thinking about peace. In reality, that is to say, in the thought of individual liberal philosophers, economists or sociologists, the two conceptions are not clearly distinguished from each other. In arguing in favour of the realistic possibility of establishing a state of peace between states, Kant has recourse to ideas taken from political economy, and Smith is by no means deaf to the need for security as a basic precondition of trade. Nevertheless, it still makes sense to talk of these two versions as separate lines of thought, since on particular issues they do give rise to different prognoses and evaluations. There is a productive tension built into the liberal discourse here. The question of whether a peaceful foreign policy is made more probable by the democratic participation of ordinary citizens, the internal rule of law or the mutual links between states created by trade is undoubtedly open to empirical exploration. The results of numerous attempts to do this are controversial in detail, but taken overall, they do not make liberal conceptions of peace look misguided and they point unanimously to the existence of a kind of special peace between liberal states. However, the present argument does not address that point. Both liberal conceptions of peace have a shadow side, as well as a bright one.

Neither is so untouched by war and conflict that it can be appealed to as an innocent idea. Both have been used to justify warlike behaviour. Now, no idea can be entirely immune to ideological misuse. But we have to inquire how far an idea actually favours misuse and how it can be modified in order to preclude it. The demonstration that these two liberal ideas of peace have their darker side is not intended as an attack on liberalism, but is concerned to explore their intellectual stock in trade in the light of the actual lessons of history.

The darker side of the *utilitarian liberal* conception of peace lies in the history of colonialism and imperialism. By this I do not mean the Leninist conception of imperialism as the logical consequence of capitalist economic practices and as the highest or even last stage of capitalism. This use of the term as a weapon with which to legitimate large-scale territorial domination by the Soviet Union, and which cast an aura of suspicion over every nation with a capitalist economy, did more to obscure the problems of international inequality in recent decades than to shed light upon them. What is meant, rather, is the ease with which liberal thinkers accommodated themselves to imperialist policies. The history of German liberalism in the Bismarck era and especially during the Wilhelminian age shows that no more than a few people articulated a critique of the economic damage caused by the state acquisition of colonies and the wasteful nature of militarism from a free-trade point of view, and that as a consequence of their criticism these commentators were relegated to the status of outsiders in the spectrum of opinion. Even those who preserved a sceptical distance from imperialist tendencies raised no objection to state support for export policies designed to gain greater economic influence abroad. What was typical of the age, however, was the tendency of liberalism and imperialism to join forces. By way of illustration, it is enough to mention such names as Friedrich Naumann and Max Weber. Britain as a model for liberals also included the idea of the exemplary ability of the British to lead an empire, politically, economically and culturally. In particular, the 'liberal imperialists' regarded 'a German imperialism as the fulfilment and logical continuation of the policy of founding the Reich'.[6] In their eyes, domestic liberal reforms were justified not primarily in terms of values such as freedom and popular sovereignty, but as part of a process of modernization that served as the precondition of an external imperialist policy. The liberals were more conscious of the links between foreign and domestic affairs than conservatives and articulated them with greater vigour. Now, at this point it could of course be objected that the imperialism of liberals in Germany does not in itself tell us anything about the dark side of liberal thought as such, but simply provides evidence of the weakness of liberalism in Germany and for the shallow roots of free-trade liberalism there. In Germany, it will be said, the impulse towards a politics of peace that springs from a free-trade liberalism did not really manage to assert itself. This is why it is necessary to look towards Britain, where the question of the relationship between liberalism and imperialism can be put more radically. In fact, the influence of free-trade thinking upon the peace movement was very great in Britain throughout the nineteenth century – a combination scarcely conceivable in Germany.[7] An author like Herbert Spencer, whom current opinion might have expected to have Social Darwinist views on the relations between peoples, turns out in reality to have been among the resolute opponents of the Boer War and of British military interventions in general. This apparent hostility to imperialism on the part of leading utilitarian liberals was the basis of Joseph Schumpeter's theory of imperialism as the product not of capitalism but of pre-capitalist influences. The question thus can be narrowed down to focus on how, precisely, the same radical liberals, the orthodox representatives of political economy and Spencerism in Britain, reacted to the question of imperialism. This is the theoretical aspect of the debate about *free-trade imperialism*. The liberals were undoubtedly severe critics of the mercantilist colonialism that lasted into the early nineteenth century, but does this make them consistent anti-imperialists? A close scrutiny of their theories and opinions shows that the majority of them had at the very least built pro-imperial provisos into their theories. The industrial supremacy of Britain, of its products, production methods and opportunities for innovation was consciously included in their calculations. The link between free trade and Britain's superiority was not just an afterthought, a contingent result, as it were, of their thinking, but was a considered and intended part of it. Their arguments in favour of free trade were not disinterested, but geared to Britain's leading role in the world, which was to be achieved by prudent, non-violent methods. This even applies to Jeremy Bentham, who, as is well known, began his essay on peace by advocating the surrender of all the colonies in the spirit of free trade. Nevertheless, he subsequently let himself be converted to regarding colonies not as a squandering of capital, but as an opportunity to invest surplus capital and to channel the outflow of excess population. His supporters and successors actively promoted imperial programmes, such as the systematic colonization and settlement of Australia and New Zealand. Friedrich List and others reacted to the ideas of free trade with the argument that the universal expansion of free trade ensured that the majority of countries would for ever remain inferior to powers that held the leadership in industry, trade and sea-power. In making this point he fully grasped the intentions of the British theoreticians of free trade. His plea for protectionism was based on powerful reasons and, naturally, it contributed to the weakness of the utilitarian liberal conception of peace beyond Britain's frontiers. We should describe as the dark reverse side of this conception of peace the dogmatization of the idea that free trade has pacifying effects, even if it exacts the price of considerable, worldwide inequalities and imbalances. This conception of peace can only be salvaged if the potential tendencies of a liberalized economy to provoke violence are not repressed or recklessly disregarded.

III

The *republican* version of liberal thinking about peace also has its less attractive side. This lies in a proselytizing universalism that itself represents a threat to peace. This problem first surfaced as early as the generation of Kant's disciples in Germany who had come under the influence of his views on peace politics. Some of these disciples were fully in sympathy with the idea that if the revolutionary French republic wished to transform other states into republics, this could be done by force because it would assist in the propagation of peace.[8] In their hands, most prominently in the writings of the young Joseph Görres, Kant's thinking was transformed into an ideology of intervention with the aim of 'republicanizing as many despotic states as circumstances of time and place allow' and of 'confining all republicanized states within the frontiers indicated by nature' – which we must presumably understand as a plea for the Rhine frontier.[9] It was Carl Schmitt who best summed up this problem, which acquired renewed topicality with the steps taken by international law in the twentieth century to restrict war, the establishment of the League of Nations and other attempts at the peaceful resolution of international conflicts. For Schmitt, the core issue raised by the League of Nations, but by extension also the true meaning of the American Monroe Doctrine, is the systematic way in which the question of the procedure by which we are to decide whether an offence has been committed against international law remains open. Despite all the objections that have been rightly lodged against Schmitt's decisionism, his exaggerated concentration on the necessity of decision-making, there can be no doubt that his insistence on the importance of who makes the decisions is a legitimate question for sociologists. 'The problem does not lie', Schmitt argued in opposition to Friedrich Meinecke, in the normative content of a moral or legal commandment, but in the question of who decides? . . . Of course, everyone wants justice, morality, ethics and peace, no one wants to do wrong; but the only interesting question *in concreto* is always who decides in each specific case what is right, what peace consists in, what the threat to peace or a breach of the peace is, how it is to be eliminated and when a situation is normal and 'pacified', etc. This *quis iudicabit* shows that within the law and the general commandment to be moral a dualism lies concealed that robs these concepts of the ability to stand up to 'power' as simple opposing principles and to swing pendulum-like towards it.[10]

However, an institution that permits an open-ended view of this question will allow a particular power to ensure that its own definition prevails. This means that the power to define is power in a pre-eminent sense. Schmitt sees the same danger in efforts to 'outlaw wars' by means of international agreements and in the use of international law to formulate a so-called 'discriminatory' concept of war.[11] What Schmitt has in mind here is the redefinition of wars into a confrontation between criminals and world police. Whereas a non-discriminatory concept of war conceives of war as a struggle between two or more states and in principle gives each participant the same opportunity to achieve legitimacy, a universalistic intention to outlaw war leads to a situation in which individual parties to a conflict are empowered to proceed against a real or supposed aggressor in the name of humanity. In this way a conflict between two different upholders of order becomes a conflict between order and disorder, the preservers of order and those who disrupt it. Schmitt backs up his fears with a creeping erosion of the concept of neutrality. Where you have a conflict between equal, sovereign states, neutrality, he maintains, is self-evidently possible. But in the dispute between police and criminal every form of behaviour must imply taking sides with order or disorder. Where the discriminatory concept of war gains the upper hand, moral inhibitions towards the enemy are said to disappear along with that enemy's legitimacy, and so does the opportunity for limiting a conflict. Wars would once again become crusades, and aim not just at victory but at the annihilation of the other side in this 'global civil war'. Whether intentionally or not, the result of attempts to institutionalize the republican liberal conception of peace was, in Schmitt's view, an ideological devaluation of the opponent and hence itself a threat to peace.

Needless to say, Schmitt's own intentions become all too clear in the course of this argument. He writes from a profound resentment towards what appears to him to be a conglomerate of Versailles, Geneva and Weimar. There is probably no point in discussing the political aims of his counter-programme: a concrete notion of an ordered society and a new community of the European nations in line with National Socialism. But this does not mean that we can utterly dismiss his line of thought. The fact is that in the American interwar debates about international law and the prospects of peace there is a controversy between universalists and traditionalists in which arguments are deployed that strongly resemble Schmitt's.[12] Here, too, it emerged with a kind of internal cogency that on the universalist side the attempt to outlaw the use of force led to new justifications for the use of force in order to uphold the prohibition of force. This dilemma and the tiny step from universal moral responsibility to a political crusading mentality are highly characteristic for the history of American thinking about peace and also for American foreign policy. Paradoxical as the concept of *free-trade imperialism* may sound at first, there is a similar paradox in the way President Wilson's policy and its intellectual background was referred to as an *imperialism of good intentions*. It follows that we should think of the darker side of the republican conception of peace as consisting of the danger of allowing one's own side unlimited scope for the definition of situations within mechanisms for the peaceful resolution of conflicts, and of casually authorizing the use of force to intervene in order to bring about liberal regimes.

IV

It would appear, then, that power-political realism is by no means as realistic as it pretends to be, but rather uses a highly problematic model of rational action for the analysis of international relations. Similarly, liberal peace concepts may be better at disclosing the realities of normatively oriented actions but cannot be pursued in an unmodified way. If this is the case, then it follows that we need to develop an integrated concept of peace. Such a concept would contain the rule of law, a reliable set of expectations, economic equity and empathy (Dieter Senghaas), and would go beyond a simple confrontation between liberal idealism and power-political realism.[13] However, such an integrated peace concept gains in realism even further if it is based on a sufficient understanding of violent phenomena. What that calls for is to avoid being misled by over-hasty moral reactions into overlooking the kernel of truth contained even in the mythologies of violence, although every step of that kind is bound to encounter emotional resistance. Thus, for example, when great German sociologists, such as Georg Simmel and Max Scheler, interpret the First World War as an opportunity to break with the tragic tendencies of modern culture and as the shattering experience of an ecstatic security that frees our personalities from all inhibitions and makes us malleable again, then we may be tempted to respond with a description of the war experience of the ordinary soldier, his blood, sweat and tears. When a voice like that of Georges Sorel makes itself heard from amidst the workers' movement, saying that strikes and the violence associated with them are legitimate not because they are a means to social reform, but because they enable the oppressed to experience the process of becoming conscious of themselves, then we may be tempted to talk of an alien fascistoid intruder in the history of socialism. When, in a similar vein, Frantz Fanon argues that the violence of the colonialized against the colonizers was necessary to overcome their feelings of inferiority and to regain their own identity, we are tempted to point to the blind alleys of violent decolonialization processes and the consequences of the concentration of military power, for example in Fanon's homeland of Algeria. When in the USA, as the model democracy, violence on the frontier of uncivilized nature and of the 'savage' Indians was the constant accompaniment of the establishment and stabilization of democratic polities, then we are tempted to react by saying that this is no more than a chance contingency that tells us nothing about the nature of the liberal social order.[14] But we might also react quite differently. Perhaps we shall only understand the causes and effects of the First World War if we make the effort to think about it from the standpoint of the enthusiastic war mentality of intellectuals and the mass ecstasy of summer 1914. Perhaps social movements can often only be understood as collective attempts to acquire an identity that do not shrink from violence, rather than as activities in the furtherance of particular interests. Perhaps the curse of establishing a democratic polity by force continues to have an impact through the way in which the myth of regeneration through violence continues to reverberate through the history of that particular polity.

If these suggestions are convincing, this means that the liberal tradition of thinking about peace can only successfully be continued if we overcome our inhibitions about confronting the internal logic of violent phenomena. The effectiveness of these inhibitions can be seen not just in the repression of violence and in the tendency to describe violent phenomena that visibly fail to conform to the patterns of means–ends rationality as 'meaningless', as a regression to an earlier stage of civilization or as unleashing the 'savage' or the 'beast' in us that lurks behind the mask of civilization. It can also be seen in the tradition of research into violence when acts of violence are subsumed into the models of instrumental or normatively oriented action.[15] Needless to say, there is no intention here to deny that it is possible to act violently from rational calculation or even from a sense of moral duty. But even where this is the case, the practice of violence is fuelled by experiences and fantasies not contained in the ideas of 'ends' or 'norms', and this is even clearer where ends and morality did not in fact unleash violent action. As a theoretical task for research on violence, we should therefore formulate the question as follows: how are we to overcome an instrumental understanding of violence without contributing to a broadening of the concept to the point where all human relations appear to be permeated by violence and all social order posited by it? Nietzsche, the 'philosopher with the hammer', proclaimed in violent tones that the smashing of the ancient tablets of the law and the destruction of ancient shrines must be the premise of all new creation. In contrast, we must insist on both the affinity and the ultimate disjunction between creativity and violence.

2

The Modernity of War
Modernization Theory and the Problem of Violence

War and violence are parts of modernity and not just of its prehistory. In this chapter, I use the fact of war in the modern age and the interpretations of this fact by intellectuals as a probe to discuss the adequacy of modernization theory for understanding the social developments of our time. Topics other than war dominate current debate on modernization theory as the most ambitious and influential project of a macro-sociological theory of social change. On the one hand, the collapse of what has been known as 'actually existing socialism' has at least temporarily given a new impetus to modernization theory and has led to a new interpretation of Soviet and Soviet-dominated paths of development. This interpretation treats the Soviet model as an unsuccessful or fake modernization and calls for a complete modernization that can and will overcome civilizational delay.[1] On the other hand, the ecological repercussions that result from successful modernization processes suggest that we should rethink our attitudes towards economic growth and ongoing functional differentiation. This has been argued by Ulrich Beck and Anthony Giddens in their influential and controversial diagnosis and in their programme of a 'reflexive modernization' that leads beyond the 'risk society'. The new self-confidence of modernization theory and the heightened awareness of ecological problems often collide under these conditions so that the supporters of rival views are reduced to sniping at each other – as, for example, during the Frankfurt Congress of the German Sociological Association in 1990.[2] An examination of the topic of 'war' in modernity might show us a way out of the stalemate of this debate. If we seriously consider the fact of war, an idyllic or completely positive view of modernity as is often contained in versions of modernization theory is not to be expected. But this does not mean that pre-modern societies appear in this perspective as a desirable alternative. The question as to what extent societies and states are able to be peaceful forces us back to possible positive meanings of modernization. From such a perspective, the theory of reflexive modernization can be said to concede even too much to traditional modernization theory. This is because it only criticizes it as outdated and inadequate from the historical point of view when the damage done to our environment by industrial economics has become obvious. In other words, it fails to question the core assumptions of traditional modernization theory as such. In my view, it is not only the topics of war and violence, but also subjects like nationalism, religion and secularization, or the development of gender roles, that could serve as the starting-points from which to rethink and re-evaluate modernization theory. Such a re-evaluation does not necessarily lead to a fully fledged alternative to modernization theory, but at least it can initiate the process by which to put it into a more balanced perspective.

The prestige of modernization theory has gone through enormous ups and downs in recent decades. Modernization theory, in its full sense, developed after the Second World War. At first, it looked as if it might offer a paradigm for a sociological and political theory of social change that could solve at least four problems simultaneously. (1) It seemed to provide a historical explanation of the emergence of capitalist economies and democratic politics in northwestern Europe and North America in the early modern age. (2) That historical explanation appeared to allow conclusions about the conditions of economic growth and democracy in other parts of the world, thus providing the guidelines for an active development policy. (3) It made it possible to trace the internal relationships between the economic, political and cultural aspects of modern societies without being locked into the scheme of base and superstructure. And (4) the theory appeared to integrate all the valuable insights provided by the heritage of classical sociological literature (that written from 1890 to 1920) and to transpose them from the level of abstract theorizing into large-scale empirical research programmes. After a phase of hegemony in the 1950s and 1960s this unquestionably fruitful paradigm came under attack from a wide variety of viewpoints. Both the conceptual means of theory construction and the implicit normative assumptions, and indeed the all-encompassing world-view inherent in this paradigm, were sharply criticized and suspected of being ideological. The paradigm of modernization theory thus not only lost its hegemony in the international social sciences, but it was completely on the defensive and, as a result, its productivity suffered. The scornful obituary, *'requiescat in pace'*, that

Immanuel Wallerstein pronounced in 1979 from the vantage-point of the alleged superiority of his 'world systems theory' over modernization theory was followed only a decade later, with the definitive collapse of Soviet-type socialism and the economic rise of East Asia, by an *'exhumetur'* (a call to bring back and revive the approach that had so recently been consigned to eternal peace).[3] In my eyes the real alternative, however, does not lie between the declaration of the death and the miraculous resuscitation of modernization theory. In positive terms, modernization theory simply was not dead enough – that is to say, because it was on the defensive, modernization and differentiation theorists developed certain revisions and additions that cancelled out a straightforward continuation of the work of the 1960s in any case. In negative terms, the refutation of Marxist alternatives to capitalist paths of development is not sufficient to cover up the internal flaws of modernization theory. There remain strong theoretical doubts about a crucial piece of functionalist theorizing, namely differentiation theory, which forms the backdrop of modernization theory. The enormous uncertainties surrounding the concept of 'differentiation', its logical status, the causes, effects, its agents and the timing of differentiation are in themselves enough to justify a new approach instead of simply positioning oneself with an untroubled mind within a supposedly viable tradition. If the debate on modernization theory in the social sciences were only a conflict of political convictions, there would be no point in it at all.

Modernization theory first of all assumes more or less implicitly that modernity is peaceful. The transition from violent struggle to a peaceful way of dealing with conflicts within societies has been essential to the definition of modern societies. But not only the peaceful resolution of major conflicts within states by way of non-violent political procedures is considered modern; individual crime is also said to have changed from spontaneous acts of violence to emotionally controlled forms, for example in property-related crimes.[4] Norbert Elias's theory of civilization, with its claim that an increase in the control of the emotions has coincided with a growth in the complexity of social relations, is a case in point.[5] Many contributions from modernization theory have relatively little to say about the role of violence between states. One of the few exceptions is Walt Rostow, who, in his classic contribution to economic modernization theory on 'The Stages of Economic Growth', dealt with colonial wars, regional aggression and the nuclear confrontation, but mainly in order to counter Marxist explanations and without really giving an alternative explanation himself. If we may be permitted to place modernization theory within a continuum not only with the classics of sociology, but even with the classic traditions of liberalism in social philosophy, then it could be argued that modernization theory still clings to the dream of a non-violent modern age.[6]

How powerful these traditions were and how crucial they are for our conception of modernization can be inferred *ex negativo*, that is, from the way the First World War was dealt with from the point of view of these liberal premises.[7] At the beginning of the twentieth century, those premises were at their most unequivocal among American intellectuals. Thus, the ways in which they dealt with the war are the most instructive for our present purpose. At its beginning, the war was considered to be a sign of European backwardness as compared to American modernity: war as a feudal relic, an expression of European senility and decadence that America intended to avoid. The Russian February Revolution and the overthrow of the Tsar, as well as the intensified debates on whether the USA should enter the war, brought another motif into the foreground: the war as a battle between democracy and autocracy. To view a lack of democracy as the reason for an aggressive foreign policy exactly fitted the liberal philosophy. In his book *Imperial Germany and the Industrial Revolution* (1915), Thorstein Veblen traced the dangers from Germany to the supposed imbalance of economic-technical modernity and political-cultural backwardness in that country.[8] He and his contemporaries, who argued more in terms of intellectual history, viewed Germany as straying from the normal path of modernity. In a sense, this is the birth of the thesis of the German *Sonderweg* in the American social sciences. It is difficult to reconstruct how this idea interacted with the self-congratulatory German version of this thesis in the context of historicism. It was the American variant in particular that via Parsons, on the one hand, and Dahrendorf and Wehler, on the other, became essential for later modernization theory and research on Germany. It seems to me that its strategic meaning within that theory has received too little recognition hitherto. The American variant makes it possible to cling to an evolutionist paradigm of permanent progress with only minor corrections in the face of the World War. If the war was due to the German *Sonderweg*, then there is no need to question other assumptions about the civilized character of modernity. Only then does it make sense to see nationalism, as Veblen did, not as a product of modernity, but as a relic from a barbaric age. Thus the World War did not prod the earlier versions of modernization into questioning the assumption of a modernity free from violence, and so what Lepsius termed the 'exoticization' of some national paths of development made modernization theory relatively immune to the world-historical events of the time.[9]

The theory of 'defensive modernization' goes one decisive step further beyond the classical liberal world-view.[10] It disposes of the notion of a mere parallelism between developments proceeding along the same path. Reinhard Bendix's historically well-informed works attempted to elaborate the insight that only the first nation to modernize has the opportunity to follow its own path autonomously, without time constraints set by others.[11] All other nations find themselves in a force field that arises out of the competition between forerunners and latecomers. This competition could be interpreted as being primarily economic and technical. As a matter of fact, since Veblen the economic advantages of a certain backwardness had already been pointed out. The theory of defensive modernization, however, addresses mainly political and military power disparities. The shock of a military defeat and, sometimes, the insight of elites into the potential danger of such a backlash are seen as triggering forced modernization processes in economic policy as well as in financing and organizing the armed forces. Even the early phases of West European modernization, for example, put pressure on the Russian and Ottoman Empires; army and bureaucracy were modernized there to alleviate this pressure. The most important process of defensive modernization for Germany took place as a result of the disastrous defeat of Prussia by Napoleon in 1806; the reforms of Stein and Hardenberg and the changes in the structures of the old German Reich were supposed to help recovery from the shame of defeat and to prevent its repetition.[12] Less clearly remembered by Germans is how much the nations that were defeated by Germany, for instance France after 1871 or Denmark after 1864, came under pressure to implement a similar defensive modernization. Modern Japanese history cannot be explained without this pressure. Examples could easily be multiplied. What is decisive in the present context is that the theory of defensive modernization relates the development of individual states to one another, recognizes that it is possible to accelerate the modernization process and assumes an interaction between a state's position in the international power structure and its internal modernity. But the theory of defensive modernization assumes all this only up to a certain point. It does not ask whether the economic-political-military competition between states might lead to consequences other than modernization. Phenomena such as the use of power to *perpetuate* inequalities in development are never addressed.

To go beyond the theory of 'defensive modernization' we have to ask: what happens if modernization does not take place or does not succeed? It is possible for states not to learn their lesson or to fail to reform notwithstanding their efforts. An answer to this question has been given by the American sociologist Theda Skocpol in her theory of revolution.[13] As is generally known, Skocpol's approach does not take typical modernization theory as its point of departure, but instead lifts off from Barrington Moore's research, inspired by Marxism, on the social origins of democracy and dictatorship. In these works the role played by violence in changes in the agrarian sector and in the so-called process of original accumulation, as well as in the transformation of the state apparatus, was brought out much more clearly than in conventional modernization theory. Although Skocpol is strongly influenced by Moore's views on rural class structure and the inhibiting role of the land-owning elite, she argues against Moore as well as against modernization theory with the same goal: to propose what she calls a 'gestalt-switch' that would replace the conception of parallel, or at the most interconnected, but mainly endogenous, development processes by a concept that from the very start promotes an *inter*-societal view. Such a view, however, for which there are precedents in the writings of Thorstein Veblen and Leo Trotsky, has to avoid economic reductionism. It stands in contrast, therefore, to Wallerstein's world systems theory, which clearly succumbs to this danger. As a consequence of such a 'gestalt-switch' as Skocpol proposes, the long-term effects attributed to the internal conditions of a society are of lesser importance. Hence, the assumption of a German or Japanese *Sonderweg* loses its force, at least in so far as it is to be traced back to endogenous causes and not to exogenous constellations. This change in perspective focuses attention on crisis situations that states are unable to handle despite vigorous efforts to modernize. Wars are a case in point because they deeply threaten the legitimacy of an existing political order *and* weaken the coercive apparatus of the state in any case, but particularly so in the event of an impending or actual defeat.[14] Accordingly, Skocpol explains revolutions not by referring to the intentions of revolutionary elites or masses as the ultimate form of mobilization, but by pointing out the connection between modernization crises and the constellations of war. Seen from this perspective, the outbreak of the French Revolution appears to have been largely determined by Anglo-French competition in the eighteenth century; in the cases of the Russian revolutions of 1905 and 1917, as well as the Chinese Revolution, the impact of war is immediately apparent. Although the Russo-Japanese War of 1904–5 ended in the defeat of Russia and caused widespread disaffection leading to revolution, the war was relatively confined in terms of location and duration and left the military's ability to function and its loyalty almost unscathed. During the World War the situation was completely different. The rural and urban population revolted, and the military became the vehicle for transmitting the deep dissatisfaction of peasant youth instead of repressing it. The changes brought about by revolution appear thus not so much as putting into practice an ideological intention to better the world, but rather as the desperate continuation of a process of defensive modernization. However, the means used by such revolutionary regimes differ from those used by their competitors and so do the effects, since they move towards the extreme centralization of state power and the total destruction of traditional social structures. Used in this way, however, the term 'modernization' becomes ambiguous. In the revolutions of the twentieth century the competition to modernize produced the opposite of the original models of modernization. And this ambiguity re-emerges in an undisguised fashion with the collapse of this path of development, or what could be called the 'anti-Communist revolution'. Was the Soviet development in itself an attempt to catch up with modernization or was there a need to catch up with modernization after the collapse of the Soviet model? Will such an attempt to catch up with modernization now advance unhindered, or will there be a repetition of the same constellation from which revolutionary forces arose during the First World War and which tried to go beyond defensive modernization? The connection between modernization, war and revolution weakens the assumption that the pressure to modernize as a defensive reaction will surely lead to a more or less successful modernization. Instead, we are made aware that new social orders may arise as a possible result of modernization crises and wars.

The constitution of a new order becomes even more obvious if we take into account the rise of Fascism and its relation to the spirit of war. The hope that the war would have a revitalizing effect was very widespread at the time, not least among such leading German intellectuals as Max Scheler and Georg Simmel. In order to understand this phenomenon adequately, we should think of it not as a continuation of an old-fashioned militarism or of the Social Darwinism of the nineteenth century, but as a highly modern search for a different modernity. Georg Simmel, for example, sees war as a break – or at least as the opportunity to break – with the tragic tendencies of modern culture. All at once, long, winding chains of means and ends can be shortened again, a true sense of time can be regained and it again becomes possible to experience the social character and the malleable nature of individuality. All cultural critics of the prewar era sense very well that modernization could not be pursued solely in terms of increased rationalization. At the same time, hardly any of them believed in the possibility of reversing the process of modernization. Hence the First World War could be considered by all these thinkers as a revelation of the solution they had desperately sought. It seemed that all of a sudden the birth of new values and social ties had taken place before their very eyes. That is why this war was equated with the greatest cultural changes in European history, such as the Reformation and the French Revolution. Apparently, there had been a fundamental change of direction within the modernization process.

For German intellectuals the euphoric cheers about the beginning of a different modernity were soon followed by a hangover. Mussolini and leading Italian intellectuals, in contrast, declared war itself to be the revolution. In this respect they differed from both the Bolsheviks, who saw it as a favourable precondition for a revolution, and from the bellicose German existentialists, who regarded it as a prerequisite for the unique inner metamorphosis of humankind. Some Italian intellectuals had already enthusiastically declared that the Russo-Japanese war of 1904–5, which set off the first Russian revolution, was proof of 'the modernity of war' (Enrico Corradini).[15] Gabriele d'Annunzio joined Nietzsche's praise of acts of violence as a splendid unfolding of Dionysian man and transformed into martial adventures what in Nietzsche had been no more than a philosopher's fantasies on paper. For Mussolini, the First World War became the occasion to break with the vision of a peaceful world that was common to both liberalism and socialism, and to rediscover human beings as 'the most warlike of all species'. Organizationally and institutionally, Italian Fascism tried to establish a warlike regime on a permanent basis. In terms of organization, the Fascist movement was based on the model of a combat group. Violence and terror against enemies in the domestic sphere were not only practised by the Fascist combat groups in an undisguised and systematic fashion, but they were also defended in cases where they clearly served no instrumental purpose. In the beginning, demobilized officers and elite soldiers plus students and schoolboys predominated in this movement. The combat groups were then transformed into a Fascist militia that, though a government agency, had to answer to the party. The wartime economy with its enormous co-ordination and mobilization of all social forces led the charismatic leader to a vision of a new order: one in which all social groups in the corporate state would obey the *will* of one individual and the whole population would form one obedient mass.[16]

As in the case of Soviet Communism, it is obviously possible to interpret Italian Fascism as a more-or-less successful form of dictatorship geared to catching up with modernity. The extent to which its development was successful then becomes an empirical question. However, we should be alert to the fact that the goals proclaimed by Fascism and German National Socialism were by no means either unambiguously modernist or anti-modernist. This is even truer of the results of the policies of those regimes. For this reason Ralf Dahrendorf has ascribed to National Socialism a kind of unintended modernizing function. Moreover, Fascists and National Socialists definitely defended their ideas as models for other countries. How would we now assess National Socialist modernization if Hitler and Nazi Germany had won? Today, this question may seem silly and absurd. But in 1940, it may well have looked as if North America would be the only democratic society left on the planet. If we take such a possibility seriously, then it becomes obvious that the fact that Fascism and Bolshevism perished when they did was highly contingent in nature. Put differently, it becomes evident that the syndrome of developments described by modernization theory might have been replaced by a model that was able to compete and survive, but was devoid of the normative values of the Western cultural tradition.

If we are willing to entertain the idea that the fall of Fascism is a radically contingent occurrence and if, as a result, we accept the proposition that the victory of Western societies over their enemies in the twentieth century is not underpinned by any philosophy of history, then this suggests that we should abandon the attempt to interpret the emergence of modernity in evolutionist terms. We should regard it instead as itself the consequence of a contingent historical constellation. It can be said that such a conclusion was by no means foreign to the German classics of sociology like Max Weber and Werner Sombart. Max Weber did not see the breakthrough of modernity as the automatic result of a cultural process of rationalization that could be taken for granted. In 1913 Sombart had tried to elucidate the constitutive role played by war in processes of bureaucratic rationalization and the cultural formation of the discipline. In his lectures on economic history Weber declared these ideas to be exaggerated and misleading because he considered them monocausal. Nevertheless, he recognized that competition between developing nation-states played a crucial role in the emergence of modernity.[17] In recent British sociology, for example in the writings of Michael Mann, John Hall and Anthony Giddens, this approach has undergone an important renaissance.[18] In a much more sophisticated way than Sombart, these scholars interpret the failure to establish an encompassing empire in Europe and the concomitant permanence of warlike conflict situations as the motor driving the European modernization process. Moreover, it was the common Christian culture that prevented this competition from leading to total mutual extermination. When the introduction of new weapons by military revolution made feudal war strategies more and more obsolete, the entire web consisting of the state, the military and the economy underwent a radical transformation. New weapons required new technologies for their production, a new organization and new methods of training for the military, as well as a new system of financing. Many rulers of small territories simply could not afford the necessary changes. Arranging the finance was more or less feasible only in places where either geographical advantages or the existence of an already advanced money economy made it possible to bring the relation of taxes and military expenditure swiftly into balance. In other cases it took an enormous concentration of resources by the state and the elimination of all intermediate social bodies if a society was to prove able to survive the military competition. England's economic and geographical situation predisposed it for a constitutional development which is often seen as the prototype of modernization. However, it is open to question whether England really went through a process of modernization or rather was spared the pressures to develop an overpowering state apparatus.[19]

Such an explanation does not set out to ignore deep-seated traditions of culture and statehood or to minimize economic and technical developments. However, it clearly aims at conceptualizing the emergence of modernity as a contingent constellation, though not as a unique and non-recurring event. In this nexus of cultural, economic, political and military developments the military revolution between 1560 and 1660 and the history of wars and civil wars played a crucial role largely ignored in sociology.[20] Actually, even this is an understatement because it does no more than express the sheer fact that wars were involved in the emergence of modernity. But wars and civil wars have shaped modernity as we know it at its innermost core. It was Stephen Toulmin, in his book *Cosmopolis*,[21] who really hit the nail on the head. The unbearably complacent image of history that is biased in favour of Protestantism and that depicts a linear upswing of commerce, cities, book printing, philosophy, natural science and national sovereignty allegedly based on the Renaissance and Reformation cannot be considered an adequate description of the early modern age, an age that was in fact characterized by the greatest confusion, religious fanaticism and 'counter-Renaissance'. The modern age can only be depicted adequately by pointing out several possible patterns of modernization, of which only one prevailed. Important aspects of the early cultural modernization of the Renaissance, such as the emphasis on rhetoric and sensuality, and the insight that all thinking takes place at a particular time and place, were more or less suppressed in the further course of modernization. Humanist ideas of a peaceful European order fell victim to Hobbes's rationalist philosophy, which gave classic expression to the vision of a world composed of sovereign nation-states *avant la lettre* and before its historical realization. In Toulmin's view,

Descartes's quest for certainty, which in the philosophic reconstructions of modernity often marks the beginning of the modern age, is an attempt to pull oneself up by one's bootstraps out of the unbearably violent confrontations of post-medieval disintegration. Rationality is not idolized because of its evident validity, but this idolization expresses the extent of the faith that desperate people place in it.

I am well aware of the fact that the overview I present here contains many aspects, but none of them in adequate detail or depth. The dream of a modernity free of violence; the role of defensive modernization; the connections between modernization, war and revolution; the emergence of Fascism from the spirit of war; the role of war in the emergence of modernity and the impact of war and civil war on the essence of modernity – all these aspects are just briefly sketched here. However, it is not by amassing details, but only by understanding their interrelationships that the analysis of war can enable us not only to find answers to specific problems of historical sociology, but also to arrive at conclusions about modernity and about the relative significance of modernization theory.[22] I hope it will be clear that I do not wish to use the formula 'the modernity of war' in order to welcome the possibility of war – be it in a new spirit of militarism or from an ideology of value-free *realpolitik*. Neither do I intend to use it in order to describe the type of war that can be justified on 'modern' universalistic moral premises. Nor do I wish to encourage anyone to project the desire for peace onto pre-modern societies. Hopefully, what this provocative use of the phrase 'the modernity of war' will achieve is to undermine the complacent equation of modernization with a decreasing likelihood of war. After the end of the twentieth century, history and our immediate present force us to combine an investigation into the conditions of peace with a sober analysis of specifically modern tendencies to war. With these thoughts in the background, I draw four main conclusions for modernization theory.

First, the subject of war demonstrates how inadequate it is to conceive of modernization as a homogeneous whole with parallel developments in culture, economics and politics. The tight coupling of social subsystems in modernization theory has changed its character from an achievement to a deficiency. The emphasis on cultural variability and the realization that political and economic orders can be connected in a variety of ways have turned our attention towards the loose coupling of societal subsystems, in contrast to both Marxism and modernization theory, which share a common, but what seems increasingly to be a problematic, assumption of their tight interconnection.[23] Accordingly, we have to distinguish different dimensions of modernization and allow for variable relations between them. Complicated discrepancies between social subsystems, attempts to supersede these discrepancies and conflicts, various repercussions springing from these attempts or the losses of modernity and the defence of old orders by new means should be noted here. Thus we always have multiple modernities, different roads to and through modernity (Therborn), and are in need of a 'comparative historical sociology of modernity'.

Second, the thoughts presented here increase the need to justify the normative premise underlying modernization theory. If modernization theory gives up its claims to linearity and teleology and drops the talk of historical inevitability, then normative goals such as democratization can no longer be justified by the evidence of functional advantages. This does not prevent us from thinking of the functional advantages that democracy has. But, evidently, functional advantages are not always realized, and the problem of normative justification is not identical with the proof of functional benefits. Thus we need a clear consciousness of the reasons that make democracy the yardstick of progress, despite the fact that we have no historical guarantee for this progress. Even when modernity is seen very pessimistically, the terms 'modernity' and 'modernization' often still express the longing for such a guarantee. I personally am not sceptical about some crucial values of modernity, but I am deeply sceptical about such a belief in the firmness of foundations.

Third, research on the role of war in social change reveals the impact of international configurations on the precise nature of modernization processes. The relapse into a debate that is restricted to endogenous factors is, in a way, sociology's birth defect, regardless of whether one's approach is culturalist or materialist. This birth defect may prove fatal for the discipline and its credibility.[24]

Fourth, the cultural importance of war reminds us of the deep ambiguity of modern culture. To increase rationality can mean very different things, and the possible counter-notions to rationality are diverse. Modernity is not an ultimate stage in which the creation of values has come to an end; we have to understand the genesis of new values and the tensions between them and existing institutions. The abstract achievements of sociological theory construction have to be combined with historians' familiarity with individual facts and a sensitivity to cultural shifts if modernization theory is to provide an adequate conception of our time and its genesis.

3

Ideologies of War
The First World War as Reflected in the Contemporary Social Sciences

> A later age will scarcely be able to comprehend the lack of will, not to
> say, the submissiveness, with which writers of every hue surrendered to
> the fact of war in the belief that they could find their way back to a new
> life there. There was no spiritual or cultural current of thought in
> Germany and outside it which was not prepared to serve the ideology
> of war. Everyone wished to use the war as a source of strength.[1]

These sentences, which were composed and published in 1915 by Emil
Lederer, the economist and sociologist, prophetically encapsulate the
irritation that persists down to the present day in the reaction to the
writings of the intellectuals during the First World War. The social
sciences were no exception to this. It was not just individual writers
or schools or disciplines or nations who experienced a kind of catastrophic lapse from the true path of scientific objectivity and placed
themselves at the service of a more or less official interpretation of
the war and a war propaganda machine. If it had been a matter of
individual authors, it would be meaningful to look for hitherto unnoticed continuities in their works or to root around in their biographies and personalities in search of the causes of any abrupt change
of attitude. We might then be able to explain why a sensitive aesthete
like Georg Simmel, for example, was able to become an existentialist
interpreter of the war; or why Josiah Royce, the venerable and vener-
ated representative of German idealism in the USA, should have
turned into a rabid pamphleteer. If it had been a matter of individual
schools of thought, then we might be inclined to consider what light
their war writings could shed on their internal problems. But writers
of every shade of opinion – rationalists and irrationalists, idealists and

anti-idealists, Neo-Kantians, philosophers of life and pragmatists – are all to be found among the intellectuals inspired by the war. Even Marxism did not make its adherents immune from the hopes that attached themselves to the war. If it had merely been a matter of individual disciplines, the inquiring gaze could turn aside from philosophy, theology or history, and hope for better things from the social sciences, which are so deeply immersed in reality, or the natural sciences, which are so remote from politics. But here, too, disappointment is not far off. The social sciences in Europe, unlike those in America, had scarcely begun to differentiate themselves from the humanities and the old-style political sciences, and the picture they present does not differ from them in essentials. And as for the natural sciences, there is an abundance of statements about the defective state of those disciplines in enemy countries and of vows to ignore their findings in the future. If we were talking only about German intellectuals, we might regretfully interpret our irritation with the behaviour of the intellectuals in the light of a thesis about the German *Sonderweg*. But the interpretation of the World War as a conflict of cultures and principles is to be found on all sides, and everywhere it was the intellectuals who were entrusted with defining the values being fought over. If we proceed from the assumption that the reaction of the contemporary social sciences to the First World War is known in its main outlines, the depressing conclusion must be that in no country did these disciplines differ in any respect from the general intellectual currents of thought. They not only failed to provide more 'scientific' knowledge about 'reality', but they did not even show that they had the will to move in that direction.

Of course, it is at best only the historians who could content themselves with such a conclusion, and not the social scientists. For historians, an investigation into the attitudes of further representatives of the social sciences would fill out the picture, but not alter it in principle. Social scientists, by contrast, would have to ask themselves two additional questions. On the one hand, they must inquire into the relationship between paradigmatic fundamental assumptions in the social sciences and attitudes towards the war. Even if the assumptions underlying the ideas of individual schools of thought do not reveal a particular affinity for the spirit of war, there may still have been theoretical premises typical of the discipline and going beyond individual schools that preformed their perception of the war in a particular manner; at the least, we may say that it is also of current interest to study any possible tension between such fundamental paradigmatic assumptions and the overwhelming events of the war, as well as any attempts to resolve that tension. On the other hand, it is reasonable to expect the social sciences to satisfy a higher standard of explanation. They cannot evade the question of why the representatives of their discipline acted and spoke just like everybody else.

I shall attempt to make at least an initial attempt to tackle the programme implied here in four stages. I shall begin with a typology of the reactions to the First World War of the sociological classics (1) in Germany and (2) in the rest of Europe. I shall then go on to look separately (3) at philosophy and the social sciences in the USA, because there the tension between the prewar assumption of a world that is becoming more and more peaceable and democratic, and the reality of war, took on particularly interesting forms. In a further step (4) I shall examine the origins of the thesis that war has a revitalizing or regenerative effect on a culture and a society that is felt to be in crisis, and finally (5), I shall present a hypothesis to explain the striking similarity in the behaviour of the intellectuals. This hypothesis is one that I shall borrow from one of the few contemporary attempts at a 'sociology of the World War' that is worth taking seriously.

I

The period of the First World War is of particular importance in the history of sociology, among other reasons because the classics and the true founders of the discipline were able to formulate their reactions to the events of the day from the standpoint of their mature life's work. It is generally agreed today that although Auguste Comte and Herbert Spencer have frequently been cited as the founders of sociology, they should in fact be treated more as academic outsiders and forerunners, while the authentic academic institutionalization of the subject really dates back to authors who produced their crucial writings between 1890 and 1920, writings that act as touchstones for the discipline to the present day.

To name names, in Germany we must think of Max Weber, Georg Simmel, Ferdinand Tönnies and also Werner Sombart; in France, the outstanding name is that of Émile Durkheim; in Italy, Vilfredo Pareto; in the USA, there are Charles Horton Cooley, William Isaac Thomas, George Herbert Mead and also Thorstein Veblen; and in Russia, Pitirim Sorokin. In Britain, where sociology had great difficulty in establishing itself as an institution, the situation is more complicated. My own discussions refer principally to the authors above, as well as to a number of philosophers, such as Henri Bergson and John Dewey, who were directly involved in the debates. Of course, by placing the emphasis retrospectively on authors who subsequently influenced the development of the discipline, I deviate from the view of people's reputations at the time and so follow a guideline that, initially at least, rules out other conceivable approaches. For example, we could study the behaviour of the organized institutions of the discipline or of all its representatives, including those who have since fallen into oblivion. On this point I would simply note that during the war the German Sociological Society followed a war propaganda line and even after the war isolated attempts at self-critical reflection were drowned in a veritable barrage of criticism.[2] Among the forgotten sociologists, we should perhaps remind ourselves of Johann Plenge. It was this sociologist from Münster who coined the catchword of the 'ideas of 1914', even though he thought about it more in terms of the totally rationalized organization of society than with the overtones of cultural regeneration that it acquired in the popular mind at the time.[3] Of the sociologists who have become classics, Sombart, Weber and Simmel, in particular, represent three clearly distinguishable types of reaction to the war.

Shortly before the war, Werner Sombart had published a detailed study on 'war and capitalism'.[4] This book, which he wrote in 1912, develops the connection between war and capitalism in sharp contrast to the materialist conception of history. He does not inquire whether wars originate from the development of capitalism, but instead asks whether, and to what extent, capitalism is itself an effect of war. He does not dispute the viability of the approach adopted by historical materialism, but simply declares it to be unproductive of further knowledge. Nor does he deny the destructive impact of war on economic life, particularly on the capitalist economy. Among its direct effects, he mentions the damage to trade relations; the excessive burden of taxation; the disruptive effects upon transport; state bankruptcies; and, above all, the prevention of capital formation by the tributes levied by the belligerent states. But all this does not add up to the essence of his argument, which is that despite all this destruction the emergence of capitalism was made possible in the period from the sixteenth to the eighteenth century by the formation of states and conflicts between states. His argument proceeds on several levels. He wishes to show that war has led to the emergence of modern armies, and that, in his words, these armies 'foster the capitalist system, (1) as creators of wealth, (2) creators of convictions [*Gesinnungen*], and (above all!) (3) as creators of markets'.[5] Modern armies create convictions in the sense that for the first time they establish on a massive scale the discipline that we are accustomed to see as a fundamental component of the capitalist spirit and industrial labour. Armies were effective as the creators of wealth and markets because the need to supply them with weapons, but also with uniforms and food, led to the growth of large production units. They indirectly accelerated mining and metallurgy and they rationalized modes of production and commerce. The state organization of the army is accompanied by the rationalization of the state itself since the state is compelled to ensure a constant supply of equipment and a continuity in administration.

Starting with Max Weber in his *General Economic History*, critics maintained that Sombart's claims were exaggerated.[6] Had they been valid, the huge expenditure on the army 'outside the West, under the Great Mogul and in China' should have led to the development of capitalism. Conversely, the increasing tendency for the state to provide for the needs of the army should in itself have restricted the growth of capitalism. At the time of the Second World War, John Nef, the American economic historian, produced a theory directed against Sombart about the harmful effects of arms manufacture on economic progress.[7] This was followed by an extensive debate.[8] One of its conclusions was the undoubtedly justified realization that Sombart fails to correlate the constructive and destructive features of war that are relevant to the emergence of capitalism. Furthermore, he makes no effort to separate the effects of war from other, long-term trends. This means that his theory can easily lead to false empirical assessments in particular instances. This is not to assert that the theory is completely without value. After all, it does draw our attention to one possible explanation for the rise of capitalism that is clearly differentiated from evolutionist interpretations, from Weber's emphasis on the specific characteristics of Western rationalism, and from Marxist attempts at explanation. In a manner reminiscent of the work of a number of younger British sociologists (Hall, Mann, Ashworth/Dandeker) of our own day, we might argue with Sombart that even if it is not the war, it is the absence of a European superstate and the resulting permanent warlike relations between individual states that could be deemed to be the essential dimension by which economic centralization and cultural discipline were achieved. According to John Hall,[9] it is well known that since the fall of the Roman Empire and despite the efforts of Charlemagne, Frederick Barbarossa, Napoleon and Hitler, it has not proved possible to establish an all-encompassing state in Europe. However, the developing competition between states was acted out in the common cultural arena of the Christian faith. The absence of strong states or a common cultural arena, however, would have been enough to block the development of capitalism.

The outbreak of the First World War did not disappoint Sombart's historical expectations. It was self-evident to him that war would retain its importance as long as – literally! – 'men shall determine the fate of nations'.[10] On the basis of his theory, the war could have led, on the one hand, to a precise study of its economic, social and psychological effects upon the societies affected. On the other hand, it could have been the occasion for taking a fresh look at the old question of the causes of war according to historical materialism. This would have meant either accepting a version of the theory of imperialism, or else positing a counter-theory. However, Sombart failed to seize any of these theoretical options. *Merchants and Heroes*, the book he published in 1915, signalled its general thrust with its sub-title, 'Patriotic Reflections'. It dismisses as superficial every interpretation of war as the product of economic interests or the aspirations to power of nation-states. According to Sombart, this war, like every war, is a war of religion, in this case, the life-and-death struggle between West European civilization and the German character. For Sombart, England, not France, is the prototype of this Western civilization. Sombart presents us with a comprehensive polemic against utilitarianism and eudae-monism, against individualism and the commercialization of all realms of human activity. Following the critique of utilitarianism that is fundamental to sociology, he denies that we can picture societies as aggregates of individuals and actions as the result of motives designed to maximize pleasure. Any notion of freedom as the space for individual free will is dismissed as just as inadequate as the reduction of history to the evolution of individualistic social relations. For the most part, this kind of argument had remained abstract in the classical sociological writers, whereas here, thanks to the identification of utilitarianism with the English character, it degenerates into a nationalistic tirade to which those of Sombart's contemporaries who had a deeper knowledge of England reacted with distaste, notwithstanding any political sympathy they might have felt for him.[11] 'Frequently, we really imagine that we are fighting against a department store.'[12] Any non-utilitarian currents of thought in Britain are traced back to the Irish blood of individual writers. However, the German spirit – which is viewed in similarly essentialist terms – resists the subjection of the world to that outlook. The war that was raging was said to be Nietzsche's war, but not only Nietzsche's. It was also the war against utilitarianism and eudaemonism, and in rejecting these philosophies and fighting against them 'the hostile brothers, Schopenhauer and Hegel, Fichte and Nietzsche, were of one mind, as were Classics and Romantics, the representatives of Potsdam and Weimar, the old Germans and the new'.[13] Sombart certainly is not completely mistaken here; but over and above this assertion of a German tradition critical of utilitarianism, he seeks to set up a positive counter-model to the self-centred individual of the British philosophical tradition. Such an individual is defined not by self-interest but by selflessness, generosity of spirit and the intensification of self; his virtues are 'self-sacrifice, loyalty, lack of guile, reverence, bravery, piety, obedience, and kindness'.[14] The individual who possesses these virtues in their pure form is the very essence of the hero, and 'to be German is to be a hero'.[15] War, however, is the fruit of a heroic world-view and is necessary to curb the mercantile spirit. Thus the unpolitical cultural patriotism of German Classicism or Nietzsche's insistently anti-nationalist pro-Europeanism, and in general the predominantly aesthetically based ideal of personality, are unhesitatingly turned into the stages leading to German militarism. At this point, then, Sombart's book becomes a travesty of history that we can only interpret as the mark of a profound feeling of meaningless-ness in the culture of the prewar period. It is true that Sombart had already produced highly speculative ideas about the psychology of nations before, for example in his attempts to trace the source of the spirit of capitalism to enduring characteristics of the Jews. But on that occasion he had armed himself against criticism by proclaiming in advance that he was consciously adopting a one-sided perspective for methodological reasons. Now, however, capitalism appears to him unambiguously as the emanation of a mercantile spirit, and this in turn is interpreted as the expression of an individual nation; the life of states is the life-and-death struggle of individual nations striving to develop their individuality; victory in this struggle belongs to *the* nation that is able to curb the spirit of commercialism that levels everything down and destroys culture.

The thrust of Max Weber's writings on war and the nation-state is clearly very different from Sombart's, although his German national-ism in the prewar period and his patriotic enthusiasm for the war were no less marked. Weber's work contains no elaborate conception of the sociology of the nation-state or of the military. It is well known that the section of *Economy and Society* entitled 'The "Nation" as a Power Structure', where we might soonest have expected to find one, remained a fragment. Nevertheless, we can find in many places in his writings evidence of the importance of the army as an institution and the interests of the nation-state as a normative reference-point for Weber's life, both public and private. For Weber, as for Sombart, military discipline is the quintessential form of early mass discipline. As a bureaucracy, the modern army becomes the prototype of an organizational tool in the hands of leaders. The idea that since the early modern age the state has progressively gained control of all our juridi-cal norms runs right through Weber's sociology of law. And what is most remarkable about this process from the point of view of theory is that while for Weber market forces are indeed the driving force of the monopolization of violence, the result of that process consists in the simultaneous expansion of the market and the strengthening of the state. In other words, his argument includes the idea that the state and the market are not simply irreconcilable opposites, but that the development of the nation-state and the establishment of market relations are all part of a *single* process. The best-known testimony to Weber's ideas about the nation-state is to be found in his Inaugural Lecture in Freiburg in 1895, 'The Nation-State and Economic Policy'.[16] In this lecture, Weber rejected, with his characteristic acerbity, any faith in immanent value criteria for science in general and economics in particular. A realistic and responsible yardstick was to be found not in the advancement of happiness or justice, but singly and solely in the survival of the nation in a Darwinian struggle for existence. What raises Weber's text above others is his clarity about norms and his distance from all particular interests, since this creates the opportunity to judge classes and parties from a higher vantage-point, even though he fails to ask whether a national interest conceived in a non-partisan or supra-partisan manner can be shown to exist. The survival of the nation and its self-enhancement, its cultivation, are the values that science and politics must cherish. The assumptions of classical economics that world trade has a pacifying effect are simply brushed aside. In a discussion of the results of his study of agricultural workers in the provinces east of the Elbe, he remarks that

> As we have seen, the economic struggle between the nationalities runs its course even under the semblance of 'peace'. . . . Yet the sombre gravity of the population problem alone is enough to prevent us from being eudaemonists, from imagining that peace and happiness lie waiting in the womb of the future, and from believing that anything other than the hard struggle of man with man can create any elbow-room in this earthly life. . . . As far as the dream of peace and human happiness is concerned, the words written over the portal into the unknown future of human history are: *'lasciate ogni speranza'*.[17]

And so forth in many variations. Economic development does not lead to the reduction of power struggles, but is itself no more than these power struggles in a different shape, struggles from which there is no escape. It should be noted that in arguing thus Weber does not distinguish *empirically* between the violent nature of an exploitative capitalism, whether imperialist or colonial, and a peaceful trade based on exports, but that *conceptually* he makes a pre-judgement to the effect that in principle all social relations are based on power struggles.

Max Weber responded to the First World War with a plethora of published statements and analyses. They tower above the published statements of the chauvinistic professors who were in fashion at the time.

Ironically, however, his rejection of pseudo-historical and pseudo-metaphysical interpretations of the war was founded on his conviction that the eternal conflict between nations called for no justification. Admittedly, his writings, too, contain signs that he believed in a German cultural mission, but such signs became increasingly feeble. His war writings are no ideological tracts, but neither are they socio-logical analyses of the causes and effects of war. They can be described in essence as the contributions of an intellectual who wished to play a direct role in the strategic debates in both foreign and domestic politics. And in fact he gradually advanced to become the leading light among the moderate university professors. In this context, some of his statements appear clear and far-sighted even today. His warn-ings that the expansion of the U-boat war would lead to the entry of the USA into the war are an example. But nothing happened to shake his conviction that the nation was the supreme value – regardless of all questions about forms of government – or to diminish his emotional commitment to the idea of politics as struggle and not self-determination. He defends the need for the German Reich to pursue a policy of colonial expansion and also its claims to continen-tal hegemony, ostensibly in the interests of the smaller states of Central Europe. There is, however, a change in his emphasis on the liberal ideal of upholding the rights of the individual. The tendency of German intellectuals to glorify the state, the notorious 'ideas of 1914', served in his eyes only to pave the way for the further expansion of the bureau-cracy. He therefore opposes the warnings against too much individu-alism or democracy on the grounds that the real question is whether, 'given the basic fact of the irresistible advance of bureaucratization, it is at all possible to salvage any remnants of individual freedom of movement in any sense'.[18] In particular, he asks how to curb the growing power of state officialdom and to control it effectively, and how the limits in principle to the achievements of the bureaucracy are to be recognized and compensated for. At this point, Weber's indi-vidualist instincts merge imperceptibly with those in favour of im-perialism, above all on the issue of how to construct and consolidate an appropriate foreign policy and mass support for a drive for expan-sion. Kant's notion of the peaceable character of a republican constitu-tion is transformed in Weber's hands into the question of the domestic political preconditions for the support of a well-calculated offensive foreign policy. His political demands, such as for the democratization of the Prussian three-class voting system and the conversion of the Reich executive to a parliamentary system, emerge from analyses in which he pioneered the study of the connections between the ability to act in foreign affairs and the nature of the domestic constitution. This is the scientific yield of his war writings. The amateurish nature of the Kaiser's foreign policy, the compliance of the apolitical civil service, the political immaturity of the German population – all this could only be changed in Weber's view by a genuine selection of leaders through a struggle for a mass following and by a powerful parliament. *'Only a politically mature people* is a "nation of masters" [*Herrenvolk*], which means a people controlling the administration of its affairs itself, and, through its elected representatives, sharing decisively in the selection of its political leaders.'[19] In short, a democracy on the British pattern as the tool of an imperial world politics – that is the formula that might well sum up Weber's thinking during the war period. For the most part, Weber heaped abuse on all those who were opposed to such thinking, dismissing them as 'literati' and their ideas as the products of 'an ethics of conviction'.[20] We can consider the converse question of whether Weber's nationalism did not lead to theoretical deficits in the core of his work. The fragment of *Economy and Society* that we have referred to might well have led him to a historical downgrading of the nation-state in the past, and hence perhaps also in the future. However, as a *transitional* historical phenomenon, it is difficult for the nation-state to serve as the ultimate normative reference-point. In the same way, the thesis of the eternally changing forms of the power struggle is in the last analysis unhistorical in conception. It is strange to accuse Weber, the great historical thinker among the classics of sociology, of unhistorical thought. But such an accusation is supported by the observation that he introduces his concept of the state in terms of characteristics – such as clear territoriality and the legitimate monopoly of the means of violence – that did not become defining features until the advent of the modern nation-state. Thanks to the war, Weber refined his analysis of the links between domestic and foreign policy. Nevertheless, it would seem that for political reasons he protected his conception of the nation-state from every revision.

In Georg Simmel's writings on the war we have a third way of reacting to the war on the part of a leading representative of early German sociology. It is true that in his celebrated *Sociology* of 1908, he claimed that conflict and struggle played an essential part in the causation or modification of social forms, and he even designated struggle as a form of sociality in its own right. To this day, he is therefore regarded as the founder of so-called conflict sociology. However, the war played no more than a tiny role in these discussions. An academic outsider whose career suffered because he was a Jew, Simmel might not be thought to be predisposed to don the mantle of German nationalism. Nevertheless, he responded to the war with a series of writings some of which were collected and appeared in 1917 in a volume with the title *War and Spiritual Decisions.* In this book 'the will to Germany' appears as an unprovable but also an irrefutable supreme value. Simmel, who had finally become a professor in Strasbourg, a town that was a bone of contention between France and Germany, interpreted the war with the aid of his theory of culture, which emerged from the contradictions of creativity caught between form and the process by which form became independent. His interpretation of modern life in the prewar period as a 'tragedy of modern culture' had emphasized how the increasing importance of money leads to the constant elongation of the chains of ends and means; the paralysis of creative activity due to the inability to assimilate the excess of cultural works and hence to enjoy the experience of perfecting one's own culture; and the emptiness of a sense of time that is familiar only with the cyclical repetition of everyday life or the ideal timelessness of meaningful values. Simmel goes on to interpret war as the great rupture with these tragic tendencies of modern culture. In his view, war transmits to us an insight into the social, 'organic' nature of our individuality – not as a cognitive insight, however, but as the deeply moving existential experience of an ecstatic feeling of security that liberates our personality from old inhibitions and opens it up to social impulses once again. In theoretical terms there is a direct parallel here with Durkheim's theory of 'collective effervescence' in his sociology of religion of 1912. Durkheim analyses religious experience as a group ecstasy that has the function of shaping identity and creating social bonds. The experience of the future efficacy of actions taking place in the historical medium of war leads, according to Simmel, to the recuperation of an authentic experience of time. Here we perceive parallels to the contemporary critique of culture in Bergson, who had regarded as crucial the loss of an authentic experience of temporality due to the spatialization of time. Ultimately, war leads us back from the over-elongated chains of ends and means to the elemental purposes of sheer survival. What Simmel hopes from this military experience is a 'gentler, less blasé, I should like to say more reverential relation to the objects of everyday use'.[21] At the start of the war, Simmel seemed to have promised himself a complete break with the culture of the prewar period. The longer the war lasted, the more subdued his tone became; his hopes become more modest and are reduced to the residual effects of individuals' experience of war. There is no sign of a sociology of the causes of war in his writings; the sociology of the effects of war is confined to socio-psychological effects, and even these contain no empirical findings but only the pipe-dreams of an intellectual.[22]

Sombart, Weber and Simmel represent three profoundly different reactions to the war on the part of German sociology. We can ask whether the inclusion of further intellectual heroes would change the picture significantly. I believe that the answer is in the negative, although I cannot demonstrate this at length here.

The most important author not to be discussed here is Max Scheler, although, admittedly, his prewar writings only belong to the margins of sociology. In his writings on the war he goes far beyond Simmel in providing an interpretation of war based on the ideas of *Lebensphilosophie*. His starting-point is the question of how it is possible for an age dominated by death and hatred not to end up in despair, but instead to inspire with enthusiasm all those whom Scheler describes as follows:

> Believers in life as opposed to believers in the machine, believers in love as opposed to believers in clever organization and legal contracts, believers in free action as opposed to believers in 'necessary developments'; believers in the person as opposed to believers in the work, believers in the individual as opposed to believers in the law, believers in the creative spirit as opposed to believers in the calculations of reason.[23]

He reckons Social-Darwinist explanations of war among the dangers of utilitarian Anglo-Saxon thought against which he mobilizes German traditions. As the war progressed, his attitude became less simplistic. The somewhat ingenuous question about the 'causes of anti-German feeling' is less marked by the self-righteousness typical of the majority of war writings, and more concerned to make the German 'idea of freedom' more comprehensible. His 'second conversion' to Catholicism, in 1916, transformed Scheler, the echo of whose German nationalism could still be heard, into a supporter of Catholic social politics and the peace programme of Erzberger's Centre Party.

Leopold von Wiese[24] is another scholar who refers to the 'homesickness of the individual for the maternal womb of the masses', but he also warns against the threat to realistic policies posed by constant enthusiasm and an emotionally charged rhetoric. His idea of a realistic policy, though, is the uprising of Oriental colonies against a hated Britain and a new European imperialism in which, after the great reckoning with the British, Germany will be able to pursue a creative world politics. Meanwhile, Robert Michels, the great sociologist of party organization, develops from syndicalism and internationalist socialism into the crassest form of nationalism – not German, but Italian nationalism, oddly enough, in his case – and as an early supporter of Mussolini, he defends Italy's entry into the war against Austria and, subsequently, Germany.[25]

Ferdinand Tönnies is concerned to arrive at a balanced moral judgement on the question of war guilt and places his trust in the ability of the neutral nations, the women's movement and the rationality of science to hold the warlike spirit of men in check. This may appear morally superior to many people today, but from the point of view of sociological theory I do not detect any great merit in it. His hostility to the 'Nietzsche cult' and his well-developed social reformist proclivities, as well as his great knowledge of Britain and its history, should have predestined him not simply to distance himself from the chauvinist publications of his colleagues, but to present his own sociological analyses in opposition to them. His book *The State in England and Germany*, which appeared while the war was still in progress, would have furnished him with that opportunity.[26] However, his assessment of the situation is also undermined by a nationalistic standpoint. In stark contrast to Max Weber, as if in an inverted mirror image, Tönnies maintains that in Britain foreign policy is conducted by a 'cabinet aristocracy' without parliamentary controls and that 'Caesarism' is a distinct danger, whereas in Germany the farmers and the middle classes are strong and independent, the urban working class clearly articulates its own political will, federal elements hamper the growth of every attempt at over-centralization, and the monarchy, together with its armed forces and its civil service, forms a welcome counterweight to the aristocracy with its plutocratic tendencies. There can be no doubt that in the climate of the time every admission that there might be defects in German constitutional life as compared with British society was scandalous and it called for personal courage. In this sense, Tönnies's critical comment that in Britain bureaucracy and respect for the police were less developed is important. But for all his criticism and his support for reforms – such as the reform of the Prussian voting system – the general thrust of his book prevents him from breaking out of the parameters of the German critique of Britain.

II

If we limit the study of the intellectual effects of the First World War to Germany, this can easily result in a distorted picture. It can give rise to the impression that enthusiasm for the war and what Hermann Lübbe called 'academic chauvinism' was confined to Germany. In truth, however, similar features can be found in France, Italy and Austria, and, to a lesser degree, in Russia, Britain and, later, the USA. However, the relations between a nationalist point of view and the enlightened, universalist ideals of a peaceful world order turn out to be significantly different from those obtaining in Germany.

For France, this can be briefly illustrated with reference to the two major philosophers, Émile Boutroux and Henri Bergson, as well as to Émile Durkheim, who was the undisputed leading sociologist, both intellectually and institutionally. All of them had been profoundly influenced by German thought and struggled with the question of how that thought was connected to German militarism. Boutroux lapses into a chauvinistic tone when he calls German culture *'une barbarie savante'* and equates it with the threat represented by the Huns.[27] His accurate and sociologically crucial insight that the war of 1914 was no longer a matter of a passage of arms between two armies, conducted according to rules, but a war that was in the process of becoming total is weakened by the fact that this new quality of the war is simply ascribed to the utter lack of restraint on the part of the Germans. Despite this, Boutroux ends with an appeal not to pay the Germans back in their own coin, but to ensure that the values of humanism should survive intact.

Henri Bergson's book on the war is particularly noteworthy because it defends the French cause with arguments drawn from *Lebensphilosophie*. Whereas Simmel, Scheler and also Sombart had called on *Lebensphilosophie* in support of German nationalism, and maintained that both Anglo-Saxon utilitarianism or materialism and French rationalism were inorganic, Bergson arrived at the very different conclusion that the 'mechanical' character of Prussia was repellent and hostile to life. This example shows how little abstract philosophical traditions predetermine for which concrete political goals they are used. According to Bergson, the Prussian state was a thoroughly artificial construct, with its core in the army and a notoriously mechanical administration. The entire character of the nation bore its stamp. In Prussia, the military had become the cultural bedrock of industrialization so that industry and the army had been able to reinforce one another ever since. Even German scholarship contributed to the mechanization of the spirit, rather than being an emancipation from it leading to a spiritualization of matter. If in this mechanized universe the need for a new vitality were to be expressed, it would take the form of an enthusiasm for one's own strength, beyond all respect for law. In that event, vitality would discard the sense of justice and truth. However, that would be an error since without a commitment to higher ideals, no moral force can survive. Everything mechanical is used up by use, 'tandis que l'énergie morale qui s'alimente à un idéal éternellement vivant se revivifie sans cesse elle-même et sans cesse aussi refait son instrument organisé, comme une âme qui reconstituerait son corps' ['while the moral energy which feeds on an eternally living ideal constantly refreshes itself and constantly refashions its own means, like a soul that reconstitutes its body'].[28] Hence with this demonstrative leave-taking from universal values, Germany had robbed itself of its own moral vitality. Thus in Bergson's thought there is no conflict between the philosophy of life and universalist validity claims.[29]

During the war Durkheim published two lengthy essays on the war, both of which were immediately translated into German, presumably for propaganda purposes. What he undoubtedly also had in mind was to defend himself against attacks in which he had been labelled a friend of Germany, the 'boche with a pasteboard nose'.[30] Nevertheless, in one essay he goes into the question of war guilt in a tone of demonstrative impartiality.[31] In the other, more important pamphlet, 'Germany Above All',[32] he criticizes German policy in the World War as the product of an attitude whose theoretical underpinnings had been derived from the writings of Heinrich von Treitschke. The turning of state authority into an absolute, the cynical attitude to international law, the glorification of war as the source of the highest moral virtues and the denunciation of the ideal of 'eternal peace' as unethical – all of this is represented by Durkheim as a blow against the Enlightenment rooted in German culture. By resisting this, France was fulfilling a mission. As emerges from letters written during the war, Durkheim did not see the war as the death-knell of the pacifist ideal. On the contrary, the victory of France could help to make of this ideal a reality and could spell the end of militarism. The end of the war and the peace treaty of Versailles were a severe test of this conviction, one that Durkheim did not live to witness.

We have no reason to cast doubt on the sincerity of Durkheim's pacifism. In theory, in his major work on the 'division of labour' Durkheim had already parted company with Spencer's simplistic distinction between 'militant' and industrial societies. The idea that in 'militant societies' individuality was suppressed by force arises in his view from projecting modern ideas of individualism onto earlier ages.[33] For Durkheim, in contrast, where conditions were primitive, the individual simply did not exist as a personality. It followed that the emergence of strong leader figures under primitive conditions should be seen not as the suppression of an original freedom, but, on the contrary, as the first step towards individualism. 'Chiefs are in fact the first personalities who emerge from the social mass.'[34] Furthermore, Durkheim takes the edge off Spencer's prognosis that war would disappear in industrial society by predicting that war would die out gradually, rather than by leaps and bounds. In various writings before the war he attempts to develop a concept of patriotism that would not conflict with the ideal of cosmopolitanism. The crucial problem that defeated Durkheim's theory of the state[35] lay in the Janus face of the state. Durkheim believed that he could posit a development between the violent and aggressive actions of the state externally and its moral, pacifying actions internally. We are, so he held, the witnesses of a progressive shift from a permanent state of war among primitive communities to that of permanent legislation in modern societies. This, then, seems to preclude theoretically a simultaneous growth of internal and external power. Without the state, Durkheim cannot imagine any way of regulating social inequality or any guarantee of individual freedom. The strengthening of the state cannot therefore be conceived as a threat. Democracy does not mean much more than the citizens' acquiescence in the actions of a strong, centralized state standing above intermediary groups. War largely eluded the categories of this analysis. For that reason Durkheim could only strive to ensure that his normative ideals were not submerged in the frenzy of nationalist ideologies.

In the Durkheim school, too, no attempt was made to produce empirical analyses and theoretical interpretations of the reality of the war, from which the specific competence of sociology might have become clear. The question of war guilt, the analysis of German war rhetoric or the study of military and political coalitions – all of that belonged to the conventional apparatus of contemporary diplomatic history and had nothing specific to sociology about it. In this respect the circle around Durkheim's contemporary rival, René Worms, was rather more successful. At least they produced studies of the effect of the war on individual sectors of society. But a study of the war itself as a sociological phenomenon was lacking here too.[36]

The British situation is different since sociology in Great Britain was distinctly less institutionalized, and arrived later, than in France or the USA. So we have to look instead mostly at the history of economics.[37] The debate about the economic consequences of modern wars and their probability or improbability was conducted in a particularly interesting way as early as the free-trade peace movement of the nineteenth century, and persists down to John Maynard Keynes's critique of the Versailles peace treaty.

A brief remark only about the situation in Italy. The three types that I have distinguished in the case of Germany (representatives of *Lebensphilosophie*, liberal nationalists and intellectuals blathering on about a war of spirits) are to be found in Italy as well. And in particular, the intensification of the war experience to the point where it gave birth to a new regime was of particular historical significance in Italy, in Mussolini's Fascism. But equally, in Benedetto Croce,[38] Italy had a leading intellectual who, like Lederer, interprets the different writings on the war not as judgements, but as mere emotional outbursts written under the direct influence of the war. He defends German thought against the over-simplified view of it as a barbaric tradition glorifying power. In his view, thought of every type must be seen historically, in the context in which it arose, but also universalistically, in its contribution to European culture and human culture in general. Like no one else he seems to me to have maintained the balance between historicism and universalism, even during the war.

III

For American philosophers and social scientists, Durkheim's problem concerning the role of war in the evolution of humankind to a peaceful world order presented itself in an even more acute form. The search for a foreign policy that was different in principle, for a peaceable way in which to settle international conflicts and to bring about a 'new world order', has had deep roots in the American history of ideas ever since the founding of the republic, and it has powerfully influenced the optimistic faith of progressive liberal intellectuals in the future.[39] For them, the outbreak of war in 1914 came as a shock that many of them tried to digest by emphasizing the differences between America and Europe.[40]

One illuminating piece of evidence is the open letter of October 1914 in which one of the most influential representatives of American sociology, Albion Small, responded to Georg Simmel's complaint to him that countries outside Germany were all too willing to give credence to propaganda lies about Germany.[41] Small bent over backwards to arrive at a balanced judgement and emphasized that the war was not simply a matter of German guilt, but a consequence of the militarism that was endemic throughout Europe, but had been systematically propagated only in Germany, where it was downright popular. What America wanted was for this war to be the last and for it to be followed by a system of international courts, backed up by police. In general, we can see that in the first years of the war an almost sentimental regard for the German university and German learning retained its power among the first generations of American social scientists. However, there was now an increasing emphasis on the distance that Americans had always felt from the state-centredness of the German university and its organization. All this notwithstanding, what predominated at the beginning was an interpretative pattern that proclaimed that war was a kind of feudal relic, the expression of European decadence and senility, and that America intended to keep itself free from contamination by it. As the war dragged on, its duration exceeding all expectations, and as the debate about whether America should join in became more heated, shriller tones began to be heard in America too. Furious polemics against the 'Goths' and 'Vandals', wild stereotyping and constructions of intellectual history came increasingly to dominate the scene. One of the pioneers of quantitative empirical social research, Franklin Giddings, published a number of articles against that 'metaphysical monster', the Prussian-German state[42] – in short, it was Sombart in reverse!

The spokesman of those in favour of demonizing Germany was the Christian Neo-Hegelian Josiah Royce, the friend of Peirce and teacher of Mead. Shortly before the war, inspired by his firm belief in a kind of Hegelian philosophy of history, he had proclaimed that the human race would grow together into a single great community. He proposed a system of international guarantees to prevent future wars. For him, as the representative of classical German philosophy in America, the war was a threat to his personal credibility among the American public. He appears to have wished to silence the widespread questioning about the connection between German intellectual history and German politics by refusing to show any sympathy for German policy, and falling over himself in his eagerness to attack Germans as the 'enemies of mankind', the Cain of the international community.[43]

However, his rivals did not let him get away with this so easily. The anti-idealist George Santayana pointed scornfully to Royce's theoretical bafflement in the face of the war, a bafflement merely concealed by the vigour of his polemics.[44] His own contribution to the interpretation of the war was contained in his book *Egotism in German Philosophy*, which appeared in 1916.[45] From the very start, in the Preface, he admits that German philosophy had always been a closed book to him, but that he had also felt it to be uncanny, both hollow and aggressive. He uses the term 'egotism' to characterize the exaggerated emphasis on subjectivity in its thought and its arbitrariness in morality. His book draws a straight line from German Protestantism via Kant, Fichte and Hegel to Max Stirner and Friedrich Nietzsche. Even Goethe is included in this tradition, and since this cannot be done without difficulty, his love life is introduced in which he used force to overcome women's resistance as Germany used force against Belgium. . . . Santayana's ignorance of the fissures and contradictions in the German intellectual tradition and of the philosophy of subjectivity outside Germany – from Locke and Hume down to William James – makes it difficult to believe that, despite isolated criticism, this book was greeted for the most part with enthusiastic agreement. In what amounts to a full-blown conspiracy theory, Santayana saw the Germans carrying out a pincer movement against humankind, 'one with the secular arm, and another by solemn asseverations and sophistries'.[46]

Among the more cautious voices we must include John Dewey, who was probably the most important progressive intellectual in America in the first half of the century. He had published a book on 'German philosophy and politics' in 1915 and in a review of Santayana he had noted the differences in their interpretation.[47] For him what was disturbing about the German intellectual tradition was not the conception of the subject in German philosophy, but the ease with which German thinkers, such as Kant, accommodated themselves to political conditions that left no room for the self-determination of the individual. Thus for Dewey, German politics is not simply an emanation of the German mind, although he, too, is not free from a misleading tendency to homogenize intellectual history. Dewey speaks instead of the 'tragedy of the German soul'; only through the democratization of Germany would the German mind be able to flourish fully and thus add something new to the intellectual life of the democratic nations. With this, Dewey strikes a note that was to become dominant in the American debate following the entry of the USA into the war: the war as a struggle between democracy and autocracy.

Both John Dewey and his friend George Herbert Mead, two outstanding representatives of pragmatist philosophy and sociology, remained loyal to President Wilson's basic line in the first years of the war. This was for a 'peace without victory' in Europe. It signified a non-interventionist policy on the part of the USA, since an American intervention on one side would settle the conflict decisively once and for all. In a brilliant study of the development of the magazine *The New Republic*, Christopher Lasch has shown how there was a struggle at the heart of the reformers between such non-intervention and an activism that felt itself unable simply to stand by and watch the Europeans fight to the death.[48] This activist impulse of reformist intellectuals found expression in 1917 in rather altered circumstances. As the war progressed, the USA had become increasingly involved in the Allied cause, both politically and economically. Then the February Revolution in Russia, by getting rid of the Tsar, also eliminated an ideological obstacle, since it now became possible to declare that the Allied cause was also the cause of democracy. To take up the cause of democracy and the abolition of war by establishing the League of Nations and guaranteeing the rights of small nations to exist and to determine their own fate – those were worthy war aims in the eyes of the reformist intellectuals. President Wilson declared that the American entry into the war was a matter neither of national interest nor of compliance with existing pacts, but of the disinterested defence of the principles of law and democracy. Dewey and Mead went even further than this justification of entry into the war as an American mission on behalf of democracy, since they regarded it as an opportunity to bring about domestic reforms. John Dewey produced the classical legitimation of war as a compelling reason to extend public control over private enterprises and for the expansion of scientifically orientated planning in general to a point where this could no longer be reversed after the war. Mead, too, in newspaper articles, presented the commitment on behalf of the Allies as the presupposition for overcoming militarism in the USA itself. In a pamphlet, he discussed the problem of conscientious objection and acknowledged the legitimacy of objections to conscription based on religious or pacifist principles. However, in the case of politically motivated objections he saw no alternative to punishment, on the grounds that the duty to obey the law knows no exceptions.

Now it soon turned out that the domestic political implications of the American entry into the war were quite different from what the reformers had imagined. Repression, censorship and the persecution of socialists and pacifists assumed vast proportions. Dewey attempted, in September 1917, to play down the importance of these effects, but as early as November of the same year he published a self-critical essay in which he deplored his own attempt to minimize their significance. Such was the speed with which the original confusion returned. It is not possible for me to trace in detail here the exciting process of the gradual revision of these expectations in Dewey's writings and those of other progressive intellectuals after the entry into the war.[49] It was abundantly clear to all those involved that their hopes of riding the tiger successfully had been nothing more than a delusion. What followed this history of disillusionment was a series of splits between academic teachers and their students, a growing silence and a retreat from politics, and an increasingly urgent inquiry into the relationship between democracy and peace. All the participants had in common a profound disillusionment with the dream of an automatic, irresistible progress, that 'fool's paradise' of the prewar age, as Dewey called it. 'We confused rapidity of change with advance, and we took certain gains in our own comfort and ease as signs that cosmic forces were working inevitably to improve the whole state of human affairs.'[50] In this sense, then, the war really did represent a historical shift in the basic assumptions of American sociology. The progressive reformist generation never quite recovered from these blows. A few modified their positions by taking a radical turn. There was a greater emphasis on the influence of the 'labouring masses' on foreign policy, since only through them could the economic motif of conquering the marketplace be deprived of the threat to peace that it contained. In 1929 Mead published 'National-Mindedness and International-Mindedness', the most mature reformulation of the opinions of this circle on nationalism and the peaceful regulation of international conflict. He rejected James's 'moral equivalent of war' as an attempt to replace the highly dangerous cult of war with the harmless, but 'somewhat fantastic cult of a youth conscripted for social labour', on the ground that cults could not simply be produced to order.[51] He arrived at his own solution, making use of his social psychology of the formation of the self, which overcomes the supposition, still virulent in James, of an innate, masculine fighting instinct. He admitted that such an instinct exists, presumably just as basic instincts to co-operate also existed. However, social integration is not produced at all at the instinctual plane, but at the level of collective will formation. The institutionalization of forms of open discussion and the rational solution of conflicts of interest at both the national and international level remains his chosen perspective.

Like Durkheim, the American authors strove to prevent their normative ideals from being totally devalued by the war. More than Durkheim they managed to distil sociologically productive starting-points from their reflections on these ideals and their relationship to reality. Such starting-points emerged, above all, from the relation between democracy and peace. This was developed at the level of social psychology and led to the contrasting of two different ways of how to achieve social integration, whether from hostility to internal or external enemies or from participating in public decision-making processes in a way that was effective in creating bonds of loyalty. In terms of norms, emphasizing a universalist plane so as to justify a national foreign policy leads to a situation in which the interests and actions of individual states, national classes or sections of classes cannot remain without such justification. All this, however, did not amount to a satisfying conception of the causes and effects of wars.

It is altogether astounding to see what little attention the social scientists of the day devoted to establishing the relative importance of economic and political, military and socio-psychological factors in the origins of the war. The scholar who went furthest in the American debates on these questions was the economist of the Chicago school at that time, Thorstein Veblen. He produced a study of the prospects for a lasting peace that emphatically thought of itself as a scientific analysis and not as an ethical programme.[52]

In harmony with the republican tradition, he declared dynastic traditions of uncontrolled foreign policy to be the chief threat to peace. The democratization of autocratic states, particularly the enemy powers, but also Japan, is therefore decisive in his view. An occupation regime in Germany and the confiscation of Junker landed estates seems to him to be an entirely appropriate way of bringing this about. He believes that the dynastic, authoritarian interest, reinforced by welfare policies, was combined in such states with a whipped-up patriotism to create a platform for a popular expansionist foreign policy. However, Veblen does not idealize the Allies or even the USA, or regard them as models of peaceful, democratic societies. He sees them as threatened from within because their capitalist economies are insufficiently restrained by a welfare state. In consequence, he fears that they, too, might be threatened by the growth of nationalism as a panic reaction to demands for social equality. Veblen made every effort to give a clear-eyed view of the strengths of the German Empire and the weaknesses of his own society. This had the consequence that, for all his loyalty, and despite his activities as a direct adviser to President Wilson's committee on the preparation of a peace treaty, he promptly placed himself between all the available stools. Whereas the propaganda agency gave a warm recommendation to one of his books, the postal censorship banned the same book as pro-German.[53]

The book in question was his *Imperial Germany and the Industrial Revolution*,[54] in which he attributed the danger emanating from Germany to the mismatch between its modernity in economic and technical respects, and its political and cultural backwardness. He differed from his more philosophically minded colleagues, who attempted to identify the specificity of the German intellectual tradition as a whole, and as a result succeeded only in producing what was in the main a superficial and grotesquely distorted account of the history of political institutions in Germany. In his account – and putting all the details to one side – Veblen aimed at a more accurate sociological understanding of German developments. However, what links him to the students of intellectual history is his labelling of Germany as a deviant special case. Whereas at the outbreak of war America and Europe were contrasted as embodying different stages of modernity, as the war progressed a view gradually prevailed that saw Germany as the special case, the maverick, as far as the process of modernization was concerned.

I am quite unclear about what interaction took place between the German origins of the theory of the German *Sonderweg* within the general context of historicism and these American variants.[55] There are no direct references on either side. But I would like to venture the thesis that the theory of a German *Sonderweg* has independent origins in American sociological understanding of the First World War, and that this American version was of crucial importance for the subsequent development of modernization theory and research on Germany.[56] The strategic significance of the American theory of the German *Sonderweg* was to enable social scientists to retain an almost unrevised evolutionist paradigm of progress. If the war could be attributed to special features of the German situation, this would not undermine other assumptions about the civilizing character of modernization. It is consistent with this theory that in Veblen nationalism appears not as the product of modernity, but as a relic of barbaric ages. It is true that the war led to a rethinking of evolutionism in the American social sciences, but the resulting corrections were of a limited nature.

IV

The development of the idea that war has a revitalizing effect took quite a different course. This idea should not be confused with old-fashioned versions of bellicosity or with the acceptance of war in a spirit of the realism of power politics or Social Darwinism. Max Scheler, in particular, has made it crystal clear what a great difference there is between the idea that war is inevitable and the idea that war can be a solution to a cultural crisis.[57]

Here, too, it may appear with hindsight that this existentially supercharged concept of militarism and bellicosity was peculiar to Germany. But this is only approximately the case, even in the war writings. If we consider the question in slightly more abstract terms and include the basic idea of the regenerative effect of violence, even outside war, then we find that this idea is astonishingly widespread in all modern societies. It starts with Proudhon and Dostoevsky and proceeds, via Sorel's idea that the oppressed gain consciousness of themselves through violence, down to the American topos of the fight against the wilderness and savages. This is why not only had the First World War been accompanied by affirmative statements of this kind, but on occasion it had even been consciously desired beforehand from such motives. Nevertheless, to note that the idea was widely held internationally is only to make the need for an explanation more urgent. We must try to understand why the cultural situation of the 'long peace' before the First World War was experienced in such a way that war and violence could appear to many as the solution to a problem. The story has often been told of the individual elements in the diagnosis of cultural malaise and how the war came as a welcome escape.[58] There is no need to repeat this story here. These diagnoses differ widely on points of detail, and are even contradictory in part. The progressive stifling of all individuality or the complete release of individual choice and arbitrariness – these things are by no means identical. This explains why analysis should not be too direct in establishing links between particular components of a philosophical or sociological cultural critique and the hopes that are placed in war. What they have in common is only a negative. What all cultural critics of the time have in common is the awareness that modernization cannot be pursued back adequately through the connecting thread of the rationally acting individual or progressive rationalization. But hardly anyone believed that the process of modernization could be reversed. This is why everyone looked for an alternative way of understanding it. It is possible to regard many such theories from the prewar era as attempts to derive the genesis of new norms and values from non-instrumental acts and non-individualistic social relations. I am thinking here of Tönnies's by no means backward-looking concept of community [*Gemeinschaft*], Simmel's writings on art, Weber's concept of charisma and Durkheim's theory of religion. After the war, American pragmatism developed a theory of art and religion from the same roots. All these thinkers in search of a new idea could think of war as the revelation of the solution they were seeking. Suddenly, the birth of new values and commitments appeared to take place before the very eyes of those involved, and this is why the war came to be included among the great transformations in European memory, such as the Reformation or the French Revolution. Within the modernization process, events seemed to be striking out in a fundamentally new direction. And the World War probably was a fundamental transformation in actual fact, but in quite a different sense from what was imagined by those living in hopes of a great process of revitalization. Unless we wish to include the rise of Fascism among the cultural achievements of the war period, we shall probably arrive at the conclusion that all that remained, once the intoxicated rejoicing at the arrival of a 'different modernity' had passed, was a hangover. The sensitivity of German sociology had made just as much a fool of itself with its cultural critique as the Americans had done with their evolutionist trust in the future.

V

Remote from reality, incapable of analysing the social reality of the war, and unwilling to show any restraint in putting their scientific reputation at the disposal of war propaganda and the construction of enemy stereotypes – this is the picture our survey presents of broad sections of the international social sciences. But there were isolated exceptions. For example, in 1914 there were a few members of the Max Weber circle in Heidelberg who stayed aloof from the universal war fever. But while Georg Lukács and Ernst Bloch converted to Marxism under the impact of the World War and the Russian Revolution, another man, Emil Lederer, the hero of this story, continued to observe the conflict of contemporary interest groups even in wartime, and attempted to make a record of the behaviour of the various collective actors under the impact of the war. Over and above that, he wanted to comprehend certain features of the war that had come as a surprise to everyone, including the social scientists and the military experts. To preserve a 'cool detachment' and 'to take up a stance outside the war even while still in it', that was his programme. In view of the gigantic complex of causes that had led to the war, he simply brushed aside in one sentence the dominant question of war guilt. In the same way, when confronted with the plethora of pompous interpretations of the war, he reserved the right to doubt that it had any meaning; indeed, he regarded it as the duty of the sociologist and the historian to assert that the war might be 'meaningless' and not deducible from cultural or socio-economic principles. What is missing from the majority of war writings is precisely what Lederer attempted to put into practice, namely to reflect upon the conditions that made the specific features of the war a real possibility. While the majority of writers simply evoke and generalize about the communal experience of the outbreak of war and the front, Lederer attempts to explain it as the product of the specific conditions of a war conducted with universal conscription. His starting-point is an account of the tension between the principles of organization at work in the army and in civilian life.

> The army turns out to be a form of society alongside society proper and independent of it. It is, moreover, a universal form of society. And with mobilization, it takes on the social form of a community, because mobilization has been decreed as a response to the threat to the existence of all, and by arousing every social force in the defence of the nation. And for this reason, combining the disparate social groups of the nation into a unified army appears in the consciousness of the individual not as coercion by the state, and indeed not even as the consequence of any action by the state, but as an overwhelming act of destiny. Society is transformed into a community, as the expression not of social solidarity, but of intensive mutual interdependence. All previously existing social groups whose existence had before been felt to be fundamental now pale into insignificance when confronted by the infinite unity of the nation that rises up gloriously to defend its native soil. We must not be so blind as to look at the unanimous solidarity that exists outside Germany any differently from the solidarity that exists within its frontiers. What it expresses is a situation that is identical for all. The community that the nations of Europe have entered is a community not of action, but of destiny.[59]

Lederer reflects here upon the experience of community, consciously including the similarities with the other nations involved, and he proceeds in like fashion with other phenomena, in particular with the way in which the machinery of war gradually makes itself autonomous, and with the seeming paradox of a state that appears to become more dependent upon society internally, while externally it manifests itself increasingly as all-powerful. Here, too, he emphasizes what the warring parties have in common, namely the increasing separation of the forms of organization from the cultures of individual nations. While the majority of social scientists were involved in the production of nationalist apologias, Lederer observed the structural homogeneity of the feuding ideologies. In his view, modern nationalism, far from bringing out the cultural individuality of different nationalities, makes them resemble each other. The very competition in the military sphere of activity brings the states closer together and nationalism becomes simply the ideology of the all-powerful state.

> We have, then, an interaction of incomparable coherence: starting in the army, technical developments and the numerical growth of the armed forces mutually reinforce each other by their very nature. And this entire dynamic interacts in turn with the growth in state power. And it is precisely this internal dynamic in the armed forces that leads to the growth in the power of the state. . . .[60]

Lederer is at pains to think of these relationships as historical and contingent, rather than determinist. The doubling of the abstract all-powerful state and community experience enables him to provide an explanation for the behaviour of the intellectuals. On the one hand, he argues, the modern all-powerful state exerts such a pervasive influence on people's minds that, even above and beyond all official propaganda, intellectual currents flow of their own accord in the desired direction. On the other hand, he believes that the multiplicity of war ideologies in one and the same country, 'the utter disarray in the intellectual analysis of the war', is quite obviously without consequence for the progress of the war. 'In actual fact the opponents pitted against each other in this war are merely the stages of organization reached by the individual states.'[61] This process, which has taken on a life of its own, however, is of course experienced and interpreted subjectively in different ways. Whoever endorses the suspension of social differentiation in the communal experience induced by the all-powerful state, he believes, thereby renounces the 'struggle for the rights of the individual and society vis-à-vis the state'. But it is precisely this struggle that Lederer would like to take up or continue. According to his pre-eminently state-centred analysis, the road to a different modernity can definitely not be said to advance via the euphoria of the war experience.

On the contrary, he perceives two alternatives. The first lies in 'shaping the economy in the common interest', though not if this economy perpetuates the domination of society by the state along the lines of a state socialism. It is only acceptable if a radical change in economic thinking leads to an emphasis on greater justice as opposed to greater prosperity as the ruling idea of economics. Lederer regards this revulsion from the tendency to increase the internal and external growth in power of the state as desirable, but also as utopian.

For this reason he finds the second alternative to be more realistic. This is that 'modern states should come together in such tightly-knit groups that they no longer have any scope for a dynamic tendency'.[62] He does not explain how we are to think about this constructively. But perhaps it is permissible to think about it in terms of a network of states linked together on a number of levels, of a post-Hobbesian order of states, as I would like to call it, following the suggestion of Philippe Schmitter. In opposition to new ideologies of war and also to the abstract denigration of the state – this solution may well provide a meaningful prospect for a peace policy for us today.[63]

PART II

AFTER WAR

4

After the War
Democracy and Anti-Communism in Berlin after 1945

Sociology in Berlin has never been an easy matter. The balance between commitment and detachment that the social sciences absolutely require in their research and the formation of their theory is doubtless difficult to preserve in a place in which the heights and depths of German history during the century that has just come to a close are so very tangible. It is true that in retrospect we can see that the lives and works of a number of now celebrated figures from the history of sociology are closely associated with Berlin. The classical case is surely Georg Simmel, who was not only born a Berliner, but was also for a number of decades and almost his whole life long one of the intellectual magnets of Berlin University and the cultural life of the city. The themes and even the literary form of his writings are permeated with the spirit of the rapidly expanding metropolis. The work of Max Weber can certainly not be understood apart from the immersion in the political and scholarly life of the Imperial capital that he had experienced already in the parental home. Similar statements might be made about Werner Sombart and Theodor Geiger or about Goetz Briefs, who is little known internationally, but who powerfully influenced the industrial sociology of the postwar period.

However, it would be a typical illusion of hindsight to merge these outstanding figures into a tradition of Berlin sociology, however conceived. As has frequently been remarked, there has never been a Berlin school of sociology. Even in the past Berlin was never the centre of academic life in Germany in this discipline. It is quite in keeping with this that there is no history of Berlin sociology that rises above the level of personal reminiscences. It is even difficult to speak of a Berlin tradition, if by tradition we mean an unbroken chain of activity. As is well known, Simmel never managed to progress to a full professorship in Berlin, and the career difficulties he experienced tell a familiar story of the narrow-mindedness of the world of German scholarship under the Empire and of the political and anti-Semitic prejudices that were commonly disguised by the rhetoric of academic autonomy. Weber's intellectual impact is associated with Heidelberg rather than Berlin. Sombart taught at first at the Commercial College, Theodor Geiger at the College for Adult Education, and Goetz Briefs at the Technical College in Charlottenburg. Variety or fragmentation, then, rather than concentration and the formation of a school, was the hallmark of Berlin sociology. At the university, where every Prussian scholar dreamed of obtaining a chair, a new discipline had a particularly hard time of it. Conversely, the new subject tended to ignore the highly significant achievements of scholars outside the boundaries of its own discipline proper – we need only think of Ernst Troeltsch or Otto Hintze.

Similarly, after the Second World War, the core schools of German sociology developed elsewhere, in Cologne and Frankfurt, Münster and Göttingen. Otto Stammer and Hans-Joachim Lieber did indeed succeed in creating a critical, sociological milieu that was to become important for the Berlin students' movement, but to call this a school would be going too far. It is true that the Eastern part of the city also had sociological aspirations after the war, but these did not survive the Stalinist ice age of the GDR. The gradual revival of the subject at both the university and the academies was subject to mistrustful controls and the insistence that scholars should abandon all attempts to establish an independent mission of enlightenment. Notwithstanding the efforts of a number of committed sociologists of integrity, only a few scholarly or political initiatives could emerge from sociology in East Berlin. This was expressed inimitably by the long-standing East Berlin principal when he said of the collapse of the GDR that the social scientists 'may even have helped to bring it about'. For a long time, ordinary scholars had scarcely any opportunity to make their name in the West; such opportunities were open only to dissidents involved in spectacular protest actions or especially reliable academics with a licence to travel abroad.

But neither did the West manage to achieve a balance between commitment and detachment. I have in mind here the consequences of the student movement for Berlin sociology, which were far from intended. The temporary *de facto* domination of the university department by junior academic staff and the missionary project to reconstruct Marxism look in retrospect like the Pyrrhic victories of a social movement. Those who believe that the deficiencies of other people's scholarly writings stem from a false class standpoint have no need to study the object of their criticism too closely to feel superior to it and to be in a position to develop grandiose perspectives for themselves and their own future research projects. Such a tendency will from the outset be jeopardized by fantasies of omnipotence, and unless it encounters some significant intellectual resistance, it will be the weaknesses and not the strengths of this approach that will come to the fore. It is no accident that in Germany the interest in social movements and literary and aesthetic or therapeutic trends has occasionally resulted in social scientists going native and changing sides. The preoccupation with lifestyles and fashions can also be converted imperceptibly into a dependency on the *Zeitgeist*. It would be a fascinating task to take Simmel's characterization of the spirit of the metropolis – from nervousness to a blasé indifference – and apply it self-reflexively to Berlin sociology. I would venture the hypothesis that Berlin sociology would exhibit the features of the ephemeral metropolis of West Berlin: the remarkable blend of big city and idyll or modernization-critical project; the simultaneous fact of its international connections and its isolation from its hinterland; its indifference to that hinterland and to its own history. Today, however, for all the difficulty in obtaining an overview, a difficulty that arises from the co-existence of several universities as well as large and important social research institutes, there is a huge potential for work in our discipline in this city. And the opportunities for making contacts and collaboration are correspondingly great.

Research in the social sciences in Berlin is by no means confined to topics with an immediate relevance for life in Berlin. It is true that neither the population of Berlin nor the social scientists working there ever repressed the reality of the division of Germany to the same degree as the West German population did. But what this meant was that in the island city people felt the need to compensate for this either by concerning themselves exclusively with West Berlin – a provisional entity that seemed to have become a permanent reality – or by donning the mantle of a larger-than-life cosmopolitanism and experimenting with every conceivable political and scientific context from anywhere in the world. Anything but reflect upon their own immediate situation. These reactions are entirely comprehensible, but they meant also that a great opportunity was lost to reflect as social scientists upon their own situation. There was less of a risk than usual that a concern with local problems might degenerate into a mere hobby. A brief list of the events and trends that have shaped the city since 1945 makes this clear: the military occupation; the unprecedented experiment of a four-power administration among whose members, moreover, a conflict broke out on a world-historical scale; the blockade of Berlin in 1948 and the consequences for the Western part of Berlin of the establishment of the two German states in 1949; the great crisis in Berlin in 1958 (Khrushchev's ultimatum); the building of an impenetrable wall through the middle of a giant city in 1961; the controversies surrounding policy towards the East and détente, the co-existence of differing social and political systems in a single city; the emergence in 1967/8 of a student movement that increasingly saw itself as revolutionary; the democratic uprising of 1989 in the GDR and the fall of the Berlin Wall; and lastly, today, the problems of integrating the two halves of the city, and of coming to terms with Berlin's renewed status as capital city.

It is not my intention to give a comprehensive survey of the research in which Berlin nevertheless figures as the object of sociological scrutiny. I would like instead to focus on a single work that in a particularly impressive way places the research on Berlin in a broader context. Because of its virtues, however, its tremendous precision and scrupulosity, this book may not have received the broader attention and degree of influence that it merits. The work I have in mind is the one produced by Harold Hurwitz under the title *Democracy and Anti-Communism in Berlin after 1945*.[1] It is perhaps no accident that the author of this mammoth work – it runs to more than 3000 pages – is neither a Berliner nor even a German, but an American, albeit one who has lived in Berlin since 1946. He lived here at first as a civilian employee of the US military government. Subsequently, he worked as a radio journalist, and then as a sociologist and an associate of Willy Brandt, Egon Bahr and Richard Löwenthal. Lastly, until his retirement, he was active as a professor at the Free University.[2] A stranger in Berlin may have found it easier to muster the blend of enthusiasm and cool expertise that is needed for research into what lies close at hand. For over twenty years he pursued a question that is of central importance for an understanding of Berlin, but that has acquired a topicality that goes far beyond this, thanks to the collapse of the post-Stalinist dictatorships in Eastern Europe. This question concerns the chances of success for democracy following the collapse of a dictatorship, in circumstances in which one cannot rely on a vital democratic tradition and in which material conditions are poor.

This does not prevent Hurwitz from basing his study on an ambitious concept of democracy. In at least two respects democracy means more in his eyes than the establishment or reform of governmental and social institutions. First, he insists that the principle of representative democracy must be supplemented by direct participation, since without it 'the representative character of the parties is functionally undermined. . . . The parties increasingly and almost exclusively become special-purpose groups: for the mobilization of the population in election campaigns, for the selection of leaders and to support the leadership, whether as government or opposition, with parliamentary groups in which a consensual discipline almost always has priority.'[3] According to Hurwitz, however, if direct democratic elements are to function, they are dependent upon a democratic culture, or, rather, a plurality of democratic subcultures. For this reason he is particularly interested in investigating the democratic potential of existing political subcultures in Berlin and in the question of their continuity and their possible disintegration. The second respect in which Hurwitz goes beyond a purely institutional conception of democracy lies in his emphasis on collective experience and learning processes. Democratic leanings are never given once and for all in any society; they are either weakened or reinforced in the course of concrete historical processes.

Hurwitz's interest focuses centrally on the emergence of a consensus to resist communism in the Western sectors of Berlin between 1945 and 1948. So as to judge this consensus, he asks the question, an essential question from a democratic point of view, on what was the consensus based? Was it the product of pre-democratic or anti-democratic attitudes, and if so, was it simply the continuation of National Socialist anti-bolshevism spreading through the population in the form of a general hostility to the Soviet Union? Or did it point to the dominance of authentic democratic attitudes, with the implication that we would be justified in speaking enthusiastically of a successful struggle for freedom and democracy in Berlin at that time?

It is not possible to give an adequate picture here of the methodological richness of this study. Nor can I deal with the advantages and disadvantages of his reliance on a 'relative-deprivation' model of the development of collective action. It is enough to mention that Hurwitz's research employs both sociological methods and the study of sources typical of the historian, and that he manages to combine these methods in a particularly fruitful manner. His work relies essentially on the secondary analysis of opinion polls conducted by the US military government, on content analyses of the Berlin daily newspapers, his own surveys on the membership statistics of the political parties and the careers of party officials. These are typical sociological methods. On the other hand, like the historians, he has also made use of archive materials, such as the records of the military governments and the reports of the Allied secret services. In addition there are interviews with contemporary witnesses and he makes use of the whole spectrum of the historical literature and that of the social and political sciences for the period he is examining. The separation of the social sciences, which frequently does more harm than good, is overcome here; the historical blindness of many writings emanating from empirical social research and the lack of theory in many historical analyses are both eliminated in favour of a complex mosaic of specialized studies.

The first volume, *The Political Culture of the Population and the New Beginnings of Conservative Politics*, is concerned with the general framework of political developments in Berlin after 1945. How are we to imagine the political consciousness of the population of Berlin following the collapse of National Socialism, given that Nazism had not been destroyed as the result of their own efforts? In the minds of the occupying forces and also of many returning émigrés, there was a widespread belief that openly or secretly the German people continued to sympathize with National Socialism and could only become mature enough for democracy after a lengthy period of re-education. But how does this chime, for example, with the many political initiatives against big capital that were in evidence in the first years after the war and reached well into the camp of the emerging bourgeois parties? Looking back on the situation today, would it be wrong to see the occupation forces more as obstacles to a new order aspired to by the German population? There is a third aspect that predominates in the memory of the German population: this is the memory of a time of complete disorientation, of the shock devaluation of values and loyalties, and the aversion to any new political entanglements.

> People who had followed the National Socialists, who had seen themselves seduced, misused and then bitterly disappointed, and who now found themselves conquered and occupied by foreign powers, reacted to the overtures of parties licensed by the occupying powers with statements like 'Never again' and 'Without me'. Because of this, even though there were also signs that the parties were accepted because their foundation members had been confirmed as opponents of the Nazis, these beginnings were very restricted. A further factor was that it was the occupying powers and not the new parties who were the new authorities. And, at the start, there was not simply a rational realization that people should accept the new configuration of power, but in addition there was a widespread tendency to submit to the new, the real rulers.[4]

The results of Hurwitz's research show us a path through this confusing terrain and permit us to make a number of surprising, but well-supported empirical statements. For one thing, the number of people with deep-rooted National-Socialist beliefs was small, and even distinctly smaller in Berlin than, for example, in the US Zone of Occupation in Germany. Berlin's cosmopolitan traits as well as the socialist, but also the conservative Prussian, traditions were still very much alive. At the same time, however, in non-political matters, these traditions were often highly authoritarian and undemocratic, as we can see from Hurwitz's analysis of answers on education and interpersonal relationships. The picture becomes even more complicated when we realize that the widespread anti-capitalist mood could be fuelled partly by sources hostile to democracy. A lengthy chapter is dedicated to the re-emergence of the bourgeois parties and in particular the tensions between the leadership elite that came from the resistance movement and the grass roots of these parties.

Volume 2 is concerned exclusively with the Social Democratic workers' movement, and places it in a broad historical framework in order to make it and its importance for the emerging democracy comprehensible. This volume is itself in part a highly innovative history of Social Democracy caught up in the conflict between – as the title puts it – 'authoritarian tradition and democratic potential'. Hurwitz is concerned here with the enormous importance of the broader subculture surrounding the SPD and the trade unions. We are given a vivid, concrete account of the typical German features of this subculture in which great emphasis is placed on the virtues of moral reliability, the value of education, and solidarity.

The first two volumes foreground the attitudes of the people of Berlin and the views of the political elites. Volume 3 focuses on another crucial participant: the victorious Allies. The chief argument of this volume highlights the 'rule of concord' between the victors. For an astonishingly long period of time the Western powers felt under an obligation to demonstrate their unity vis-à-vis the defeated Germans. Since the Soviet Union had been the sole occupying power in Berlin in May and June 1945, it was able during that time to fill important posts in the Berlin administration and the media with its own nominees.

> The attempts by non-communists to use a mixture of criticism and complaint to resist Soviet-communist endeavours to disadvantage them and force them into line were consistently met by the officers of the Western occupying powers with distrust, which helped to make democrats look like 'divisive forces'. The victors took the view that it was in the interest of the Germans to play the victorious powers off against each other.[5]

As Hurwitz is able to show, this attitude persisted even while every day doubts increased about the possibility of collaborating with the Soviet Union within the framework of the Four-Power Agreements. Only at the end of a lengthy and contradictory process were the Americans able to overcome their distrust of the vanquished Germans to the point where they could start to perceive them as potential allies and the Berliners not as unruly, but as heroic.[6]

With this development the ground was prepared for the analysis, presented in narrative form, of the first decisive act in the anti-Stalinist struggle for freedom in West Berlin. This was the conflict concerning the merging of the two parties representing the German workers' movement, the Social Democrats (SPD) and the Communists (KPD). They had been separated ever since 1918/19. Immediately after the end of the war there was a powerful desire for an alliance, or even a merger, among the ordinary members of both parties. The aim was at long last to put an end to the old split, which was regarded as one of the reasons for the victory of the National Socialists. Initially, however, the KPD rejected the idea. This changed in autumn 1945 and the so-called merger battle lasted from November 1945 until April 1946. In the Soviet Zone of Occupation and in East Berlin the union led to the establishment of the Socialist Unity Party (SED), which subsequently exercised dictatorial power. In West Berlin, on the other hand, the vast majority of Social Democratic party members rejected the merger in a ballot. Hurwitz inquires into the factors determining this decision and its historical significance.

The findings of Hurwitz's study of Allied policies have already enabled us to exclude one possible interpretation. It was not the Western occupying powers that led the Social Democrats to their rejection of a merger. On the contrary, in their distrust they even missed the opportunity to hold the ballot (which the Soviet authorities had banned in the Eastern sector of Berlin) under the auspices of the Four Powers, or at least to attempt to do so. To be sure, there were individual officers, principally British, but also some Americans, who understood and were sympathetic to the motives of the left-wing Berlin democrats and anti-Stalinists, but the latter were hampered rather than assisted by the military governments. We must also eliminate an interpretation that claims that resistance to the KPD and Soviet plans for unifying the two workers' parties is to be explained by the people's authoritarian, anti-communist resentments. The population of Berlin was in part detached from all politics and, until well into the period of the Berlin blockade of 1948, it kept its distance from active resistance to Soviet policies. A third interpretation might attribute resistance to the merger to the vested interests of Social Democrat officials who feared that they might lose out or be disadvantaged by a merger. This explanation, too, has become untenable following Hurwitz's research. The Party apparatus of the SPD was largely ready for a merger, albeit with reservations. All the simple reasons for distinguishing between the opponents and supporters of the merger fail to convince. It is by no means the case that left-wing Social Democrats tended to favour unification and right-wing members were against it. According to Hurwitz, many right-wing Social Democrats accepted the merger in the spirit of authoritarian submissiveness, regarding it as the inevitable consequence of the occupation and the strength of the Soviet occupying power. Hurwitz goes out of his way to be fair to all sides in his analysis of their motives. He has absolutely no wish to portray the supporters of the merger as irresponsible, corrupt or narrow-minded. Both the Social Democrats who resisted and those who yielded to the pressure for the merger shared the same goal. This was to prevent the division of Germany in the prevailing circumstances.

In contrast to these erroneous interpretations, Hurwitz's analysis shows that the resistance to the merger can only be understood as *the result of a rebellion of the ordinary members of the Social Democratic Party*. These ordinary members had noted with increasing bitterness the undemocratic manipulating tactics of the Communists and Soviet military officials in the Berlin administration and in internal party affairs in the Eastern sector of Berlin and in the Soviet Zone of Occupation. It was above all the pressure exerted by Soviet officers in favour of the merger, the naked threats and even the use of force, that made clear to the party members throughout Berlin that agreeing to the merger might well be the first step *en route* to a new dictatorship. But the yoke of the National Socialist dictatorship had only just been cast off, thanks to foreign assistance; the lesson from that period could only be that it would be wrong to acquiesce in the rise of a new dictatorship without a struggle. As we know today, the pressure and the punitive measures of the Soviet Military Administration towards Social Democrats who resisted the merger extended to re-using the grounds of the former Nazi concentration camps. Hurwitz gives the story of the successful struggle against the merger in the Western sectors of Berlin the breadth of an epic – and this is only fitting. He enables us to understand how these conflicts could lay the foundations of a democratic consensus in Berlin. To be sure, the Third Reich was not toppled by a revolution and democracy in Germany was not created by a social movement. However, in West Berlin at least, the conflicts over the merger were the start of a period of successful social struggles for democracy that anchored democratic ideas in the minds of the population.

In the volumes of this giant project that have so far appeared, Hurwitz has not yet broached the question of how this emotionally underpinned democratic consensus developed in the following decades. Thanks to its existence, the SPD was able to enjoy several decades of undisputed political leadership in the city. This leadership became increasingly precarious, however, and at ever greater risk of missing the larger meaning of its own struggle. Its rigid concentration upon its own trauma of past threats made it conservative, inert and a hostage to 'vested interests'. The clash that took place at the end of the 1960s between the student movement, with its insistence on an expansion of democracy, and a social democracy with its fears of a new communist movement was nothing short of tragic. The mutually distorted perception of other points of view led to bitter conflicts, although, fortunately, these also resulted in a further pluralization of the democratic consensus.

I should like to single out one further insight from the almost unmanageable richness of Hurwitz's findings. The strength of the Soviet Union was definitely 'experienced' more powerfully in Berlin than in the Western Zones of Germany. This is true of all political camps and attitudes. Furthermore, in Berlin there was always a more lively interest in the possibility of closer relations – whether economic, political or cultural – with the peoples of the Soviet Union. This may even be said to apply to the opponents of the merger among the Social Democrats and to many bourgeois politicians. This fact has given rise to many misunderstandings in West Germany, and all the more so further west. Every attempt to come to an arrangement with the Soviet Union was all too hastily interpreted as a sign of a faltering democratic commitment. That could be seen in the way the German peace movement in the early 1980s was perceived in the West, or in the reactions to the paper proposing dialogue between the SPD and SED, even though that paper was concerned to overcome the silence between them, not to promote the acceptance of an undemocratic regime. Whatever developments take place in the near future in the territories of the former Soviet Union, they will undoubtedly have a particularly powerful effect in Germany, and above all in Berlin. Not only the themes of a politically conscious social research, but also the conditions in which they are negotiated, will be more influenced by such developments in Berlin than elsewhere.

5

After the Cold War
The Collapse of the German Democratic Republic

Present and Past

The collapse of the GDR is gradually shifting into a different time dimension: that of the past. It has ceased to be what we saw unfolding before our incredulous eyes, creating new, unexpected experiences by the day. Instead, it is acquiring the contours of a self-contained event; in other words, it is becoming part of history.

Admittedly, the essentials of this history are far from being understood. It will keep the social sciences busy for a long time to come. The first analyses – commentaries on events as they unfold – have been published in considerable numbers so that gradually the web of interpretation has become denser and interpretations are starting to become repetitive. But most of the work still remains to be done. And the fact that the events lie in the past does not ensure that they are accessible to us in an unproblematic way. The collapse of the GDR forms the starting-point of a future that is as uncertain now as ever, and makes for uncertainty in our interpretation of it.

No doubt, the social sciences must count among their pre-eminent tasks the need to examine the changes undergone by the society of the former GDR and the emergence of a united German society, and to work out both the most likely paths of future development and the alternatives available in this process. The experience of a fragmenting social framework should be no obstacle here, but should instead sharpen our sense of the assumptions about stability on which such projections depend and *must* depend.

A study of the collapse of the GDR is the necessary starting-point for any judgement about the present potential for development. We should begin by asking what exactly has collapsed and what has not. This question cannot be answered independently of the chosen theoretical framework. What is clear is that both the institutions of the state and most of the formal institutions of society and the economy – which were scarcely to be distinguished in this 'nationalized society', to use Claus Offe's expression – had completely broken down. On the other hand, many of the underlying social structures, forms of life and mentalities are still at work and will remain so. What this amounts to can only be discovered after a careful analysis of the historical situation. For a long time to come, the society that is coming into being may be described as a specific form of 'the synchronicity of the non-synchronous'.

Perhaps the best way to understand our theme would be to explain the formulation that we have chosen. The use of the word 'collapse' – with or without a question mark – is by no means self-evident. Many people speak instead of the 'revolution' that is said to have taken place, qualified by such terms as 'catching-up' (Jürgen Habermas)[1] or Protestant (Ehrhard Neubert),[2] as a non-violent or late-bourgeois revolution. Nothing could be further from our thoughts than the wish to belittle the achievement and the personal courage of the individuals and groups who ventured to take a stand in autumn 1989. It is not the pathos of the victors and the self-opinionated gloaters that nevertheless makes us speak of collapse. What is crucial, rather, is that we attach greater importance to foreign policy factors, on the one hand, and the failure of the regime to offer any resistance, on the other. That a state should respond to pressure by collapsing like a house of cards is hard to reconcile with our normal understanding of the term 'revolution'. Thus to ask the question 'revolution or collapse?' expresses the fact that the events may be subjected to a variety of interpretations. This is even truer of the developments that preceded the events.

The Improbability of Collapse

As far as the past is concerned, controversy starts with basic principles, namely with questioning the accuracy of earlier prognoses about the stability of the GDR. We see today a tendency to pretend that we always knew that the system was destined to collapse, and to collapse in short order. Of course, it is always easy to guess with the aid of hindsight, or to make predictions without definite dates, and we have not yet found a contemporary commentator who had predicted – say, in 1988 – that there would be a collapse or revolution in the GDR in the immediate future.

Those who lose sight of this now are not only intellectually dishonest, but also deprive themselves of the opportunity for an unpre-

judiced assessment. They fall for a view in which a determinist explanation is constructed from results – a philosophy of history in reverse
that in reality is no more than the old way of thinking in a different
guise. It is morally questionable because it is a philosophy of history
according to the victors, and it is analytically false because it is based on
an excessively narrow frame of reference. It turns the historical choice
of one possible option into the foundation of its own reference system.
To analyse the GDR backwards, using its collapse as the first premise,
is a teleology in reverse that (unwittingly) makes use of the same
dogmatism that characterized official state Marxism. Looking back into
the past, this teleological approach sees only the indicators that develop
into insoluble contradictions; in short, it perceives only a process of
decay governed by natural laws. The theory underpinning this has
been missing up to now, but is now being supplied retrospectively.

It is important to remember, however, that the collapse of the GDR
came as a surprise to everyone, even the secret service, as Klaus von
Beyme has sarcastically noted.[3] This reminder documents the constantly renewed astonishment of us all at the fact that this state, and
with it the entire institutional system of the socialism installed there
(we can evidently no longer talk about 'actually existing socialism',
even in retrospect), should have collapsed so quickly and utterly.

This point is constantly reiterated in the present contributions to this
topic. Rolf Reißig shows that the GDR was for the most part perceived
to be not just stable but also capable of development within certain
limits.[4] As Claus Offe points out, the collapse of the GDR is in great
measure to be understood not in categories of the will, or even those
of structure, but only according to categories of chance.[5] However, we
must enter the caveat here that 'chance' is also a question of perspective. From the perspective of the GDR, on the periphery, perestroika
and its consequences are a matter of chance; from the perspective of
the Soviet Union, that is, from the centre, they are a problem of structure. The self-confidence of having possessed the theoretical tools with
which to predict the collapse of societies in the strategic ambit of the
Soviet Union is at its greatest among the exponents of geopolitical
theories (such as Randall Collins).[6]

So the question is rather whether the presumption of stability was
always an error, or from what point in time it became one. We may
legitimately ask sociologists whether they should have been able to
predict the collapse of the GDR. For sociologists in the East, this was
not even on the agenda, for obvious reasons. It could not even be
contemplated as a possibility. For its part, Western sociology showed
little interest in the GDR; it was hardly a fascinating topic. Even worse,
the GDR triggered feelings of acute discomfort on the West German left
(including large sections of the SPD). Even when people distanced

themselves from the actually existing socialism, providing a convincing theory to distinguish it from other forms of socialism was a tricky task, one that was avoided wherever possible. The only exception were the small minority who excused all the failures of the GDR by referring to the terrible conditions at the time of its establishment and placed all their hopes in the future. For the right wing, too, the GDR failed to provide any cause for satisfaction. From the time of the political compromise between the leadership of the CSU and that of the SED at the latest, right-wing commentators found themselves in a cleft stick, caught painfully between their principled stand and their sense of reality. Political dilemmas of this kind and the effective sealing-off of GDR society from sociological scrutiny were enough to marginalize Western research into the GDR.

This does not license us to pillory sociology. The assumption of stability may not have been misguided after all – it may have been right not to predict the collapse on the grounds that it was too implausible (too much of an unpredictable concatenation of contingent events) and not sufficiently 'home-made' (too dependent on external factors). In this sense, the failure to predict the future is not necessarily a sign of weakness. Sociology must reconcile itself to the fact that there are limits to its predictive powers and that it has no gift for prophecy. Indeed, to accept this can even be a source of strength. It is the mark of a mature discipline that it does not need to have exaggerated explanatory powers foisted onto it.

Where no prognosis was possible, a retrospective reconstruction may yet be achievable. Where an event is partly or wholly determined by chance occurrences, it can only be explained historically. It is the endpoint of a chain of events, in other words, it is not the product of a social transformation to be comprehended in terms of laws, but rather the product of a history – and not just a structural history, but a history of events.

A history always contains the emergence of the new; it is open to surprises. It could have had other endpoints, but these alternatives have been gradually closed off in the course of history. The task of a 'historical explanation' is not to naturalize this process of selection with the aid of hindsight, but to keep an eye on the points where the alternatives bifurcate. Bifurcation points are 'structural breaks' or caesuras that interrupt a continuous development.

If sociology is conscious of these necessary limits and does not remain exclusively fixated in its analysis upon the perspective of collapse, it will be in a position to tackle the task of shedding light on the structural problems and contradictions in the society of the former GDR. Its tempo is slower than that of writers and essayists who claim to reveal the truth without too much empirical or theoretical fuss. The difficulties of a retrospective reconstruction of past conditions and their dynamics are substantial, but much is easier today than it was in the past, because the veil behind which relevant information was concealed has now been lifted.

A Typology of Explanations

In order to obtain an overview of the controversial interpretations of this historical event, it will be helpful to arrange the available explanations according to a typology. In many contributions, use is made of a variety of different types, and this is entirely justified, since sometimes using a single type would merely highlight the fact that a particular approach has been misleadingly privileged at the expense of others. The types are arranged here along a continuum that extends from the microlevel to the macrolevel.

The *first type* declares the *psychological attitudes* of the population of the GDR to be the crucial determining factor of social processes. This refers to explanations that attribute the stability of the GDR regime over many years, including the absence of broadly based oppositional movements, to the mentality of the GDR population. These explanations look to this mentality for the causes if not of the *Wende*, the turning-point of 1989, then of what they see as the swift end of the *Wende*. Among the general public the best known of these attempts is the psychogramme of the GDR, *The Emotional Blockage*, produced by Hans-Joachim Maaz, a psychotherapist from Halle.[7] But we may also include the statements of a number of GDR theologians about the pathological lack of self-confidence and commitment on the part of the citizens of the GDR. Such diagnoses may be regarded as the 'subjective' corollaries of structural theories that talk about the total 'de-subjectivization' of people living in a totalitarian state. Of course, we have at once to inquire about the origins of such a mentality. Should we think of it as the continuation of a mentality and a political culture that were already present at the foundation of the GDR, a mentality that is perhaps specific to Germans, or should we see it as something produced by the GDR itself? But by what means could this mentality have been produced and maintained? Is it the systematic product of totalitarian manipulation, or of the resignation of individual generations who were forced to endure the forcible suppression of the uprising of 1953 and the building of the Wall in 1961? Or is it the effect of the process of selection resulting from the steady drain of sections of the population? Questions such as these give an idea of the ambiguity and inconclusiveness of hasty psychological explanations. It could of course also be the case that all these interpretations are based on false premises. Measured by its own goals, we might think of totalitarianism as a failure, while the mentality of the populace could be seen as a rational technique for survival.

The *second type* of explanation is more sociological. It foregrounds the *people's belief in the legitimacy* of the GDR regime and the SED's efforts to establish such a belief. What calls for investigation in this case is not the irrational conformism or a teeth-grinding acquiescence in an imposed regime, but an at least partial acceptance of it. Now, on the basis of the data available hitherto, it is difficult, if not impossible, to form a precise picture of the history of the belief of the GDR population in the legitimacy of the regime. Rolf Reißig believes that he possesses empirical evidence of the rapid decline in legitimacy during the 1980s and a simultaneous increase in democratic demands.[8] But this may exaggerate the extent of the belief in the regime's legitimacy before this process of erosion. For this reason it would obviously be a good idea to study the SED's attempts to strengthen its own legitimacy. This is what Sigrid Meuschel has attempted to do.[9] In her work, she distinguishes between the different phases of 'anti-fascist Stalinism', the idea of the technocratic reform of Stalinism and, finally, 'actually existing socialism'. In the first phase, legitimacy was derived from anti-fascism; the strong state established itself with a view to the future abolition of the state and treated deficits in legitimacy as acceptable because they were considered a consequence of the deformation of the German nation, which, after all, had been the agents of the Third Reich. In the second phase, by contrast, it was the promise of reform itself that became the basis of the loyalty of the population. In the third phase, the loss of utopian expectations could already be discerned in the use of the term 'actually existing socialism'. Similarly, the idea of peace as a further instrument of legitimation was unable to eliminate the deficits of legitimacy that by now had become plain for all to see. We may also mention a kind of postmodern type of explanation focused on legitimation that is to be found in Heinz Bude's attempt to investigate how the way in which societies define themselves provides one of the sources of legitimation problems. In the course of his study he makes particular use of the dichotomy between 'tragic' and 'ironic' conceptions of self.[10]

Explanations concerned with legitimation also include all attempts to proclaim as essential the great systems with which to interpret the world, and their institutional incarnations. The progressive undermining of Marxist-Leninist ideology is undoubtedly important. As a result of its increasing dogmatism, the latter could not possibly retain any great attraction for scientifically minded intellectuals; but the loss of a utopian dimension also spelled the demise of its quasi-religious potential. And the idea that the future belonged to communism, one common even among many non-Marxist intellectuals, had likewise dissolved. There is no debate about this loss of credibility and of the power of Marxism-Leninism to fascinate. What is controversial, however, is the precise role of the Churches in the collapse of the GDR, in particular that of the numerically more significant Protestant Church. Was the 'revolution' a 'Protestant revolution' or was it merely the fact of the breach created by the Church in the monolithic structure that was decisive? Detlef Pollack believes that the role of the Church has been overestimated in explanations of the historical events.[11] He emphasizes that the part played by the Churches was, and had to be, highly ambivalent.

Lastly, there is an especially lively debate about the part played by national identity.[12] On this issue there is considerable disagreement among commentators. When Rolf Reißig declares that there was no marked national identity in the GDR, he is referring to the failure of the attempts to imbue the population of the GDR with the feeling of being its 'own socialist nation'. However, this fails to address the question of an overall German national identity. Claus Offe's contribution, also contains a succinct assertion on this topic.[13] For him the emphasis on a nostalgia for German national identity is artificial and instrumental. In his view, West German elites had made an offer on unification that was based on cool calculation; the GDR population had accepted it just as coolly. Offe is undoubtedly right to counter claims that Germany had experienced a sudden uprising of a highly emotional and nationalist kind. But does this really permit such a far-reaching conclusion? Many phenomena not inspired by West German elites point in a different direction. Instances include the visibly spontaneous resurgence of regional identities, right down to the re-establishment of the historical *Länder* (Saxony, Brandenburg, etc.), as well as a leaning towards the West German state that had never disappeared.

A *third type* of explanation seeks the causes of the rapid transformation neither in long-term traditional attitudes, nor in systems of political legitimation, but in the *dynamics of social movements themselves*. Jan Wielgohs and Marianne Schulz give a 'description' of the popular movements in the East and their social origins.[14] They interpret these movements less as evidence of political opposition than as countercultural tendencies with a strong socio-ethical content. By comparing them with the 'new social movements' in Western societies, but also with other popular movements in Central and Eastern Europe, the picture they give gains in depth. The methods they use stand in sharp contrast to the study by Karl-Dieter Opp, which is based on the theory of rational action and rational choice.[15] He is concerned to explain the quantitative growth in the numbers of people participating in the spectacular protest actions of autumn 1989. In his contribution Wolfgang Zapf focuses on structural social changes and highlights a peculiarity in the dynamics of the East German protest movement.[16] This is its interaction with the simultaneous growth of the 'emigration movement'. What is striking is that although many studies that focus on the dynamic of social movements stress the collapse of the regime's ability (or its will) to suppress opposition, they lack a thorough analysis of the internal contradictions of the security organizations. The taboo on the security apparatus that was ubiquitous in the sociological research of the GDR has evidently not yet lost its hypnotic power.

A *fourth type* of explanation – the most prevalent one – is concerned to uncover the profound *deficits in the political organization of society and the state in the GDR*. The yardstick for judging the GDR is frequently given by the different versions of differentiation theory. Everyone stresses the central role of the Party and the monopolistic power structure of the GDR state and sees this as the source of learning difficulties. In the absence of channels through which to articulate deviant views or of opportunities for organizing conflicting interests, adjustments to changed circumstances could only be achieved with difficulty. On the basis of his long-standing research into the GDR, Gert-Joachim Glaeßner gives a vivid description of the unintended consequences of centralized power.[17] Rainer Weinert's case study of the East German trade unions (FDGB) illustrates this with reference to one of the most important mass organizations.[18] In addition to the undifferentiated nature of the political system, Manfred Lötsch[19] and Sigrid Meuschel[20] point to the levelling out and elimination of difference in the structure of society. The most varied tools available to the sociologist are deployed in order to define the specific nature of GDR society. Thus Glaeßner speaks of 'Party patrimonialism', Meuschel of 'party-bureaucratic rule' ('partyocracy') and Artur Meier goes so far as to see in the GDR a 'corporative state with caste rule',[21] a claim to which Manfred Lötsch advances weighty objections. For all the deficiencies of differentiation in GDR society, we ought not to be completely forgetful of the modern features it undoubtedly possessed.[22]

The *fifth type* of explanation is *economic*. For decades controversy has raged over the achievability of global economic planning and the consequences of the state monopoly of foreign trade and state ownership of the majority of the means of production. The inadequacies of consumer goods, both in quantity and in quality, and the scarcity of services were obvious to even the most superficial observer. Above all, however, the new wave of technological innovations in the West brought onto the agenda the problem of the technical and economic capacity for innovation under 'socialism'. In his contribution,[23] Heiner Ganßmann focuses especially on the 'chaoticization' of the economy to which the attempt at total economic planning had led. Questions related to foreign trade, such as the role of debt or insufficient integration in the international division of labour, are the subjects of other studies centred on the economy.

The *sixth explanatory type* corresponds closely to the proof of the lack of differentiation, the inability of socialist societies to learn and innovate. In addition, however, these diagnoses are imported into a *scheme of global evolution* the consequence of which is that the upheaval can be seen simply as the correction of an error. A representative example of this approach is Habermas's formula of a 'catching-up revolution'. The experience of the long duration of this error and the fact that even the Russian Revolution and Bolshevik ideology were a reaction to a specific form of modernization should alert us to the need for caution. Not every step towards modernization leads to a stable form of modernity. The long-term effects of the upheavals of 1989 are as yet very unclear; the normative superiority of certain institutions does not mean that there is any greater probability that they will prevail in practice.

A *seventh explanatory type* regards the *external circumstances* of the GDR rather than the internal ones as decisive for its collapse. Most discussions feature references to the impact of 'perestroika' and 'glasnost' in the Soviet Union, the changes in Poland and Hungary and the unwinding of the Eastern bloc. On the periphery, mention is also made of the growing importance of international cultural links and the 'Conference on Security and Co-operation in Europe'. For the most part, however, such mentions remain unsystematic references to contingent features in the penumbra of society. A radical exception is the case of Randall Collins. For him, as early as the beginning of the 1980s, the demise of the Soviet empire was only a matter of time.[24] He regarded the empire as having over-extended its powers – when compared, for example, to the USA – bearing in mind the far smaller resource base of the Soviet Union. In his contribution he emphasizes not only that his theoretical assumptions enabled him to predict what had now occurred, but that other theories had also pointed in the same direction, without their exponents having had the courage to make the same prediction.

Collins's thinking is anything but monocausal. Rather, he calls for 'geopolitical' theory to be combined with the results of research into social movements and legitimation analyses. As noted above, many writers combine elements from these different types of explanation. The next step towards integrating them convincingly probably lies in extending our purview beyond the single case of the GDR.

The Need for a Comparative Perspective

The end of the GDR immediately raises the question of the reasons for the GDR's 'special path' (*Sonderweg*). Among the socialist countries of East and Central Europe, the GDR was the only one in which (at least since 1953) there were absolutely no real signs of a developed opposition. The mass protests of the autumn of 1989 had no precedent – aside from a few small civil-rights and environmental groups that had formed in recent years. The collapse came all the more suddenly and surprisingly.

Of course, there is an obvious answer here, one that is connected to the GDR's external relations, and in particular its relationship with the West German state. This relationship prevented the formation of a national reference-point for the identity of the GDR society. The GDR leadership had attempted to create a national identity, on the one hand, with their policy of anti-fascism and their self-stylization as 'the better Germany' and, on the other hand, by differentiating themselves from the exploitation and moral depravity of capitalism. These efforts turned out to be futile in the long run. The official denigration of Western capitalism ultimately helped to create the impression that it was a consumers' paradise and even a utopia. The relevant GDR saying ran: 'People in the West no longer have any ideals. People in the East have one ideal: the West.'

It is obvious that the collapse of the GDR should also be viewed in the context of the socialist camp. Does this mean that no great acuity is needed in the analysis of the social and economic causes of the collapse? Perestroika in the Soviet Union, the drawn-out processes of transformation in Poland and Hungary, and, finally, the opening of the Hungarian frontier all played their part in overturning a system that had never been based on the loyalty of the masses. In fact there was no immaculate conception of the socialist idea in the German East, but only a close association with Stalinism and the Soviet military occupation from the very beginning. But to leave matters there is again to over-simplify. The fact that the chief impulse came from the (Soviet) centre does not mean that the search for internal causes of collapse is superfluous. The question must be reformulated for the particular situation of the GDR. The question is not 'Why did the GDR collapse?', but 'When the external support of the Soviet apparatus of domination disappeared, why was the GDR regime unable to offer greater resistance to the collapse?'

This question points back to the particular circumstances of the GDR, as compared with those of the other socialist societies. Such comparisons, however, are still in their infancy. Even where the need for them is not disputed, it will take time before they can be pursued since West German social scientists are far more ignorant about the societies of East Central Europe than about the GDR.

Such a comparison would have to focus on the social structures in existence at the time of the transition to socialism, and the way they were modified by the socialist regimes. The closest comparison to the GDR is Czechoslovakia (or at least its western part). The different dynamics in the two countries point up the difficulties that need to be resolved. Even if we inquire into possible organizational nuclei that might have served as a basis for an opposition, and emphasize, for example, the role of the Church, the difficulties facing such a comparison (with Poland, Czechoslovakia or Hungary) are obvious.

The relationship between social and political dynamics can be seen most succinctly in a comparison with Hungary. Hungary is an instance of relatively steady development without the collapse of the state. The decades following 1956 witnessed a process of social and economic modernization that gradually produced a need for political change that was visible to the Hungarian political elites and was promoted by them. Why was Hungary able to produce this process of rather steady modernization on the basis of a series of political compromises? An analysis of social structures alone would not yield a sufficient explanation. It would have to be supplemented by a history of the various phases of the political opposition and their relation to the state – we might also say, by a history of the different phases of the social contract between the people and the regime.

Theoretical Implications

While we may be unwilling to make do with partial explanations, the task of constructing a unified explanatory framework appears hopeless in view of the multiplicity of competing reasons and explanations for the collapse of the GDR, from the impact of international influences down to psychoanalysis. But this cannot be our final word on the subject. Without wishing to present the reader with an all-inclusive 'master interpretation', a few pointers to possible theoretical implications can perhaps be permitted.

We might attempt, with some prospects of success, an explanation analogous to classical Marxist explanations. That is to say, we might regard the collapse as the consequence of a new historical intensification of the contradiction between the forces and relations of production. In this instance we are dealing with forces of production in an age of increased scientific and technical complexity and where production is increasingly a matter of information flows. These productive forces rely increasingly on decentralization and individualization, while the relations of production were concerned to inhibit them. The GDR and the other states in the socialist camp were unable to effect the transition from extensive to intensive growth. Employing the concepts of industrial sociology that were developed for the transformation of the structures of production in the West, we can say that socialism had some success in coping with the problems of Taylorist production methods, but the transition to post-Taylorist, post-Fordist methods of production was altogether beyond it. With the emergence of new production concepts and of decentralization as part of the new industrial division of labour in the West, the GDR's goal of catching up with the West receded into the distance. The need to conceal this failure gradually gnawed away at its substance.

At this point, we need to consider a problem of theory construction. It is not easy, nor is it particularly productive, to seek what Reißig calls the 'root cause' of collapse. Even in relation to the impact of external events, it does not greatly advance matters to keep extending the causal chain further and further until the ultimate, the original, cause has been found. It cannot possibly be perestroika, since that, too, calls for further explanation. If we pursue the question in that way, we can easily end up with Helmut Schmidt or Ronald Reagan, with the NATO twin-track decision or the forced participation in the arms race.

This suggests that we should look at a more general level for a theoretical reference-point that would render superfluous the unproductive search for ultimate explanations. We might find this in a theory of differentiation and open systems. What is at issue here is the stock of structural conditions and institutions that ensure that a system has the requisite ability to adapt itself. This would enable us to reformulate the question of the collapse of the GDR, as follows: If there were dangerous bottle-necks and difficulties, why were they allowed to grow unchecked to the point where they threatened the survival of the entire system? What caused the failure of all the mechanisms designed to repair defects and compensate for them? This question, which is directed towards internal structures, remains meaningful even if, as is not disputed, the immediate stimuli and perhaps even the major causes of the collapse came from outside. What characterizes open systems is that chains of events can be interrupted, that is to say, they do not harden out into causal chains operating like laws of nature.

The question can also be formulated in terms of evolutionary or learning theory. Why was the GDR unable to learn from its mistakes? What were the institutional deficiencies and cultural scleroses that prevented mistakes from being perceived, perceived mistakes from being put on the agenda, and solutions to publicly debated mistakes from being discovered?

By 1961 at the latest, the GDR had become a 'closed society' – much can be explained by this simple formula. Closed, of course, to the outside world, but also not sufficiently open in its internal attitude to information. There were too few opportunities for societal self-observation and self-evaluation. This is well known as far as the economy was concerned. Here the role of markets and prices in furthering the process of self-observation and self-evaluation was missing. But even in politics and culture, there was a lack of the relevant institutions. There were no early warning systems. On the contrary, alarm signals were systematically stifled. 'Blockade' seems to be a consistently apposite metaphor when we speak of the GDR; 'blockage' [Stau] another: 'conflict blockage' (Niethammer), 'emotional blockage' (Maaz), 'blocking the future'. Such blockages are particularly dangerous for a society that, as Heinz Bude makes clear, only ever thinks of its present in terms of its future. For this reason, the loss of credibility of Marxism-Leninism, even among its supporters, could be of importance. For many years one of the most powerful experiences of dialogue with the social scientists and philosophers of the GDR was the impression that no one, literally no one at all, seriously 'believed' any more, and that individuals were distinguished from one another only in the degree of their budding scepticism. With us, individual and social disinterest coincide, as Volker Braun put it with a touch of gallows humour.

When Claus Offe speaks of a 'nationalized society', or Detlef Pollack of an 'organization society', what is meant is the basic problem of insufficient differentiation between political, economic and cultural systems and their specific criteria of rationality. Politics invaded everything; within politics it was the Party, and within the Party, the Politburo. Political rule and an economic system based exclusively on a centralized monopoly of organization and force in a political hierarchy are evidently not efficient enough.[25]

Shortly before the events discussed here, Immanuel Wallerstein put forward the claim that the movements of 1968 had represented a revolution in the world system.[26] In the context of Wallerstein's general theory, this claim does not come as a surprise, but the consequences of this revolution, which are indeed becoming clear to us, are different from what he described. In the West, the '68 revolution ushered in an overdue thrust towards modernization; it was living-cell therapy for an ageing society. In principle, the cultural revolution in the West might have threatened its existence, but empirically, it seems to have had the opposite effect: it promoted the necessary adaptations to the changed conditions (including the transition to a 'post-Fordist' mode of production . . .). In the East, this revolution was suppressed until, two decades later and in different circumstances, it broke out with an annihilating explosive force.

This reduces the value of an explanatory method based on the Marxist model. We should not seek an explanation for the collapse of the GDR in the fact that contradictions have emerged between the forces and relations of production, in other words, that these societies have not succeeded in making the transition from extensive to intensive production or from heavy industry to electronics and services. We should inquire instead why they could not make this transition and why they were unable to react flexibly enough to a deepening contradiction. In other words, we must ask why they did not possess the institutions that are needed for a flexible adaptation. The same may be said of the political crisis: what is crucial is not that these societies proved incapable of channelling changed political aspirations and the emerging protest movements, but *why* they were incapable of doing so, that is to say, why their institutional repertoire was so disastrously restricted.

For indisputable reasons, this situation leads to a renaissance of modernization theories and thereby to those theories that for about twenty years had been considered representative of the 'orthodox consensus' of Western sociology, to the point where they had even become the objects of ironic obituaries. This renaissance has been articulated not just by writers who find their old views confirmed, such as Wolfgang Zapf or the Parsonians, but even by authors who were known to be critical of modernization theories, like Dieter Senghaas, or were seen as sceptical reformers of the paradigm of modernization theory, like Edward Tiryakian.[27] But the situation is complicated, for two reasons. On the one hand, history should teach us that we must show the greatest caution in attempting to resolve theoretical controversies on the basis of current events. On the other hand, the internal theoretical reservations about modernization theory have not just suddenly become irrelevant. At the very least, the inability to clarify the question of the origins and agents of the processes of differentiation, the exclusively positive value placed on those processes, the use of functional explanations, and many other factors, justify a major corrective to modernization theory − and not a simple resuscitation.

What is needed is a confrontation and an attempt at a synthesis with macro-theories based on theories of action.[28]

Future Prospects

This chapter is not the right place to deal with these questions. By way of conclusion, we prefer to direct our gaze elsewhere. It is possible to ask whether the lesson of the GDR is that an unviable system collapsed and the Western way has been vindicated, or whether both paths end in blind alleys and we have merely failed to notice it. Given the huge problems piling up in Western societies, as well as in the international system, this is by no means an absurd question. Will the West's ability to learn prove itself yet again?

In the postwar era, Western societies have developed a range of institutions that can basically be reduced to a 'magic square': pluralist democracy, the rule of law, the market economy and the welfare state. This repertoire determines the social contract (which in the main is still a contract between capital and labour) and with it the modernization coalitions on which the success of Western societies has rested up to now. At the same time, they are anything but uniform. At the beginning of the 1980s it was customary to regard Western European societies as ossified systems that were facing acute threats to their survival ('Eurosclerosis'). In the meantime, this perception has been reversed. The collapse of the socialist societies took place at a time when Western European societies, with Germany in the lead, were held up as astonishing models of social and political stability and economic dynamism. Their advanced welfare states seemed not only not to hamper their economic dynamism, but even to reveal themselves as a new productive force. The most advanced welfare states (Sweden above all) gave rise in the East to widespread and misleading hopes about a possible 'Third Way' – misleading because it went unnoticed that all these societies had private enterprise at their core and for that reason are only variant forms of the 'First Way'. But the differences between them are considerable, for example where the regulation of the labour market and the size of the public sector are concerned.[29] With the collapse of socialism, Western societies find themselves in a new situation. On the one hand, competition between different systems simply lapses, and in the long run this could have dangerous implications for the pressure to innovate.[30] On the other hand, there is the problem of integrating the Eastern societies in the process of transformation. Of particular importance for the German federal system is the question whether its institutions are equal to the task of adjusting to the process of unification, a very demanding test of the system's ability to learn. What is at issue is more than simply the ability of the institutions imposed on the former GDR to function satisfactorily. In addition, we have to ask whether the central institutions and the political and economic participants are open and flexible enough to avoid a colonization of the East by the West. Only if they succeed in correcting such dangerous imbalances in the unified society, and only if they are able to create the foundations for a new, stable social contract, will it be possible to claim that West German institutions have proved equal to the tasks posed by the uni-fication process. The same problem is replicated on the European plane. If the integration of Europe proves incapable of *including the East*, the West, too, will find it impossible to survive as an Island of the Blessed in the ocean of growing global problems.

6

Sprayed and Betrayed
The Experience of Violence
in the Vietnam War and
Its Consequences

Wars have destructive consequences that continue long after they have finished. After the end of a war there is not only mourning for human lives ended by violence, social relations torn asunder, cities and countryside destroyed. Even the survivors of wars have not remained unscathed, since separation and loss, as well as the experience of mass destruction and violence, have wrought changes in them that will last their entire lives. As the violent resolution of disputes between states, wars represent the most extreme experiences of violence for all participants, both perpetrators and victims – and in war many perpetrators are transformed into victims, just as many victims are transformed into perpetrators. Admittedly, social life is never entirely free from violence or the threat of violence, but in war the degree of this threat and the fear that accompanies it surpass for the most part all imagination of it entertained by people who grow up in peacetime.

The war-wounded are like ruins casting their shadow over the subsequent peace, reminding us of the destructive power of war. The sight of them makes it harder for the survivors and those born after the war to repress the events of war or to indulge in unthinking glorification of it. But they do fit an interpretation according to which one's own side can be seen as the innocent victim of enemy violence. The pain is sharper, however, when we become aware that the men of violence include our own sons, brothers, fathers and husbands, especially when the degree and kind of violence exceeds what is held to be the reasonable use of force in the circumstances. War crimes committed by one's own side and acts of violence by war veterans can, therefore, if there is any goodwill at all, become the occasion for a nagging soul-searching about the justifiability of a specific war or of war in general.

The extensive American sociological research on Vietnam veterans offers an impressive example of such a public self-questioning using scientific methods. It builds a bridge between the investigation of external and internal violence.

With the Civil War of 1861–5, the historical memory of the USA remains fixated on a war that was marked by a brutality carried out with modern weapons of destruction. In this respect it went beyond previous history and many historians regard it as the first modern war and the prelude to total war. However, since the Civil War came to an end, the USA has been spared further wars on its own soil. It is in all probability the trauma of the Civil War, rather than the long peace in its own country, that has made the vision of a victimless war – of war without fatal casualties of its own and won through supremacy in the air or in rocket warfare – so very attractive, above all in the USA. The failure of this vision in the jungle, the rice-paddies and the cities of Vietnam led to a profound crisis of the American self-image and of the legitimacy of the political system. In what follows, we shall take up some of the questions raised by social-scientific research on the effects of the Vietnam war. In doing so, we shall keep the effects on the USA of the experience of violence in that war in the forefront of our minds. Our intention, however, is not to strengthen the ethnocentric tendency to pay more attention to even very subtle effects of the war on the American public than the very palpable acts of destruction in the country of their Asian enemy. Having said that, an examination of the existing sociological research from the USA about the USA can only focus on matters raised in that research.

Every more scrupulous study of the consequences of soldiers' war experiences in the postwar period must be preceded by the question: who exactly are we talking about?[1] Global talk of 'the' soldiers or even 'the' Vietnam generation conceals the different degrees to which individuals are affected and all too easily gives rise to misinterpretations and misleading inferences. The impact of the Vietnam war can be gauged in stages as far as the American population is concerned. If we take the years between 1964 and 1973 as the actual period of the Vietnam war, 53 million young Americans reached the call-up age of eighteen during that time. Of these, as is demographically normal, something over a half were men (26.8 million). In the Vietnam war, women were scarcely involved in military operations; however, they did play an important role in the medical services. Nevertheless, numerically they did not exceed 15,000.[2] Of the men liable in principle for service, only around 40 per cent (that is to say, 11 million) were actually called up; the rest were declared unfit or were deferred on the grounds of education or their profession, or they managed to evade the call-up illegally. Overall, around one quarter, that is to say, 10 per cent of all young men of call-up age, actually went to Vietnam (2.7 million). Of the troops stationed in Vietnam only about one in five saw active combat (540,000 men). Hence every generalization about the consequences of the experience of violence must concentrate on this group, which amounts to around 2 per cent of all young men in the relevant age-group. While it is true that an entire generation lived in the shadow of the war, only a small minority were involved in the sense that their own lives were palpably at stake.

Even during the war, and also after it, both the soldiers and the general public discussed whether the call-up, the posting to Vietnam and engagement in actual fighting had been shared in a socially just way. Social inequality with regard to the risk of being killed on behalf of the state stands in fundamental contradiction to the notions of justice in a liberal social order. But in the social reality of all modern states, even in liberal democracies like the USA, there are powerful institutional traditions that facilitate the evasion of military service by making financial payments, by the right to nominate substitutes or by taking into account participation in ('higher') courses of education to which access itself is not distributed in a socially just way. The conclusions of sociological studies on this point are quite unambiguous in their general thrust. Young men of the white middle class were more successful than their black contemporaries and members of the lower social strata in their efforts to avoid military service altogether; if they were called up nevertheless, they succeeded more often in avoiding a posting to Vietnam; if they were sent to Vietnam after all, their exposure to danger in combat was significantly smaller. The social selectivity of the armed forces during the Vietnam war is revealed in all its brutality in a breakdown of the casualty figures. One vivid finding relates to the comparison between the graduates of elite institutions like Harvard University and MIT (Massachusetts Institute of Technology), on the one hand, and their contemporaries from South Boston, a district close to those institutions but with a predominantly working-class population, on the other. Of the over 20,000 graduates of the two elite universities from the years 1962–72, fourteen fell in Vietnam. Of the roughly 2000 young men who reached the call-up age in South Boston during the same period, twenty-five lost their lives in Vietnam. This means that the risk for the young men of the lower class was around twenty times greater. An abundance of other findings point in the same direction.

Of course, it is interesting to inquire how such stark inequalities in a matter of life and death can come about in a situation of formal equality. To begin with, an important factor was the regulation according to which a college education allowed call-up to be deferred. Such a regulation directly benefited the sons of the educated middle classes, who are disproportionately represented in higher education or who were able to decide in favour of such an education in the light of such favourable treatment. Knowledge of these and other exemptions, moreover, presupposes a particular receptivity to information that is more frequently encountered in the better educated sections of the population. Of course, this trend could be countered by an active information policy on the part of the state. However, since the armed forces identified the middle class as the class where the tendency to protest was most marked, they were probably not too unhappy – from an organizational point of view – about this unjust social distribution. A further gateway for social disadvantage was to be found in the local draft boards, whose composition was not socially representative, but who were recruited instead from among the local worthies. Their familiarity with the sons of people from their own circles increased the latter's chances of avoiding being sent to Vietnam. In general, the ease with which doctors, psychiatrists or lawyers could be approached via informal networks played a not insignificant part in the selection process for military service. In addition, the illegal ways of dodging the draft, such as taking refuge abroad, were also taken chiefly by members of the middle classes. Despite a few spectacular cases of sentencing and imprisonment of conscientious objectors, the state tended to deal with them rather leniently. Since the age-groups had no problems in principle in supplying additional young men, the illegal methods, too, tended to shift the balance of social distribution further to the disadvantage of the lower strata.

Greater precision is also needed in dealing with the question of the age of the US soldiers sent out to Vietnam if we are to obtain a more accurate picture of the war veterans. What is decisive here is the way postings to Vietnam were organized. American soldiers were sent to the theatre of war for precisely one year. For the individual soldier this had the advantage that his own commitment was limited regardless of the overall duration of the war. Furthermore, the rotation after 365 days served the general sense of military fair play, since it distributed the risk of death in combat over a greater number of men instead of confining the risk to soldiers who, once committed, had to stay put. These advantages, however, were counterbalanced by grave drawbacks. Since the soldiers posted overseas were for the most part young conscripts who had just finished their basic training, the average age of the soldiers stationed and fighting in Vietnam was extremely low. It was in fact nineteen years and thus differed significantly from the average age of American soldiers in other wars. In the Second World

War, for example, it was twenty-seven. Even the officers were for the most part often very young and relatively inexperienced. What was typical of soldiers in the Vietnam war was not just their low average age, but also the uniformity of the age-group. Where the age-range is greater, a military unit will bring together men with a varied experience of life and combat, and this will facilitate the socialization of the younger soldiers. In this respect the US soldiers of the Vietnam war were forced to rely on themselves. The *individualization* of soldiers is seen most strikingly in the practice of making up for losses not by replacing entire units, but by filling the gaps with individual soldiers. This procedure actively undermined the growth of social cohesiveness between the soldiers and the formation of a collective identity. The rotation system of the Vietnam war did meet the complaints about the feeling of hopelessness experienced by soldiers in the Second World War who were condemned to combat duty for an indefinite period, but at the same time it flagrantly ignored the lessons that military sociologists had learnt from the Second World War. In that war the emotional maturity of the servicemen, their respect for the professional abilities of the officers and the social cohesion of the combat units had been identified as the crucial preconditions for high morale. In contrast, the rotation principle produced an extreme individualization of the temporal perspective of each soldier. Enduring and surviving the one, long year in Vietnam of necessity became the one fixed orientation point of soldiers who were still adolescent.[3]

A further feature of the Vietnam war needs to be borne in mind if we are to understand its subsequent impact on the lives of the war veterans.[4] The Vietnam war was no typical, conventional war in which army stands against army, but a war in which regular troops are opposed by a guerilla army. Without wishing to suggest misleadingly that all wars are much the same, it can be said that in war the combat situation and the intensification of war to a life-and-death struggle have mostly been exceptions limited to short periods of time. These exceptional situations were modified, above all, in the positional war on the German western front in the First World War, in the sense that combat was constantly present as a possibility and hostilities failed to yield any clear decision. Despite this, for the majority of soldiers there were long periods of relative quiet during which, even for those at the front, let alone those behind the lines, there was no immediate fear of death. The situation of American soldiers in Vietnam was fundamentally different from this. The enemy was not clearly identifiable, nor was it possible to perceive clear outcomes from fighting with him. The Vietnamese allies were frequently felt to be unreliable; an attack might come at any time even from the Vietnamese civilian population, though the soldiers were convinced that they were risking their lives to protect them and to defend their liberty. Thus, danger was not confined to a formal battle situation, but lay in wait everywhere and at all times of the day and night. What produced the actual fighting was not as a general rule the servicemen's own military strategy; instead, they found themselves forced to fend off an enemy whose attacks came quite out of the blue. No territory could be considered to have been conquered ('liberated') definitively. In the absence of territorial gains, success was increasingly measured in the figures showing the enemy's losses. Members of the civilian population were thus included in the tally of Vietnamese killed. You could never be sure which of them secretly belonged to the enemy guerilla forces. For this reason, the year in Vietnam represented a year of constant, diffuse danger, even for those personnel who ultimately were never involved in combat. This is not to say that it is after all irrelevant to delimit the number of people with direct experience of danger and violence. But the kind of experience they had and the experience of those not directly involved was decisively influenced by the war's specific character as one waged against a guerilla army.

Needless to say, the contrast with the classical war of army against army should not be overstated.[5] Otherwise we shall create the impression that classical warfare truly is exactly as it is portrayed in a large part of the literature on strategy and the history of war, that is to say, a co-ordinated movement of masses under the leadership of a superior will, who coolly face up to the possibility of their own death in total discipline and commitment to their own cause – as if marching in step were the rhythm of battle. In reality even classical warfare represents a highly contingent situation in which strategic intentions can provide no more than a vague guideline. When facing a threat to your own life and the compulsion to kill, the fear of the enemy and one's own superiors takes precedence, as does the need to take instant decisions in conditions that could not be anticipated and are confusing, if not chaotic. This extreme contingency combined with the enormous stake explains why discipline as such cannot be the decisive factor in achieving success. Success calls for a collective spirit that enables the individual to perform risky actions on his own initiative. The outcome of every battle is determined not just by numbers and resources, or even by pure discipline, but in essential ways by the 'moral' force of each side. For this reason, ideas about rational action fail to do justice even to classical warfare; such warfare, too, drives the participants into realms of experience that affect the foundations of personal stability. The war of an army against a guerilla force, therefore, represents not the antithesis of classical warfare, but an intensification of what is already an unbearable experience of violence and danger there.

'If you start a man killing, you can't turn him off again like an engine.'[6] This statement applies initially to war itself, where violence against civilians or prisoners of war and atrocities against the enemy go beyond what is strategically necessary. In the case of the Vietnam war, alongside spectacular war-crimes, like the massacre of the inhabitants of My Lai, it was above all the acts of violence committed by returning soldiers that aroused the interest of the public. In the media veterans were portrayed as ticking time-bombs who could explode at any moment. The fear of reimporting violence from Vietnam reached a climax in May 1971 when Dwight Johnson was shot dead by police during a robbery in Detroit.[7] Johnson had been decorated with the highest military honours for his heroism in Vietnam; he had even been used by the army in their recruiting campaign. Admittedly, the hysterical accounts in the media were contradicted by the soothing official figures that showed that the tendency to violence was no greater among war veterans than among other young men of the same age who had stayed at home. Initially, it was hard to resolve this contradiction. Had the media overreacted or were the official figures a fabrication? Further research was needed to shed light on this darkness. Three findings, in particular, have turned out to be illuminating. First, it is necessary to overcome the fundamental fallacy that figures about all the troops stationed in Vietnam enable us to draw inferences about the behaviour of the combat veterans. Since only a minority actually had experience of fighting, what was specific to them was lost in global statements. Second, it is necessary to include the consequences of being involved in maltreatment alongside the consequences of combat experience.[8] In doing so, it is necessary to distinguish between active participation in acts of mistreatment and mere presence, even though this distinction may be difficult to sustain, since interviewees may be disinclined to confess their active involvement in the presence of the interviewer. But it is precisely cases of maltreatment that turn out to have consequences for the personality of the perpetrators. Lastly, a certain distance in time is needed in order to be able clearly to recognize the consequences of the experience of violence in war. From this distance, various indicators show that the experience of violence does leave lasting marks. The incidence of suicide is significantly higher, and even that of fatal car accidents, poisonings and drug overdoses, as well as arrests and acts of violence, all distinguish the combat veterans from comparable groups. The supposition that there are causal connections here is therefore no longer in dispute today.

What continues to be unclear, however, is where exactly we should look for the explanation of these effects. The question of the connection between war and acts of criminal violence has a long sociological pedigree.[9] From among the conclusions of the various studies, one emerges strongly. This is that the increase in acts of violence in the aftermath of war cannot simply be reduced to such acts performed by war veterans, but, going far beyond this, it has to be explained by a general lowering of taboos against violence and a greater tolerance towards the use of force among the public as a whole. But this finding does not constitute a denial that the tendency towards violence of war veterans is higher than in comparable persons. In fact this conclusion is confirmed not only by individual case studies but also by quantitative analyses.[10] An explanation could conceivably be found in the possibility that combat veterans had shown a predisposition to violence even before their military service or had acquired it during their training. Studies that include these alternative explanations do indeed arrive at the conclusion that previously existing tendencies to violence are maintained; they can also show that the increasing tendency to violence that arises from military training does decline with the passage of time. However, one finding towers above all others, namely that of the people who did not originally possess violent tendencies, it was those who were deployed in combat who subsequently often became violent. That is to say, they acquired violent tendencies in war irrespective of whether they had any predisposition to violence or not. Thus combat is not simply a field of action for a pre-existing readiness in men to behave in an aggressive and violent manner. Rather, it transforms the soldiers' personality so that their relation to violence is changed over the long term.

Furthermore, the greatest tendency to violence is to be found in those combat veterans who display several of the symptoms of the so-called PTSD syndrome (post-traumatic stress disorder). According to the diagnostic manual of the American Psychiatric Association, this concept brings together the effects of a traumatization in which (a) the trauma recurs in nightmares, obsessions or sudden, irresistible feelings of being transported back into the traumatic events; (b) tendencies to emotional rigidity and to retreat from the external world become evident; in addition, (c) permanent restlessness, severe insomnia, inability to concentrate, impatience and guilt feelings torment the traumatized subject. Interestingly, the construction of this syndrome and its catalogue of symptoms is itself the product of the Vietnam war. PTSD was only admitted to the official vocabulary of psychiatry and from there to the consciousness of the public in the wake of the observations of Vietnam war veterans. As late as the First World War, the symptoms of trauma were interpreted by all the participating armies in terms of guilt and intention.[11] Soldiers shot for cowardice included instances of clear nervous breakdown. But with the introduction of concepts like 'bomb neurosis' [*Bombenneurose*] and 'shell shock' we can see the first attempts to label these phenomena as psychiatric pathologies.[12] The fact that psychopathological concepts were used so readily on the American side in the Vietnam war tells us clearly how far the penetration of psychology had advanced in the USA. The distance between the war and the normative expectation of warlike attributes, on the one hand, and the progressive dissemination of psychological knowledge and the civilizing of civilian life, on the other, had perceptibly increased. An important role was played also by the war veterans' *rap groups*. Mistrust towards the armed forces' psychiatrists and the Veterans' Administration led to the formation of numerous self-help groups in which participants in the war looked for dialogue about their experiences. The self-confidence of these groups made it possible for critical psychiatrists[13] to elaborate the stories told by the veterans and to bring the 'hidden wounds' in their souls to the attention of the public.

In these studies we are able to perceive the contexts of meaning out of which the experience of combat can so often lead to new acts of violence. Even in conversational situations rage and violence are more or less continuously present. Many veterans report how even minor disagreements or unintentional jostlings release violent reflexes in them. Here it is the simple habit of violent action that makes the veterans dangerous and even leads them to genuine criminal violence. In many cases, however, we find not just an almost routinized tendency to violent action, but a fundamentally altered self-image. Coming to terms with one's own capacity for violence, and even for killing another human being, changes a man's idea of his own identity. To define oneself as a violent 'monster' allows one to commit acts and even to feel that it is natural to commit acts that would have been incompatible with one's earlier self-image. Questioning this new self-image is painful, since it once again reminds a man of the moral dimension of his own acts of violence. Such a questioning process can also be violently repressed. Excessive demands going beyond the slow work on one's own self-image, or the rejection of an offered self-criticism, are felt by many veterans to be typical of the situations that produce violence.

The most frequent motive mentioned by veterans as triggering rage and violence is their feeling of betrayal. There are evidently many rational justifications for this. Many soldiers felt that they had been betrayed by the armed forces and by their superior officers. This began with the injustices of the call-up. Moreover, military service and war were portrayed so unrealistically that this subsequently led to desperate complaints against the people whose misleading accounts were now held responsible for the present traumatization. But behind the armed forces stand the entire political leadership, the political system and the cultural values of the United States, whose war aims, conduct of the war and propaganda were all felt to be integral parts of the betrayal. The feeling of having been betrayed was also directed at the entire American population. The disappointment felt on return to the USA encapsulates this feeling symbolically. As is well known, there were no victory parades for the soldiers returning from Vietnam. Even worse, for sections of the American population they became the scapegoats for their own feelings of guilt. There are numerous reports of returning soldiers preferring to remain silent about their tour of duty in Vietnam in order not to expose themselves to criticism. Many report having been spat at and attacked. The extreme individualization of service in Vietnam because of the rotation system was repeated on their return. You secretly take off your uniform in the airport toilet and put on your civilian clothes – and then no one wants to hear about your incredible experiences in the war!

The veterans' sense of betrayal is summed up in the social discourse about the effects of 'Agent Orange'.[14] In order to combat guerilla bases in the jungle, and also presumably to destroy the enemy's food supplies, chemicals were sprayed in Vietnam until 1970/1 with the official aim of defoliating the jungle. Initially, the military were probably unaware of the catastrophic side-effects of the substance, which contained dioxin and which became known as Agent Orange from the colour of the containers. The substance had been previously used in American agriculture. This meant that the chemical was spread indiscriminately over large areas. Since the spraying operations took place without regard to the direction of the wind and since the empty drums were then used for other purposes, the effects extended to the spraying personnel: American soldiers. The relatively unspecific medical symptoms that then appeared after a considerable lapse of time made it difficult to make a credible case for a causal connection. All the claims put forward by Vietnam veterans for compensation for damage to their health were rejected by the extremely influential Veterans' Administration as products of their imagination. From 1977 on, the year in which the first claims were made, there was a struggle lasting several years about the legitimacy of these demands. This struggle reflected the mutual alienation of American society and the Vietnam war veterans. Only after a number of journalists had taken up the matter and the interest of the media had gradually spread did the campaign finally culminate, after a delay lasting years, in hearings in the US Congress. Because of the apathy of the quasi-official veterans' organizations, independent organizations of Vietnam war veterans sprang into being, and under pressure from them the former organizations were finally dragged along in their wake in 1982/3. Hampered by administrative and political delays of all sorts, the veterans' groups finally succeeded, in 1985, in agreeing a settlement that gave them at least a part of their claims. The experience of the war veterans was encapsulated symbolically in the bumper sticker 'Sprayed and Betrayed'.

But alongside the sense of being betrayed by others that we have described, there is also the feeling of having betrayed oneself. We have already spoken of the transformation of one's self-image under the pressure of committed acts of violence. The feeling of self-betrayal makes its appearance in guilt-feelings of two kinds. In the first place, many a soldier in a combat situation comes to realize that he can derive pleasure from committing acts of violence, and from torturing and killing other people. If it is not taken as a reason for a negative redefinition of his own identity, this experience persists as a frightening insight into the dark side of one's own character. It is a feeling of guilt that refers not just to an evil action, but to an unacceptable side of one's own character. In the second place, even the experience of combat leaves behind the feeling of 'survival guilt', which has been recorded in survivors of the Nazi concentration camps. What we must understand by this is not the feeling that one has been guilty of the death of one's own people, as is the case with officers who have made wrong decisions, for example. Instead, it is a matter of the much deeper guilt-feeling that arises when you feel that your own life has been preserved for radically contingent reasons. Precisely because you do not remain alive through your own merits, your survival is felt to be accidental and meaningless compared to the infinite sufferings of those who were not similarly fortunate. The feeling of betrayal here is not blamed on others but is related to the loss of the meaning of one's own life. Simply to have survived is the betrayal. The horror arising from the enjoyment of violence and the pain resulting from the guilt at surviving means that the experience of violence in war leads a man to the feeling that he has missed the meaning of his own life. A man loses the confidence that he is, or can ever be, the person he wanted to be or to become. In this way violence makes victims even of the perpetrators.[15]

PART III

WAR AND VIOLENCE IN SOCIAL THEORY

7

Between Power Politics and Pacifist Utopia
Peace and War in Sociological Theory

When Václav Havel received the Peace Prize of the German Booksellers Association in October 1989, a matter of weeks before the government in Czechoslovakia was overthrown, he was not able to give his acceptance speech in person, as he had been denied an exit visa. In the speech, entitled 'Words on Words', which was read on Havel's behalf by an actor friend of his, he spoke of the allergic reaction that the mere mention of the word 'peace' provokes among many inhabitants of Eastern Europe – even today, incidentally.[1] Owing to its constant use and the shameless way in which it was employed to justify a foreign policy that was not at all defensive, and a repressive domestic policy, the word had become so devalued that it was hardly possible any longer to gain serious-minded theoretical and political attention for the threat to peace. This was the case despite the fact that in recent decades the annihilation of humanity by the catastrophe of a nuclear war has undoubtedly been an unimaginable, yet real, prospect looming on the horizon. Although it can be said that the events of 1989 have clearly diminished the probability of a nuclear confrontation in Europe between heavily armed military blocs, this cannot be regarded as reason now to herald the dawning of an age of eternal peace and to perceive the danger of unintentional self-destruction to be something that stems exclusively from the ecological consequences of our economic life.

If we as social scientists do not wish to forgo using the means that only rationality and science can make available to investigate the causes of these immense dangers and the possibilities of banishing them, then we must distance ourselves equally both from the desperate optimism of psychological repression nurtured by some of our political leaders and from the fascination that horror exerts, a fascination that paralyses any ability to analyse and act. We must, instead, examine what our respective disciplines and our personal abilities can contribute when facing such a task. Such a line of inquiry involves two questions. First, what do sociology and the social sciences tell us about the genesis and causes of war and about the effect of war on the development of humanity? And second, what light is shed on the major theoretical projects generated by our disciplines and on these disciplines themselves if they are viewed in the light of the first question?

In this context, if we cast an initial glance over the social sciences at present, all we get is a highly contradictory impression. On the one hand, it looks as if pressing current global problems have had little if any impact on the conferences, teaching and everyday research of the profession.[2] The major theories that are the subject of general discussion today – let us take Habermas, Luhmann or the poststructuralists as examples – contain hardly any mention of war and peace. On the other hand, approaches derived from the social sciences are of considerable importance both for the development of nuclear strategies and for the peace movement. Game theories and conflict theories often constitute the core of lines of argumentation employed in strategic analyses, and as soon as the various trends of the peace movement go beyond the level of appeals to personal ethical convictions, they argue almost exclusively in terms of global analyses in the social sciences. The contradiction between these two observations resolves itself once it becomes clear that the social sciences have to a certain extent delegated the concern with war and peace to a separate area of its own. Peace research or military sociology, the study of international relations or the analysis of nuclear conflict scenarios in terms of game theory – none of these fields has had any noteworthy effect on the general development of the social sciences. The reasons for this segregation are by no means coincidental. Rather, they are closely linked to the definition of the concept of 'society' that is constitutive for the social sciences. Alain Touraine and Anthony Giddens have both criticized classical sociology for employing a concept of 'society' that expressed only the reality of the nineteenth-century European and perhaps also North American nation-state.[3] All the alleged regular laws of development thus refer covertly to the reality of a state whose territories are clearly delineated, which is bound by a body of law and administered in a modern manner, whereas the dynamics of the relationships between these states is regarded as a purely historical contingency and otherwise hardly warrants interest. Consequently, such an approach cannot adequately thematize either the particular internal characteristics of a nation-state as opposed to other historical structures, or the dependence of intra-societal processes on global economic, political and military processes. There are exceptions, though not so much with regard to the nation-state, but in the central treatment of war and peace. The chief example of this is a specifically German tradition of historical human and political science. Yet this tradition cannot easily be drawn on, given its proximity to the glorification of power and chauvinism.[4] If we criticize classical sociology for neglecting to deal with international relations, we must at the same time ask whether the Enlightenment's optimism with respect to peace (and that optimism has contributed to the neglect) was a worthless illusion that had necessarily to be abandoned in favour of a realism based on power politics, or whether it can be made the subject of a serious reconstruction.

Thought on the conditions for peace began, of course, long before the Enlightenment. The late Middle Ages, at least, engendered a series of attempts to make the Christian religion, which linked the peoples of Europe, the core of a peaceful order patterned after the model of the ancient *Pax Romana*. Such attempts, of course, hardly focused on the non-Christian world; and when they did, the conditions of a Christian peace would seem not to apply to it. It was the Renaissance and a few of its harbingers, as well as the radical sects that emerged in the age of the Reformation, that represented the first thrust in the direction of a universalistic orientation towards peace. The historical impact of this way of thinking was widespread and left its mark on many aspects of life in the North American colonies. The predominant line of development, however, lies in the subsequent period, namely in the consolidation of the territorial and/or nation-states of Europe and the development of the ideology of *raison d'état* and the balance of power. The discourse of peace can to a certain extent be regarded as a relatively quiet outsider's voice raised against that way of thinking for which standing armies and perpetual conflicts of interest between the states became ever more a matter of course. The re-emergence of the issue of peace in France during the early Enlightenment was perceived by contemporaries as abstruse rumination.[5] Although the author of the early Enlightenment's most famous utopia of peace – the Abbé de St Pierre – could not complain that his proposals failed to attract any attention, crude and polemical retorts were initially clearly the order of the day.

Nevertheless, it was the Enlightenment that generated the first serious attempts to base the possibility of lasting peace on a change in the internal nature of states, attempts that continue to have an influence on the social sciences even today. A total of at least five such approaches can be discerned; they set their sights on guaranteeing peace respectively by means of the expansion of free trade, the founding of republics, the development of industrial society, the establishment of socialism and, lastly, the existence of stable nuclear alliances. All of them have been discredited by historical events, at least in the stark form in which they were initially presented. This is not to say that they were falsified in some simplistic fashion. Their overall claims, however, were dashed by the emergence of wars that they had not foreseen, the causes of which apparently contradicted the expectations that had been nourished by theory. An adequate treatment of the subject at hand would require that all of these approaches be reviewed in order to identify the precise point in the context of events at which each exhausted its respective claims. Needless to say, this would exceed the scope of the present discussion. I will therefore outline each of them here as briefly as possible. I will only go into somewhat more detail with regard to the assumption, which is constitutive of sociology, of the peaceful character of industrial society and the inherent tension between this assumption and the realism of power politics as well as developments in theory since the end of the Second World War. Borrowing vaguely from ethnomethodology, I refer to the method I have devised as that of a 'historical crisis experiment'. What is meant by this is the choice of a historical nexus of events that was of course not produced by an experimenter, but in which social orders nevertheless changed in such a way that the faith of the participants in the theories was shaken. The study of such constellations of events and the participants' ways of reacting to them can thus serve as a methodological means of shedding light on deep-seated and often unarticulated theoretical assumptions.

The two oldest relevant models in the social sciences are associated with the names of Immanuel Kant and Adam Smith. Adopting motifs from Rousseau, Kant established a link between the capacity of states for peace and their internal structure, and spoke of the peaceful nature of republics. His concept of the republic, however, was not at all aimed at deposing the monarch, but rather signified the constitutionalization and juridification of the power of the monarch. The well-understood interest of the citizens would have the effect of helping to avoid war and promote mutually beneficial relations between states, if only the citizens' interests were taken into account when making foreign policy decisions. The 'republican' model corresponds on this point to the other great peace model that was represented in the emerging political economy. Adam Smith set his sights on the pacifying effects of free trade. It was, after all, possible to effect a peaceful exchange of needed goods instead of mutual threat, destruction and pillage; the expansion of these exchange relations would serve the interests of both sides and render war superfluous.

However, both models soon ran into difficulty in view of historical developments. This became glaringly obvious in the case of Kant's position, which was totally in keeping with 'republican' thinking in general, in both Germany and France. Just after 1789, there were high hopes in France that the Revolution would also be a step towards eliminating the cabinet wars of the eighteenth century. Thus, a republican victory in the wars that were being waged against France by the monarchies of Europe would have been a contribution towards the emergence of a peaceful world. Consequently, the increasingly offensive character of the French war campaign plunged the republican model of peace into a severe crisis. It was in particular German intellectuals of the time who discussed the consequences of this state of affairs.[6] Was it right for revolutionary France also to use bellicose means to convert other states into republics, and should intellectuals who sympathized with the Revolution support this expansion of the Revolution by armed force? After Napoleon's victory over Prussia in 1806, this issue necessarily became even more acute. It was now precisely the progressive intellectuals who began to regard the strengthening of a German national consciousness and, to an increasing degree, also armed struggle against the occupying forces as the political conclusion to be drawn from their convictions. This justification of national consciousness still contained universalistic elements, yet the hope for a future peaceful world no longer played a role. As a result, in a peculiar about-turn, the side that gained the upper hand in the peace debate was the one that expected peace to come both from eliminating France as a source of unrest by reinstating the legitimate monarchy, and from a new balance of power and a concert of nations in the spirit of a reinvigorated Christendom. This raised the question as to the extent of the break between this justification of war and a philosophy of peace that had been derived from natural rights and the universalistic ideals of the Enlightenment. This question remains important for an assessment of the further development of German thought in the nineteenth century.[7]

Smith's theory of replacing war with free trade was not at all as simple as it may sound in this abbreviated formula. He was well aware that even communities engaged in trade still remained indefinitely dependent on military protection; just as he was conscious of the question of how trade between states that were totally different in terms of military strength could be kept free from the influence of this military strength. On the whole, however, his optimistic belief in peace-making policy surely predominated. After all, free trade was itself suited to bolstering those strata within society that opposed the traditionally warlike nobility. The free-trade liberalist model of peace, however, had a covert particularistic undertone. For the hopes of peace it nourished were usually not truly universalistic, but rather limited to the circle of 'civilized' peoples. Thomas More had already declared that a war was just if it was waged against a people that leaves land untilled while denying another people the use of the land. In many cases, it was stated explicitly that regulations proposed would not apply to 'savages'. As a consistent free trader, Bentham was an exception in demanding, as early as the end of the eighteenth century, that the colonies be dispensed with; were that not done, it was to be feared that conflict over the colonies would give rise to ever more wars, even if the power of war-mongering aristocrats had been curbed. In Britain, thought that focused on peace and the appeal for free trade remained closely linked. For this very reason, it was felt outside Britain that in many cases free trade merely served the interests of what was economically and technologically the most advanced nation, namely Britain, and that it was therefore by no means simply an outgrowth of universalistic thinking.[8]

In the nineteenth century these two models of peace were joined by two further models, both of which were closely linked to the two strands of Enlightenment thought about peace. Marxism took the polemic against non-constitutional states' lack of a capacity for peace and levelled it at capitalism: it was not the republic but socialism that provided the social conditions for peace. A violent and expansive character is ascribed to capitalism; the struggle to overthrow capitalism could thus go hand in hand with the struggle for peace. This is why the Marxist-inspired movement always regarded with a fair degree of arrogance pacifist tendencies that did not give priority to the critique of capitalism or efforts to reach a peaceful settlement of international conflicts through international law. Friedrich Engels, however, in later years, showed a new receptivity both to a non-violent upheaval within society and to the prospects for European disarmament. More recent Marxist attempts have been able to draw on this and have attested to the capacity for peace that capitalism exhibits in the nuclear age, at least in principle.[9] The mainstream of Marxist thought, however, is shaped by the diverse attempts to draw up a theory of imperialism; this line of argument was developed above all immediately prior to the First World War, which seemed to confirm its view that capitalism inexorably drifts into an imperialistic *stage* – in which conflict between the major 'imperialist' powers is inevitable. This view of things determined the way Marxists thought after the First World War and extended far into the social democratic camp, where admittedly older Enlightenment models of peace also continued to have an effect. It was fuelled by the impression that the foreign policy of the USSR, being the only socialist state, was – regardless of what one thought of the precise nature of this socialism – defensive and orientated towards peace.

Outside the socialist and communist movements, the fear of a revolution within society allied itself early on to the fear that such a rebellion could be incited or supported by the Soviet Union or the Communist International. Within the working-class movement, however, the Hitler–Stalin Pact of 1939 was the event that first undeniably shook the foundations of beliefs that had hitherto been taken for granted. This was not only true for members of the resistance who were fighting the Nazis within the Third Reich, nor was it limited to the abrupt cessation of all contacts made with a view to possible co-operation between the German Social Democratic Party and the German Communist Party. It applied above all to the exponents of Marxist thought. The entire range of reactions can be grasped by taking a look at the famous controversy between Rudolf Hilferding, the Social Democrat and theoretician of 'Finance Capital', and Walter Ulbricht. At the end of 1939, convinced that Hitler's Germany and the Soviet Union of Stalin were hand in glove, Hilferding concluded that both had totalitarianism in common and that social democracy consequently had to take up the cause of supporting Great Britain and France in the fight against them. Ulbricht reacted to this with a vitriolic attack that attracted international attention; in it he characterized British imperialism as the principal enemy. Precisely because of its willingness to establish a pact with the Soviet Union, Nazi Germany, as Ulbricht saw it, had become the less aggressive form of imperialism. This, of course, demonstrated not only the bankruptcy of the Marxist theory of imperialism, which was completely functionalized to serve as a justification for Soviet foreign policy, but also its profound disregard of the autonomous significance of democracy and constitutionality for an assessment of the capacity of states for peace.[10] It is true enough that the German attack on the Soviet Union in 1941 led to a renewed shift in emphasis, as now the fact that Fascism was the chief enemy was again undisputed. Yet Soviet policy in Eastern and Central Europe after the Second World War, and especially the instances of military intervention to repress internal reform movements in socialist states (Hungary, 1956, and Czechoslovakia, 1968), provoked far-reaching discussions on both occasions about the capacity of socialism for peace. The simple thesis that eliminating the interests of the capitalist military-industrial complex would result in peace was, in any case, put to a hard test and gradually lost all credibility.

For the generation that rediscovered Marxism for itself in the 1960s and 1970s and in so doing helped it to undergo a renaissance, the events mentioned here, with the exception of the suppression of the 'Prague

Spring', were already too far back in time to leave their mark on political perceptions. For this generation, the military conflicts between socialist states (above all, between China and the Soviet Union), as well as the Soviet intervention in Afghanistan in 1979, played a decisive role. For many former Marxists this meant a simple switch, for they adopted a realism of power politics, or even one of geopolitical power. This transformation is not all that plausible, since, despite all the evident gaps in the explanatory power of a peace model centred on capitalism or 'imperialism', it is not possible simply to abandon the basic question as to the internal economic, social and political prerequisites for a capacity for peace in foreign policy.

The theory of the peaceful nature of industrial society was constitutive for sociology. Auguste Comte and Herbert Spencer, as academic outsiders who propagated sociology as a new science without being able to give it institutionalized academic foundations, undoubtedly perpetuated the peace-orientated thinking of the Enlightenment by attempting to prove the peaceful character of the nascent industrial society. An influential role in this context was played, in particular, by Spencer's distinction between two types of society, namely the 'militant society' and the 'industrial society'. According to Spencer, in the society of the militant type primacy was accorded to the collective capacity for violent action towards the outside. Such a society, he claimed, as a consequence, completely subordinated the weal and woe of the individual to collective purpose; domination was structured around a unilinear hierarchy. By contrast, industrial society unfolded its potential by tolerating relationships between individuals that were entered into on a voluntary, contractual basis. In such a polity, individualism and the market flourish; the structure of domination is decentralized and multipolar. Such a polity aims externally at entering into contractual relations with other polities for the purpose of mutual benefit. The evolutionist assumption that the 'militant society' will inevitably die out may seem incredibly optimistic to us today; however, these assumptions were representative of the nineteenth-century social sciences, especially in Britain and the USA. Even classical Marxism is more closely in tune with the optimism of these assumptions than may appear at first sight. It merely moves the dawning of the age of peace up one step in history, as it were: in this system, not the capitalist, but only the socialist industrial society is in itself peaceful in principle. The path leading to such a state leads via internal social changes, the violence of which is specially emphasized; the success of these changes, however, – as Engels put it in the *Anti-Dühring* – is thought to be guaranteed in an evolutionist manner, for example by the internal dissolution of capitalist militarism owing to the increasing inability to

finance the arms burden and the arming of the class-conscious proletariat that goes hand in hand with compulsory conscription. The
period between 1815 and 1914, which was disrupted by only a few
small wars, could serve as evidence supporting the assumption that
industrial societies were peaceful. For this reason, the outbreak of the
First World War was a severe shock in that it called into question the
philosophy of history behind the social sciences. Even if the war as such
did not contradict expectations, the course it took was the source of
profound irritation.

The reaction of contemporary German sociologists to the First World
War is extraordinarily interesting with regard to the various ways in
which the cult of war and chauvinism deformed the glorious tradition
of German historical thought in the humanities and political science.
However, it is least revealing with regard to the intrinsic problems of
the thesis that industrial society is peaceful. For this thesis was least
widespread in Germany; generally speaking, the German founders of
sociology took a contemptuous view of Comte and Spencer and were
far removed from liberalism and positivism. Werner Sombart, Max
Weber and Georg Simmel can be treated here as three, clearly distinguishable types.[11] Whereas Sombart had put forward a substantial
social-scientific theory about the connection between war and capitalism prior to the outbreak of the war, during the war he boiled this down
to the fateful struggle between British utilitarian commercialism and
German anti-utilitarian heroism. Although Max Weber steered clear of
such inflated interpretations of the war in terms of the philosophy of
history, he, too, failed to develop any sociological analyses of the emergence and impact of war. Those of his publications that were directly
intended to have a political influence are pioneering achievements in
the analysis of the link between the internal constitution of a state and
the capacity for action in foreign policy. Georg Simmel, in turn, interprets the war only in categories of aesthetics and the philosophy of life
and believes that the experience of war offers a possible escape from
the tragedy of modern culture. Nor do the other authors of the period
offer anything that overcomes this failure on the part of sociology; the
sole exception is the work of Emil Lederer, for he does not fall prey to
unrestrained speculations about either the question of war guilt or the
meaning of the war. Rather, he attempts a sociological interpretation of
the surprising features of the war, namely the amalgamation of total
war and an increasingly autonomous war machinery.

The positions taken by the major sociologists of other countries were
just as favourable to their own respective national causes as they
understood them. Yet the relationship between such nationalistic positions and the universalistic Enlightenment ideals of a peaceful world

order took a different form there than was the case in Germany. In his political writings, Émile Durkheim, as the representative figure of sociology in France, does not maintain that the war sounds the death knell for the pacifist ideal; rather, he regards a victory for France as a contribution to the end of militarism and a step towards the ultimate triumph of this ideal. Theoretically, Durkheim had long since toned down Spencer's prognosis that war would disappear in industrial society by his assertion that this would be a gradual rather than a rapid process. Yet, given that the stance he took was nevertheless completely optimistic and evolutionist, Durkheim believed that he was able to speak of a progressive adjustment from the continuous state of war in primitive communities to the permanent legislation of modern societies. He failed to face up to the problem that a state internally governed by laws could very well take a stand towards the outside world as a power-state bound by no law. The events of the war largely eluded the grasp of his categories. This explains why he could do no more than attempt to prevent his normative ideals from being sucked into the vortex of nationalistic ideologies.

American thinking of the time was characterized less by a belief that followed Spencer in promulgating the pacifying effects of individualistic contractual freedom and more by taking a specific understanding of republic and democracy and transposing them into an international context. According to this view, the steadily advancing process of internationalization in the economy and the sciences would no longer permit a mere coexistence of states. The only alternative to solving conflicts without institutions, and this would always tend to be a violent solution, consisted in establishing a moral and legal sphere in which international disputes could be settled peacefully. For these thinkers, the outbreak of war was especially shocking, since it contradicted their assumption of orderly progress and their virtually evolutionist belief in a decided trend towards the dissemination of democracy throughout the world. And indeed, the events of war in Europe were initially interpreted and repressed as being an anachronism, as the expression of European backwardness; it went without saying that America would stay out of such a war. In the course of the war, however, an ever more prevalent line of argument advocated that America enter the conflict on the side of the Allies, for which it perceived a universalistic justification. Joining the cause of democracy and abolishing war by setting up a League of Nations and guaranteeing the right to self-determination for the small nations were, however, entirely noble war objectives in the eyes of American reformist intellectuals.

The consequences for domestic policy of America's entry into the conflict, however, dashed all hopes that the war would prove to be an opportunity for reform. The analysis of the war gave rise to a few productive approaches in the social sciences that were derived, above all, from the assumption that a relationship obtained between 'democracy' and 'peace'. However, for the most part these approaches were pitched at the socio-psychological level: here the possibility of achieving social integration by fostering loyalty through participation in public and effective processes of will formation was contrasted with integration via opposition to external or internal enemies. With a few exceptions – such as Thorstein Veblen's book of 1917, *The Nature of Peace and the Terms of Its Perpetuation* – the relative weight of such socio-psychological factors was only seldom considered in relation to economic, political or military-technological factors in the American social science of the day. It is interesting that Veblen quite clearly assumes that a tension exists between democracy and capitalism. He views this as one of the causes of modern nationalism, to the extent that nationalism is promoted by interested circles out of a fear of demands for social equality. On the whole, however, he, too, considers nationalism obsolete and not modern or promising for the future. His socio-psychological considerations are not developed into an analysis of modern nationalism and the significance it had in the war.

The four models of peace mentioned – namely the peaceful character of free trade, the republican order, socialism and industrial society – continued to have a great deal of influence in modified form even after the end of the Second World War. However, all of them increasingly gave ground to the realism of power politics. Just as the nuclear superpowers and the alliances they set up had confronted each other since the beginning of the Cold War, so, too, did the 'proletarian internationalism' of the one side and the democratic universalism of the other appear to be diametrically opposed, hostile, mutually exclusive alternatives. In reality, both positions increasingly degenerated into legitimatory ideologies that served the objectives of realists who believed only in power politics.

Although numerous social scientists made various declarations of their personal beliefs with regard to the problems of war and peace during the Cold War or confessed that they could at best beat a retreat in the face of the intimidating horrors of nuclear strategies, they only rarely contributed more extensive analyses. The representative theorist of the time, Talcott Parsons, made little if any comment on the Cold War in the framework of his studies, and when he did the statements did not go much beyond noting that international relations had only been institutionalized to a slight degree. As leading representatives of neo-Parsonianism themselves concede, Parsons had difficulty in integrating the present or historical role of war within the framework of his evolutionary model based on the theory of differentiation. For in this theoretical framework, wars, like social movements, are only the agents of overarching processes of differentiation; at worst, they can divert or hinder the courses of these processes in a minor way, but cannot really have any decisive influence on them.

The two most important voices in sociology during the 1950s and 1960s who consistently addressed the social meaning of war and the effects of the nuclear arms race were Raymond Aron and C. Wright Mills.[12] Today, Aron is being rediscovered in France and Britain with such enthusiasm above all because for decades he did not submit to the thematic repression of war-related problems and made an abundance of important contributions to the topic, both in his theoretical work and in his extensive political journalism. In his theories he always remained a neo-Clausewitzian strategic realist whose work can be helpful as an antidote to economic reductionists; but in my view it cannot open up any avenues of research that take us further. Mills was the real dissident in the 'orthodox consensus' of an American-dominated sociology. His warning as to the 'causes of the Third World War' still has the power to stir us today. It was based on his analysis of the power structures of American society, in which he identified an elitist complex that controls military-strategic and general foreign policy decisions. This thesis, of course, proved to be too simple in empirical terms; his analysis of contemporary society focused too strongly on the opposition of the two superpowers and did not go into sufficient depth to warrant being adopted. Nevertheless, here was someone protesting against the complacent belief of the public and, implicitly, many social scientists in the stability of the system of deterrence.[13] This belief was indeed very widespread. At most, people called solely for arms control agreements that might eliminate isolated elements that threatened the stability of deterrence. Moreover, the interest in the possibilities of conventional warfare below the nuclear threshold was kept alive in order to maintain the political scope for action.

This situation changed fundamentally from the early 1980s on. For postwar theory – that is, the belief that peace is guaranteed through stable nuclear deterrence – this change plays the role of the 'crisis experiment' that can, like the First World War, serve to make us aware of hidden assumptions. Innovations in weapons technology have reduced the stability of deterrence or have at least made us realize that radical destabilization is a possibility. This applies to the vision of a protective shield over the USA (Strategic Defense Initiative, SDI), as well as to new possibilities of a first-strike or limited nuclear war. The rapid escalation of international tensions in the early 1980s sensitized the populations of many European countries to the military nexus of conditions under which they lived. The extent of ecological problems that crossed all ideological bloc boundaries (for instance, Chernobyl) foregrounded the need for global co-operation and the question of links between the economy, ecology and armaments. All of these developments suggest that we must look beyond the deceptive security of this fifth model of peace, which in many ways of course is not unlike the old notion of the balance of power. From this viewpoint, the peace movement's most important contribution may be that it once again undermined the self-evident nature of this power-political realism and generally reopened a public discourse about peace and war among citizens in an international context.[14]

This debate was opened up, moreover, in a theoretical situation in which Marxism did not present itself as a convincing alternative. Major contributions by Marxists diverged greatly from the traditional ideas of Marxism. This is true of E.P. Thompson's thesis of an 'exterminism', in other words, of an arms race that was escalating primarily because of its own intrinsic dynamic and not because of economic or political interests, and it is equally true of Mary Kaldor's thesis of the 'Baroque arsenal', with which she questioned the economic and military benefits of the new military technologies produced by the arms race. Most of the younger intellectuals in sociology, however, began, as already mentioned, to look more in the direction of Clausewitz and Aron or even to search for rejuvenated 'geopolitical' views. The point is, however, that here all the elements of the peace models that are potentially worth preserving – even though these models certainly cannot be upheld in their entirety – are lost in the process.

One way out of this situation is to undermine the implicit identification of social order and nation-state. Indeed, as we have already mentioned, Alain Touraine and Anthony Giddens in particular have called attention to the fact that tacit identification of the abstract concept 'society' with the concrete reality of territorially delimited nation-states tends to obscure rather than shed light on the dependency of social processes on economic, political, military and cultural complexes of an international nature. In classical sociology, the relationship between state and society is not reflected upon in terms of its historical and geographical particularity. However, if we dissolve this false identification, a new assessment of the central meaning of action theory emerges. Relativizing the concept of society implies that the widest variety of social processes can be analysed using the category of action, and thus suggests that the degree to which they exhibit a 'systemic' character should not be prejudged in conceptual terms but rather be taken into account as being empirically variable. An approach that centres on the interweaving and intermeshing of actions and the consequences thereof yields a more differentiated picture than is afforded by the concept of system.

It is only possible in the present context to note in passing that I consider those current attempts that make use of action theory in order to create non-functionalist foundations for macro-sociology to be the most fruitful, also with regard to the peace issue. I am thinking here, for example, of the early transformation of Parsons's work in Etzioni's theory of the active society; or Giddens's development of a theory of structuration via a critique of Marxism; Castoriadis's and Touraine's contributions to a theory of institutionalization as a creative process; and the approach, albeit not free of voluntaristic undertones, taken by the Brazilian Roberto Mangabeira Unger.[15] What all of these theories have in common is that they proceed from a concept of action that is not limited to the level of the individual, and thus provide the basis for models of social order that, unlike the functionalist systems models, are appropriate to the specifics of human sociality. To this end, the models of rational and normatively oriented action must be spanned at the level of action theory by a more comprehensive model that embraces the creative, institution-generating dimension of action.

For all these theories, wars or uprisings are 'crisis experiments' not only of traditional assumptions, but also of the social structures themselves. They are interested in societies in a state of mobilization because they aim at thereby gaining insights that will contribute to an understanding of social structures. This finds expression in Giddens's concept of (active) structuration as well as in Etzioni's thesis that the 'active' society – which is to say, a society capable of conscious self-transformation – is the only alternative to deterioration in the postmodern age. And lastly, the same is true of Unger's emphasis on the contingency of institutional innovations and the advantages of the 'plasticity' that in his work is derived from the current perception that industrialized capitalist societies are emerging outside the Western cultural sphere and from historical cases of military modernization effected in order to adapt to one's opponents. Of course, mobilization in this context is also taken to mean the nationalist enthusiasm for war, but without ascribing to it a positive value. The question is also left open, empirically speaking, as to whether the extreme technification of nuclear and conventional state-of-the-art warfare makes it possible to dispense with mobilization on a massive scale.

To my mind, however, the fact that economic, political or psychological reductionisms can only be avoided if we forgo resorting to
comprehensive models of systems, structures or orders is still more
important than this opportunity for social analysis that the action-
theoretical approach affords. In the work of Giddens and Castoriadis,
but even in the specific link to Weber's thought such as is inherent
in Michael Mann's theory of the sources of social power, societies
are analysed in various dimensions that refer to one another in a non-
'functional' way.[16] What all of these writers have in common is that
they renounce the attempt to attribute some privileged status to one
particular domain of society that then supposedly holds the key to
understanding the totality of society. Giddens, for example, attempts
to separate analytically the dimensions of capitalism, 'industrialism'
and the organization of military power as well as internal 'surveillance'
and control and to retain them as possible variables to one another.
Castoriadis stresses especially that democracy is not to be viewed as a
superstructure of capitalism, but rather represents an autonomous
dimension of the history of humankind. Etzioni wants to show how
additional strata of international or supranational regulations are
established above the level of the nation-states; against this background
he made an early appeal for a dismantling of the military blocs by
means of regulated forms for their co-operation, as opposed to their
renewed disintegration into rival nation-states.

The programme of such a theory permits us to set our sights on integrating the assumptions underlying the models of peace in the social
sciences and social philosophy discussed thus far. Even though all of
them were shaken by historical events, this is no reason to cast them
aside. The theory of the peaceful character of industrial society has,
after all, largely been proved correct today, as far as it concerns the
process of internal pacification, which extends all the way to 'civilizing' the military complex. Even today, Kant's idea of republicanism still
raises important questions with regard to the public control of foreign
policy as a condition of its defensive nature. The Marxist assumptions
regarding the interests of the capitalist defence industry are not mere
figments of the imagination. Free trade and the prevention of both
protectionism and export monopolies have essentially contributed to
peaceful relations between the Western industrial societies. However,
it is necessary to reflect in theoretical terms on the relative accuracy of
every single explanation and to bring it to bear in the narrative totality of the analysis of the causes of a war. Thus, it is surely too simple
to explain the First World War in terms of the conflicts of interests of
various imperialist powers, the autocratic character of the German

Reich, the existence of distinct export monopolies or Europe's backwardness in relation to the USA, as various voices did at the time.

The outbreak of a new 'Cold War' at the beginning of the 1980s also shows, however, that we must not allow ourselves to settle back comfortably into the normative lack of imagination characteristic of the realism of power politics. On the contrary, it is necessary to respect and utilize the rational core of the historical models of peace even with regard to future dangers that we cannot as yet foresee.

8

Is There a Militarist Tradition in Sociology?

The neglect of war and violence in the social sciences and the link between this problematic omission and the world-view of liberalism has been repeatedly discussed in this book. For this reason it is undoubtedly appropriate to cast a glance also at non-liberal currents of thought and at older sociological approaches that can certainly not be criticized for their insufficient emphasis on the role of war in history or of violence in social life. The question to be asked is whether these approaches can be gathered together into an alternative tradition of its own, however forgotten or suppressed.

The existence of such a 'militarist' counter-tradition has been proposed most explicitly by Michael Mann, currently one of the leading representatives of historical sociology. This thesis is to be found in several of the writings[1] that prepare the way for his major and impressive project of a sociological history of the world, and explain it methodologically. Admittedly, it is always only expounded *en passant* and never really explained in detail. In his influential essay 'War and Social Theory: Into Battle with Classes, Nations and States'[2] he unequivocally contrasts two schools of theory with each other, one of which he calls 'liberal/Marxist' and the other 'militarist'. Guided by its belief in the pacific character of industrial society or of capitalism, the liberal theory, which Mann finds embodied in Adam Smith, Saint-Simon, Comte, Spencer and Durkheim, did not so much unintentionally neglect war as consciously relegate it to the second rank. With the familiar qualifications, Marx is then said to have shared the premises of the liberal tradition in this respect, as in a number of others. What we may to this extent call the common tradition of liberalism and Marxism is said to stand opposed to another tradition, which Mann calls militarist. What is meant by this is an attitude and an institutional structure that regard war and arms building as normal and indeed desirable social activities.

Both traditions are related to different historical experiences in different countries and are provided with a geographical index. The liberal tradition is said to have corresponded to the so-called century of peace (1815–1914), in particular the experience of Great Britain and, to a lesser extent, France, and to have been consonant with their goal of universal hegemony. However, the experience of other countries was quite different. Mann points to the well-known situation in economics where, depending on the national context, there were wide differences in the degree to which the classical doctrine of *laissez faire* appeared plausible and was able to prevail in institutional form. In Germany and Austria, in particular, he claims, the attempt at state-aided economic growth was closely interwoven with the expansion of military power – and parallel with that, militarist approaches became highly influential in the social sciences in both countries. In this process Social Darwinism is said to have played an important role.

In the essay I have referred to, Mann mentions as the exponents of this intellectual trend the early Austrian sociologists Ludwig Gumplowicz and Gustav Ratzenhofer; elsewhere in his writings[3] we also find the names of Franz Oppenheimer and Carl Schmitt. Again and again there are references to Alexander Rüstow's theory of 'over-stratification'. Among non-German-speaking authors, mention is made of Gaetano Mosca and Vilfredo Pareto, and, on one occasion, of William Graham Sumner of the USA. Lastly, Mann refers frequently to Otto Hintze and Max Weber as liberals who were influenced by the political climate of militarism – and also to Marxists who on occasion tended to move in the same direction in the debates on imperialism.

The thesis of a predominantly Austro-German militarist counter-tradition in the social sciences is further developed historically by Mann. Thus, according to him, there is a great irony in the fact that this tradition has been forgotten precisely because the history of the twentieth century is so rich in wars and violence. Whereas the history of the World Wars and of Fascism might have given the militarist tradition an additional plausibility, that tradition in fact disappeared along with the empires in which it was dominant.

> ... unfortunately for the militarists, their armies lost. The Austrian Empire disintegrated; Russia was conquered by Marxism; Germany lost two wars and its militarist theories were outlawed from civilization. Finally, the United States became a super-power and rediscovered the usefulness of British transnational *laissez faire* for its own global

hegemony. As liberalism and Marxism divide up the geo-political and geo-economic world, they naturally dominate its sociology. Since 1945 the militarists have been forgotten, the waverers purged of their more violent side (e.g. Weber . . .), and the 'classic tradition' of liberal/Marxist pacific transnational sociology has been enshrined in pedagogy.[4]

Thus this thesis of the militarist tradition has now been expanded to include an explanation for its demise. Of course, Mann's purpose in expounding it is not to plead for its revival. What it represents for him is the over-emphasis on power and violence that is the obverse of their neglect by liberals and Marxists. But this corrective to the weaknesses of the liberal tradition is hampered by the association of the counter-tradition with Social Darwinism, racism, the glorification of state power and Fascism, and these connections led to its expulsion from the canon of the social sciences. However, this renunciation of a counter-weight had consequences, in Mann's view, not just for the study of war in the narrower sense, but for every theory of the state in general. This is because the autonomous role of the state, as opposed to the conflict between interest groups and individuals and also as opposed to their normative consensus, was constantly lost from sight, notwithstanding all criticism and self-criticism. For Mann's own project and also for his assessment of the tasks facing a sociology adequate to the demands of the present, this is a catastrophic consequence of the well-intentioned repression of a tradition.

This thesis of Michael Mann's is sketchily presented for the most part, but is evidently ambitious intellectually. What are we to make of it? To begin with, it is certainly not outlandish to think of the social sciences as being shaped through and through by deep-seated cultural 'programmes' and historical experiences. For example, one of the most important recent accounts of the history of sociology divides the material largely according to the principle of national traditions.[5] This structuring principle is to be understood not as a dogmatic statement, but rather as an empirical assumption. There is no suggestion that each nation has a unified national spirit that merely individualizes itself in different epochs and particular thinkers. Instead, there is a network of participants, capable of being documented empirically, in a discourse extending over a number of generations. This applies especially to the phase in which sociology was established as an academic discipline, which, according to Donald Levine, the author of this history of sociology, took place from 1890 to 1920. During this period, long-term national intellectual traditions demonstrably existed in the relevant countries, and these were more important than international intellectual cross-currents.

There is one further aspect of Mann's thesis about the history of sociology that we should approach with an open mind. In recent years we have become increasingly aware that historiography, including the history of scientific disciplines, is subject to the conventions of narrative genres. The history of academic disciplines undoubtedly involves more than the mere rehearsal of an irresistible accumulation of facts and the advance of knowledge. Such historiography plays a role in the formation of a collective identity for the members of an academic discipline and for the process of socializing subsequent generations into that discipline. We cannot dismiss out of hand the suspicion that if many once-influential figures have been forgotten, it was not simply for cognitive reasons. Indeed power politics may have played a part in ensuring that entire national traditions have lost or acquired their influence. To this extent, Mann's thesis about the militarist tradition and its fate must be taken very seriously.

Nevertheless, the first doubts about it do not take long to emerge. One is immediately struck by a curious relationship between Mann's thesis and the war propaganda of the First World War. The First World War was the epoch when the coexistence of what were unquestionably national traditions of thought was suddenly elevated on all sides into an irreconcilable struggle between competing national characters.[6] Even scientists and philosophers whose own thinking had been shaped by a national tradition that was not their own began to deny it or to place themselves in the vanguard of those eager to criticize the allegedly pernicious ideology of the enemy. Even where, shortly before the war, and in some cases as recently as the first half of 1914, scholars had given even-handed accounts of the strengths and weaknesses of other national intellectual traditions, people started to feel, once the war had begun, that any such impartial treatment was high treason. Intellectual traditions, both native and foreign, were hastily robbed of their internal contradictions and complexities; they were violently essentialized, and partly even biologized – so that national traditions sometimes appeared to be natural rather than cultural givens. As a reaction to these shocking and absurd intellectual constructs, in which frequently even major scholars lost all sense of proportion, the existence of national traditions in the social sciences was later frequently denied altogether, especially after 1945. 'German sociology' was deemed to be just as impossible as 'German physics'.

Thus Mann's thesis touches a sore point in the cultural relations between Germany and the West. During the First World War, Germany had constantly stood accused of having placed might before right, reversing the tradition of natural law and the Enlightenment – first intellectually, and then, as an inevitable consequence, politically and militarily. In this context three names were mentioned in a single breath again and again as the representatives of this way of thinking: Treitschke, Nietzsche and von Bernhardi – a chauvinist historian, a philosopher who had coined the maxim about 'living dangerously' and a warmongering writer on military matters. It was undoubtedly the war propaganda that established the link between these thinkers in the public mind and postulated their intellectual dominance. Even so, it remains true that in their war writings many German professors were led by feelings of defiance to adopt the stereotype of them created by the enemy. When it comes to understanding intellectual traditions, I would maintain that none of us have been able to free ourselves completely from the after-effects of that disruptive period with its posturings and stereotyping of ourselves and others. For this reason the question has to be asked whether the thesis of a specific German (and Austrian) militarist tradition is itself an after-effect of those misleading homogenizations and mythopoeic tendencies from the time of the First World War, or whether it is justified in fact.

The initial doubts to emerge, thanks to the affinity between Mann's thesis and the war propaganda of that period, are reinforced by additional, but still superficial observations. As far as the German tradition of the historical and political sciences and of philosophy is concerned, it is usually said to have placed the emphasis on quite different matters than conflict and power struggles. Conversely, the national tradition in which power and national egoism are most frankly avowed, namely the Italian tradition, is one that Mann barely mentions. Social Darwinism was by no means a specifically, or even predominantly, German phenomenon.[7] For this reason, Mann's argument must be scrutinized more closely. When we talk about a militarist tradition, are we really dealing with a tradition here if, by tradition, we understand at least a minimum of uniformity and the possibility of showing that thinkers have a sustained influence on each other? Is such a tradition, if one indeed exists, a specific German tradition? This question will not go away even if no unified militarist tradition could be found, because even then, over and above the different currents of thought, there might be common political continuities that differentiate this country from others. Finally, we should ask whether we can learn something today from this counter-tradition, or from individual strands of thought wrongly subsumed under it, that might shed light on the blind spots in liberal thinking.

Our present examination of Mann's thesis will concentrate exclusively on the writers and currents of thought explicitly referred to by Mann. This restriction is necessary in order to establish a common empirical platform; it is worthy of mention because in principle it might well be the case that Mann's thesis is true, even though his evidence is inadequate. Our treatment of the individual thinkers will vary in thoroughness. In no case will the full spectrum of an author's writings be dealt with; each will only be discussed from the point of view of his position in Mann's militarism thesis, and the length of treatment will depend on my assessment of each writer's importance for present-day sociology.

Social Darwinism

The first component of Mann's thesis consists in his reference to the role played by Social Darwinism. This theory had its roots in Darwin's epoch-making theory of organic evolution and involved the transfer of some of its clichés to the realm of social life. These clichés included, above all, 'adaptation', the 'struggle for existence' and the 'survival' of the 'fittest', that is, the best 'adapted'. It was an international phenomenon, highly developed in Great Britain and the USA. There was nothing specifically German or Austrian about it. At first glance, it may appear as if Social Darwinism really did approve of violence and war, or at least favoured a trend towards moral neutrality. But even here caution is advisable.[8] Even in Darwin's theory itself it always remained unclear whether the concept of the 'struggle for existence' referred exclusively to antagonistic modes of behaviour or whether it also included all forms of social dependency among organisms, and hence, too, the communal, co-operative struggle to survive. This ambiguity was significantly reinforced in the subsequent, often popular, scientific literature of the late nineteenth century. Even if we confine ourselves to the narrower, 'antagonistic' interpretation of Darwin's theory, there are wide divergences between different Darwinist interpretations of war, that is to say, of its effects on the processes of selection. The non-militarist Social Darwinists argued that it was precisely the lives of the biologically fittest that were placed most in jeopardy by war. Armies are composed of healthy, physically and mentally fit young men in the best age for reproduction; their death could do nothing but harm to a nation's biological stock. The opposing sides in a war often made it their task to destroy the enemy's elite, thus improving the prospects of the less courageous in the reproductive stakes. In addition there are the consequences of injuries and mutilations, the negative impact of the war on the health of the entire population and the spread of sexually transmitted diseases through the lifestyle of the troops. The most radical exponents of this way of thinking even regarded war as one of the causes of the biological degeneration of peoples and the decline of nations.

These anti-militarist Social Darwinists were of course opposed by the better known representatives of this way of thinking. These maintained that war, at least prior to the mechanization and industrialization of warfare, had indeed been a method for selecting those who were biologically superior. This is held to be true of battle itself, but must also be applied much more generally to the harsher conditions of life in wartime. Over and above this, the opportunities for the successful war heroes to reproduce improved, thanks to their position of power and their sexual attractiveness. Some of the proponents of this view attempted also to prove that in modern wars, too, a biologically favourable process of selection retained its validity, since even modern war is said to reward the manly, warlike virtues. But even if the workings of selection have turned negative for men, they remain positive for women because the death of many members of the male sex reduces the opportunities of the biologically less valuable members of the female sex to bear children. This is because the lack of men means that not all women have the opportunity to form a couple and hence usually to reproduce themselves, and this improves the quality of the next generation.

This kind of discourse seems very remote from us today. However, the first finding of our investigation is that Social Darwinism was very divided regarding the question of militarism and that there can be no question of a particular prevalence of this mode of thought in Germany or a special preference for a militarist interpretation of it.

Ludwig Gumplowicz and the 'Sociological Idea of the State'

We should note that the arguments of the Social Darwinists we have looked at hitherto were all concerned with the impact of war on the selection of biologically superior *individuals*; a few authors, however, did take account of the selection of *groups* and interpreted war in that context. For them war unanimously represented the selection of the biologically superior group; indeed it was the only way in which, by measuring their respective strengths directly, one group could demonstrate its superiority over another. There is here a fluid transition to the first of the early sociologists mentioned by Mann, namely Ludwig Gumplowicz. Gumplowicz was, to be sure, no Social Darwinist in any precise sense, and nor was he a racist, despite his talk of the 'race struggle', since for him races emerged not from biological characteristics, but from socio-historical differences. His central idea was the 'sociological idea of the state'; he promoted it with a single-minded obsessiveness, believing that it was of decisive importance for the still-to-be established discipline of sociology. In this 'sociological idea of the state' he put forward arguments that were very similar to those promulgated by the wing of Social Darwinism that focused on group selection.

Gumplowicz first put forward this 'sociological idea of the state' in 1883, in his book *The Race Struggle*, and then again in 1885, in his *Outlines of Sociology*.[9] He subsequently expounded and defended the idea again and again. At its core was the belief that the state originally arose from a primordial struggle between groups and tribes. The victors in such struggles had discovered as far back as the dawn of time that the destruction of their enemies was by no means the most beneficial solution for them. The best solution lay instead in forcing the vanquished into service so as to satisfy their own needs. They made the transition, therefore, from exterminating their enemies to subjugating them. This relation of the group of victors to the vanquished group is, according to Gumplowicz, the origin of all domination and of a class antagonism rooted in primordial violence. For Gumplowicz, the state is nothing but the partly mitigated and habitualized authority for the subjugation of the vanquished by the victors. In this sense it has been a class state from the very outset and will remain so for all time. The law is the instrument of this class state. Where the viewpoints of the losers enter the legal system, this merely expresses the nature of the long-term armistice between the antagonists. Morality does not precede the law, but emerges from it through the internalization of the means of domination among the dominated. However, no armistice lasts forever. Beneath the surface of the state-regulated order the struggle continues, so that we must constantly reckon with new attempts to overthrow the prevailing arrangements. Such upheavals can indeed change the identity of the group that rules and that is ruled; but they do not change the fundamental nature of the class state.

Gumplowicz flanks this so-called sociological idea of the state with a no less resolutely argued thesis about the polygenetic origins of humankind and with a strictly determinist sociology that banishes all individual freedom of action to the realm of illusion. These two components of his thought make clear that the 'sociological idea of the state' takes a stand against both the Enlightenment universalism of a unitary human species and the German idealist tradition. If humankind does not descend from one single root, then in Gumplowicz's view the original plurality of the different races is beyond doubt and is proof of the fundamental role of racial conflict. If the central axis of all social processes is the race struggle, then individuals are incapable of rising above it; they can absolutely not escape from the conflicts between the different collectivities; their motives flow from the group they belong to with the force of the laws of nature. The term 'sociologism' is misleading as a description of Gumplowicz's radical anti-individualism, in so far as he definitely does not defend a homogenized and hermetically sealed conception of society, but rather 'history as a succession of conflictual inter-group relations'.[10] In terms of the categories currently in common use, we might call his sociology a *naturalistic collective utilitarianism*. In the view of Gerald Mozetic, one of the few sympathetic critics of Gumplowicz today, even if the 'sociological idea of the state' has turned out to be completely untenable, at least his emphasis on the permanence of group conflicts may well continue to be found stimulating.

In our present context, however, we are not concerned with whether the authors under discussion have made a stimulating contribution on other topics, but only with whether they constitute a militarist tradition within German-speaking sociology. So if we cast a glance at the reactions to Gumplowicz by his contemporaries in Germany, we can only speak of the catastrophic failure of his work. For example, in a review of two of his books in 1892, Otto Hintze actually takes as already proven 'the untenability of this system whose one-sidedness and consistency has something grotesque about it'.[11] And decades later, he refers to Gumplowicz's 'materialistic monism of repellent dullness'.[12] Hintze's utterances are representative of the echo of Gumplowicz's work among German scholars in the humanities and social sciences. 'The political sciences, which are derived in the main from idealist sources, could indeed tolerate a certain degree of positivism, but not this crass materialism, which is death to all individuality.'[13] There are only two exceptions to be found from among the more or less well-known authors in Germany and Austria. One was Gustav Ratzenhofer, who is also mentioned by Mann. He shares with Gumplowicz the idea that war is the authentic condition of nature and the state is the mere dominance of the victors over the vanquished, but he does not accept Gumplowicz's sociologism and many of his other conclusions. Instead he defends an old-fashioned militarism with additional arguments.[14] The other exception, Franz Oppenheimer, will be discussed shortly.

Outside the German-speaking world, the reception of Gumplowicz was much more active than in Germany. His writings were translated into many languages and exerted a considerable, if short-lived, influence on sociology. Admittedly, in France the young Durkheim, at the very start of his career, attacked Gumplowicz in a scathing review;[15] but in the USA especially, his writings were taken up with great interest, particularly by Lester Ward and Albion Small. Here, his naturalistic collective utilitarianism encountered like-minded thinkers.

Thus there can be no question of his thought being representative of a German militarist tradition. In addition, the experiential background of his sociology certainly cannot be said to have predestined him for such a role. By origin he was a Polish Jew who had started out with an intense commitment to the cause of Polish nationality. After some painful experiences of anti-Semitism in this context, he had then developed his theory in a spirit of resignation and the profoundest historical pessimism. Given his own personal history, Gumplowicz is a highly improbable candidate for the role of spokesman for a German (or Austrian) belligerence or militarism.

Franz Oppenheimer's Liberal Anti-Statism

The other early sociologist who took up Gumplowicz's ideas – so it was said – was Franz Oppenheimer. Yet there is some dispute about whether Gumplowicz's theories were really crucial for Oppenheimer's thought or whether the decisive influence on him was not Eugen Dühring, whom Friedrich Engels had set out to refute in his famous book (the *Anti-Dühring*).[16] However that may be, at a strategically crucial point Oppenheimer built the 'sociological idea of the state' into his own sociological system, his universal developmental history of humankind, as well as his campaign for land reform and the establishment of rural co-operatives. He, too, was an academic outsider in Imperial Germany, although after the First World War, as a professor at the newly established University of Frankfurt, he was very much one of the influential representatives of German sociology. In the Weimar Republic his ideas were taken much more seriously than before, even though he had not changed them significantly. There were internal and external reasons for this. Among what we might call the external reasons, we should list above all the fact that with the collapse of Imperial Germany a certain process of rethinking was initiated among some of the exponents of the traditional German idealization of the state, and this led to an unprejudiced appraisal of the 'sociological idea of the state'. 'Why should we not examine without prejudice a doctrine that regards violence and injustice as the starting-point of all class-distinctions, politics and the formation of the state?' This was the question asked by Otto Hintze in one of his two extensive discussions of Oppenheimer's work.[17] Both his original lack of interest in Oppenheimer and the visible effort, beneath the sudden expression of interest, to overcome his instinctive indifference point likewise to Oppenheimer's unsuitability as a representative of a strong militarist tradition.

The internal reasons lie in Oppenheimer's actual superiority over Gumplowicz.[18] He incorporates the 'sociological idea of the state' into a wide-ranging philosophy of history and refines its content. For him the establishment of the state was preceded by a pre-historical epoch in which groups of people lived together without internal structures of violence and without external contacts. The authentic historical age is then described with the tools of the 'sociological idea of the state'. However, this age can be overcome, in Oppenheimer's view, in a new era in which human beings will once again live in free co-operatives and the epoch of the state will be superseded. Furthermore, unlike Gumplowicz, Oppenheimer depicts the historical era between mythical pre-history and utopian post-history not as an aimless cycle and never-changing despotism, but as an articulated, inevitable process of development. Violence drives the different groups to expand, but the expansion enlarges the realm within which an internal morality of solidarity operates, and in this way it creates increasingly extensive, violence-free social orders that could ultimately encompass the whole of humanity. There is evidently a homology between this philosophy of history dressed in the guise of empirical science and that of Marx, even though in Oppenheimer it is violence and not the economy that is the driving force of history.

In the course of his exceedingly fair attempt to analyse Oppenheimer's historical scheme and assess its empirical and theoretical value, Otto Hintze dismisses the obvious objection that we are dealing here not with an empirically based theory, but only with a speculative philosophy of history. He compares the logic of Oppenheimer's scheme with schemes of a state of nature and an original social contract of the kind to be found in theories of natural law.

> No one today will regard the 'Contrat social' as an acceptable explanation of the origin of the state, and yet it retains an abiding theoretical value as the construction of the ideal type of the pure constitutional state. Could we not say of the 'sociological idea of the state' that, even if we reject it as a historical explanation of the origins of the state, it might similarly claim to be an attempt to construct an ideal type of the actual power state with its characteristic combination of imperialist politics and social class struggle?[19]

For Hintze, Oppenheimer's theory has genuine merit as an example of such an ideal type. This consists in the fact that he once again brought to the attention of his age the fact that economic needs are often satisfied by political means, that is to say, by the use of robbery, plunder and violence in general for economic ends. In Hintze's view this is a crucial dimension for the understanding of imperialism given the fact that imperialism can arise not just from capitalism, but from every historical formation. Today – after our experience of the economics of the National Socialist concentration camps, the Stalinist Gulag and the predatory elements of Hitler's strategy in the Second World War – this point must in my view be emphasized even more strongly. However, Hintze immediately qualifies his praise. He concedes that, unlike Gumplowicz, Oppenheimer takes note not just of the 'dominating' features of the state, but also of its 'co-operative' nature. However, he was incapable, according to Hintze, of combining these two components in a historical theory of state-formation and distributed them among completely distinct historical periods instead. 'Oppenheimer's whole theory of the state is a theory of imperialism. But alongside the imperialist principle . . . there is a further state-building principle: that of federalism.'[20] Hintze gives numerous historical examples of the efficacy of this principle, from the tribal leagues of antiquity, the Germanic tribes and the Iroquois, to the classical city-states, the medieval cities and city-leagues and the Swiss confederation down to the representative democratic constitutions of modern nation-states. For Hintze, the 'sociological idea of the state', even in Oppenheimer's version, represents simply an antidote to the idealization of the state as a 'product that has developed organically from the original "community." '[21] But it is far from being a satisfactory way of integrating the diverse components in a theoretically coherent and empirically tenable analysis of state-building processes.

The political point of Oppenheimer's scheme of history was not to support militarism, or to acquiesce in it with a shrug. It was an idiosyncratic combination of a life-reforming utopia of a co-operative type with a radical liberal struggle against a land-owning monopoly and on behalf of the consistent introduction of a market economy. Among academic scholars in Germany it was primarily Oppenheimer's radical liberal ideas that were taken up. For example, Alexander Rüstow, who is also singled out by Michael Mann, continued Oppenheimer's ideas, particularly in his period of emigration during the Third Reich and also after it. Rüstow transformed Oppenheimer's sociology into a theory of world history that could serve to bolster the economic liberalism of the postwar period in Germany.[22] Rüstow does not even fit into Mann's framework chronologically. But it can now be seen quite unambiguously that Franz Oppenheimer, too, the *liberal, anti-statist utopian with his emphasis on co-operatives*, is not the representative of any militarist tradition.

Carl Schmitt's Political Existentialism

The next great name on Michael Mann's list of representatives of German militarism is Carl Schmitt. Obviously, there are difficulties here, too, in co-opting him into a militarist tradition of German sociology before the First World War, since he was no sociologist, nor had he made any great mark as a writer before the war. However, as one of the leading experts in legal theory in the Weimar Republic and the Third Reich, he undoubtedly belongs among the most influential political figures on the anti-liberal wing and must for that reason be discussed in this context. The emphasis on his correct place in the chronology does indeed go to the heart of his thought, since it cannot be understood without the experience of the First World War and its aftermath – the profound shock to the whole idea of the state in Germany, the Bolshevik revolution, Italian Fascism and the changes in international politics with the establishment of the League of Nations. We must seek to discover whether the work of this writer, who is by no means repressed and forgotten, but, on the contrary, enormously influential and almost the stuff of myth, can serve as evidence for the thesis of a militarist counter-tradition.[23]

Of central importance for this question is *The Concept of the Political*.[24] This was first given as a lecture in 1927, then published in book form in 1932, and it has been continually reprinted down to the present day. Schmitt feels called upon to define the political instead of leaving it in a vague relation to the state, since in his view we are at the end of the era in which the state had a monopoly of the political and the political could be unproblematically defined in terms of its relation to 'statehood'. 'That was the case where the state had either (as in the eighteenth century) not recognized society as an antithetical force or, at least (as in Germany in the nineteenth century and into the twentieth), stood above society as a stable and distinct force.'[25] But this equation of politics and the state becomes untenable because increasingly 'state and society penetrate each other. What had been up to that point affairs of state become thereby social matters, and, vice versa, what had been purely social matters become affairs of state – as must necessarily occur in a democratically organized unit.'[26] When that occurs the specific nature of the political can no longer be discovered in its relation to the state. Schmitt seeks a more abstract definition of 'the political' in an 'ultimate distinction' that serves as the foundation for specifically political action, and he finds this in the 'distinction between *friend* and *enemy*'.[27] This does not mean – as Schmitt explicitly remarks in an attempt to avert misunderstandings – that all politics is nothing but a struggle, but it does mean that delimitation from others and the possibility of a struggle with them even to the death is constitutive of a political entity. War does not have 'to be common, normal, something ideal, or desirable. But it must nevertheless remain a real possibility for as long as the concept of the enemy remains valid.'[28] Thus it is not the 'everyday' experience, but the 'extreme case'[29] in which the political is revealed to our gaze as being the distinction between friend and enemy. This distinction is that of an extreme possibility from which 'human life derives its specifically *political* tension'.[30]

What is decisive in Schmitt's eyes is not the fact that members of a group should share specific common features or identical motives – for example, a common religion or nationality, or agreed economic interests – but exclusively the 'intensity of an association or dissociation'.[31] Whatever forces may determine the everyday life of human beings and their understanding of themselves, Schmitt detaches 'the political' from all of them, since his gaze is fixed only on the crucial situation of conflict to the death, and only in that situation can we recognize what determines the substance of the political entity and what, therefore, is the decisive authority to which all other bonds must defer. He ascribes 'sovereignty' only to this authority, since in his eyes sovereignty consists exclusively in this ultimate ability to make decisions in the state of emergency, indeed to make decisions *about* the state of emergency, which means to decide when the state of emergency is present at all.

Schmitt's book is indeed illiberal in the extreme. It is shot through with long tirades against liberalism, which he accuses of failing to perceive or of concealing this very essential meaning of the political. Liberalism is said to misapprehend the political because it subordinates it to the typical liberal polarity of business and the spirit, economics and ethics, while reducing conflict to economic competition, on the one hand, and normative discussion, on the other. Thus a clear distinction between war and peace is replaced by a picture of the world defined by 'the dynamic of perpetual competition and perpetual discussion'.[32] This misapprehension becomes obfuscation when liberalism mobilizes its arsenal of demilitarized and depoliticized concepts in order to use them for political purposes. For Schmitt, it is self-evident that this has happened and happens constantly. Every argument about values in his view is nothing but an attempt to exercise power. This holds good for both domestic and external politics. Referring to Hobbes, he interprets the 'rule of law' within states either as an empty phrase or as 'the sovereignty of men . . . who draw up and administer this law'.[33] He treats foreign policy in an analogous fashion and interprets the doctrine of the just war as 'the political aspiration of some other party to wrest from the state its *ius belli* and to find norms of justice whose content and application in the concrete case is not decided upon by the state but by another party, and thereby it determines who the enemy is'.[34]

By completely subordinating the normative to the question of its political meaning in specific situations where decisions are required, Schmitt robs the political of every inherent normative dimension. He believes that there can be no normative rationale for people's readiness to kill other people, or allow themselves to be killed. This assertion, however, is not intended to have a pacifist message in the sense that it claims that there are absolute limits to all antagonistic actions, but, on the contrary, it is intended to eliminate every normative limitation of the 'existential meaning' of struggle. In such a struggle, two forms of existence stand opposed to each other in an excluding, hostile way, and there is no third party, no higher plane on which their 'right' to exist could be debated or decided.

> There exists no rational purpose, no norm no matter how true, no program no matter how exemplary, no social ideal no matter how beautiful, no legitimacy nor legality which could justify men killing each other for this reason. If such physical destruction of human life is not motivated by an existential threat to one's own way of life, then it cannot be justified.[35]

Only if we recognize the centrality of this existential dimension of struggle for Schmitt's thought will we be in a position to grasp the specific nature of his (rampant) anti-liberalism.

Schmitt is perfectly clear about the differences between his way of thinking and those of others. He stresses that his definition of the political favours 'neither war nor militarism, neither imperialism nor pacifism'.[36] He expresses his disappointment (in the preface of 1963) that Otto Brunner has interpreted his theory as the endpoint of the development of the doctrine of *raison d'état*. As the epigone of Max Weber and exponent of the Age of Imperialism, he rightly feels himself misunderstood.[37] Against Franz Oppenheimer, he points out how arbitrary and implausible it is to set up an opposition between society, as 'a sphere of peaceful justice', and the state, as 'a region of brutal immorality'.[38] In contrast, we can glimpse the true origin of Schmitt's conception when he establishes a connection between the experience of the First World War and his fundamental idea that political 'association' is not one thing that exists alongside others pluralistically, but that it suddenly forces all others into the second rank, arching over them by means of a newly constituted communality. He cites Emil Lederer's statement that 'on the day of mobilization the hitherto existing society was transformed into a community'.[39] We should not overlook the irony that Schmitt makes no appeal to any of the countless enthusiastic proclamations of this community feeling from the war period, but to the only sober, sociological analysis by a contemporary who identified the artificiality and ultimate fragility of this autosuggestion.[40]

Obviously, it is possible to criticize the exaggerations in Schmitt's concept of the political; once again it was Otto Hintze who did this in

his review of Schmitt's *Constitutional Theory*. He cautiously drew attention to the fact that Schmitt's concept of sovereignty differs from the
dominant theory by its misplaced concreteness, since it designates
a living political will and not an attribute of abstract state power.
Conversely, by lopping off all ethical dimensions, Schmitt reduces the
constitution to a formal juridical concept.[41] Acute though such criticism
is, if Schmitt is to be discussed as a legal theoretician, it does not touch
the more vital question for our context, namely what is the logical
source of his exaggerations and over-ingenious formulations? This only
becomes comprehensible if we recognize the continuity between
Schmitt's thought and the 'existential interpretations of war' of a Georg
Simmel and a Max Scheler.

Contemporary readers were very well aware of this and were quick
to label Schmitt's thinking as 'political existentialism'.[42] Schmitt's
polemics were directed not only against liberalism, but also against
romanticism, two trends he conflated contra-intuitively, identifying
them as a sphere of bourgeois anxiety about decision-making that
he contrasted with the world of the political (as he defined it) in
which hard existential decisions are unavoidable. We gain a real insight
into Schmitt's true concerns when we contemplate the passion in
his emphasis on hard decisions and struggles, insulated from all the
particular values that these struggles are supposed to be about. What
concerns him is the value of decision-making and struggle as such, as
opposed to debating and doing deals. It is true enough that for Schmitt
such a struggle has to be imposed by others, and not to be initiated
arbitrarily. But it has been yearned for, and when it becomes inevitable,
it is welcomed with a sigh of relief. For only struggle can redeem us
from the agony of indecision and constant reflection, from the absence
of a strong commitment to values and from scepticism, and so restore
inner stability to the individual.

But this is an aporia, not a solution. For in this way the individual
can experience a liberation from the compulsion to reflect and an end
to his constant doubts about values. However, it will provide him with
a commitment not to particular values, but only to the medium in
which these doubts are silenced: namely, struggle as such and politics
as struggle. 'In this way politics becomes the idea of his own lost substantiality. He is not concerned with the essential content of the political, but only with the political as a test of existentiality. This explains
why, instead of the entire phenomenon, he grasps only a marginal
aspect: the struggle.'[43] The structure of Schmitt's argument closely
resembles Georg Simmel's euphoric interpretation of the war as an
'absolute situation' in which rational appraisal is unable to make any
impact upon the affective experience of the unconditional validity of

one's own right to exist.[44] Under very specific historical circumstances, the war appeared to Simmel as the revelation of a path leading to an alternative modernity. Schmitt stylized this exceptional experience into a constantly present possibility and necessity, into the 'concept of the political'. Thus his thought, too, would be misunderstood if it were to be interpreted as an example of militarism or belligerence. It is quite true that there are lines of continuity between the old-fashioned emphasis on the positive moral effects of war, its contribution to the preservation of manly virtues, and the existential militarism of Scheler, Simmel and, of course, Ernst Jünger. But even these writers do not simply praise war as an antidote to softness and effeminacy, but celebrate it as an opportunity to overcome the excesses of intellect and individuality. Schmitt goes even further and during the period of the run-up to the Third Reich he transforms the existential militarism of the period of the First World War into a *fascistoid political existentialism*.

Otto Hintze and Historical Sociology

The last figure to be examined is the great Prussian historian Otto Hintze. Mann describes him as a liberal (like Max Weber)[45] who was infected by the alleged militarist tradition. However, since Hintze's 'liberalism' is even less immune to doubt than Weber's, and since a 'militarist tradition' cannot have proved infectious if it did not exist, it is not possible to avoid a precise examination of the Hintze case. We have already encountered him in our present discussion as a critic of Gumplowicz, Oppenheimer and Schmitt, so it will come as no surprise if his mode of thinking turns out to differ from all those we have already described.

Unlike Mann, hardly anyone in German sociology would have entertained the idea of including Otto Hintze in a discussion of sociological traditions. The history of Hintze's influence is remarkable. Whereas in Anglo-Saxon sociology his name frequently crops up in such important writers as Barrington Moore, Theda Skocpol, Anthony Giddens and Michael Mann himself, he has as good as no influence at all in German sociology. By contrast, he has had a significant impact on the school of German historiography that calls itself the 'historical social science'. It is from this direction, particularly from Jürgen Kocka, that we have seen the most focused appreciations of Hintze as the 'methodologically most advanced, if not indeed the most important German historian of the late Empire and the interwar period'.[46] Hintze's origins in the traditions of Prussian historiography are of course obvious; but from the outset he showed that he had an open mind for questions of economics and social movements, and he developed a strong interest in the emerging discipline of sociology, an interest that was expressed especially after the First World War in extensive debates with sociological theories. His great theme was originally the history of administration in Prussia. But he gradually broadened this to include constitutional and social history, on the one hand, and international comparisons, on the other, so that we can say that he established the foundations of a historical sociology of the state 'in the development of its external power and its internal modernizing function'.[47]

But how does Hintze get into Mann's sights in the first place? What is 'militarist' and what is 'liberal' about Hintze? Hintze derives from a tradition of historiography that places great stress on the influence of foreign politics upon internal political processes. He claims that he has always maintained that, 'as opposed to both the historical school of national economy and the historical school of law, it will not do to construct constitutional history as a purely immanent process free from violent interventions from outside'.[48] And in fact as early as 1897, in his criticism of Wilhelm Roscher, he had reproached Roscher's theory with its failure to take sufficient note

> of the fundamental fact that all unprejudiced historiography makes clear, namely that the internal life of individual states is largely dependent upon relations between states, upon the pushing and pulling that prevails among them, upon the growth and decline of neighbouring states, the higher or lower pressure – so to speak – of the overall political atmosphere, in short, upon what Ranke calls the major world conditions.[49]

But this emphasis on foreign policy in the tradition of Ranke and Droysen has nothing to do with a naturalistic view of violence; nor is it a paean of praise to the pure power-state. And it does not spring from any concession to a putative 'militarist' spirit of the second half of the nineteenth century. It has its roots, rather, in the experiences of the age of the Napoleonic wars. The Ranke School from which Hintze borrows this motif is actually characterized by an anti-naturalistic idealism, and it therefore looks at history in terms of action, though admittedly the action of supra-individual totalities. This explains its concentration on 'the history of political events based on the principle of the primacy of external policy'.[50] This school of historiography is indeed keenly conscious of the fact that 'the state is based on the principle of power, and that its origin is linked to war and military organization'.[51] However, this is initially only to be understood as a corrective to the idea of the state as a matter of purely juridical relations, not as the opposite, no less one-sided, idea. Admittedly, it is quite true that the precise relation between power and the law, between historicism and universalism, remained unclear. In the exuberance of the founding of the Empire and the wars that preceded it, individual exponents of this tradition enjoyed the pathos of cold-blooded *realpolitik*, and established a link between the popular slogans of the Social Darwinists about the struggle for existence and a myth about Old Prussian history. This applies particularly to Heinrich von Treitschke, who in this way gained a prominent role in Western war propaganda against the German mentality. But Treitschke had never been representative of German historiography as a whole. A historian like Otto Hintze cannot be understood as a liberal who made hesitant concessions to a dominant militarist spirit, as Michael Mann imagines. He is rather the authentic representative of a tradition that resisted the latter's emerging one-sideness. He thinks it absurd to deny the role of law in the internal life of the state and to view the law merely as a function of power, or even the use of force; where this happens, as with Oswald Spengler, whom Mann ignores, it amounts, in Hintze's view, to endorsing the programme of the National Socialists.[52] And as for foreign policy, Hintze believes that strategically, at least, we have to take the law and public opinion into consideration. The state cannot be understood if its essence is simplistically and one-sidedly declared to be power or the law.

Moreover, even with respect to the primacy of foreign policy, of which so much is made, Hintze's position is very subtle. Neither in theory nor in practice does he ascribe any unconditional validity to the primacy of foreign policy. He is preoccupied with the interaction between foreign and domestic policy since for him there is no universally valid formula for the precise relationship between them and so everything 'depends upon individual conditions and the tact needed to understand and connect them'.[53] No doubt, Hintze showed greater interest in his writings in the way in which domestic policy depended upon geopolitical influences and foreign policy constellations than in the constitution of the system of the powers itself or the internal political factors that led to attempts to expand the power of the state. In this respect, his thinking was marked by its subject of choice, the age of absolutism. There are valid empirical reasons justifying his approach to that period. But even if Hintze was led by this background to make errors of judgement about other historical periods, this still does not amount to the proof that he had 'militarist' leanings.

And to what extent was Hintze a liberal? Certainly only in the sense that German National Liberals were liberal. That is to say, as Kocka has shown, there is a greater emphasis on the 'national' than on the 'liberal'. It is true to say that individual freedoms and legal security were important values in Hintze's eyes. But he did not speak out in support of a fully parliamentary system in Germany since it appeared to him to be irresponsible, and even impossible, for reasons of foreign policy that 'a continental Germany, threatened on many sides and dependent upon land forces, strike power and firm leadership, could afford a fully parliamentary system'.[54] The First World War undermined the confidence in the constitutional monarchy's superior handling of foreign policy implicit here, and the idea that, with regard to democracy, Germany could defend its own brand of modernity that differed from that practised in the West. Correspondingly, Hintze's scholarly interests came to focus more strongly on the factors determining democratization and the history of representative constitutions. But it is certain that even then democracy did not seem to him to be a valuable thing in itself.

Hintze's increasing sensitivity to the specific features of democracy enables us to see him as an interesting contrast to Max Weber – whom Michael Mann mentions in the same breath as Hintze, as yet another liberal influenced by militarism. In his essay on Weber's sociology, Hintze found fault with Weber because he had never provided an adequate account of modern democracy.[55] According to Hintze, it is true that Weber's work contains important passages dealing with classical and medieval democracy so that this gap may be due to the fragmentary nature of his life's work. But a deeper reason is probably the fact that Weber's entire sociology of the state is derived from his sociology of domination and thus is one-sided from the outset. Hintze makes use here of the distinction between 'domination' and 'co-operation', dating back to Otto von Gierke and already encountered in our discussion of Oppenheimer. It is 'highly characteristic of Weber', he writes 'that the element of leadership and government from above, in a broader sense, the element of domination, is very powerfully emphasized, while the element of co-operative solidarity is very weak.'[56] Thus democracy appears in Weber as a democracy of leaders; the doctrine of the form of a state recedes in favour of the analysis of the bureaucracy as the 'machinery' that characterizes the state as an enterprise, whether democratic or not.

In this greater openness to modern democracy one can see Hintze's theoretical superiority to Weber. The same may be said of his greater ability to observe forces for change within the bureaucracy and not, as Weber does, to extrapolate from the specific bureaucracy of his age and his country to epochal tendencies of bureaucratization as such.[57] One can see a further advantage of Hintze as against Weber in connection with the emergence of capitalism, since Hintze is more consistent in taking account of the military dimension in his reconstructions of history. In my view these strengths of Hintze's are far from having been fully utilized in contemporary sociological theory. However, the connection between them and his political views is considerably more complicated than emerges from Mann's thesis. And much the same thing may be said of Weber. What is decisive is not the question of more or less liberalism, or a greater or lesser proximity to 'militarism'. In his comparison of Hintze's and Weber's theories of bureaucracy, Jürgen Kocka makes a distinction in both cases between their political goals and their analytical perspective. He comes to the conclusion that in political matters Hintze is much more measured than Weber in his support for German aspirations to world-power status. Analytically, however, Weber is prepared to go much deeper than Hintze into the economic, social and internal political factors determining the Age of Imperialism. Weber was 'in a sense the more modern figure, politically in his nationalism, analytically with his awareness of the role of mass phenomena in contemporary politics, which he attempted to gain a purchase on with his concept of charismatic leadership, and through his analysis of the modern mass party'.[58] Weber made connections between liberalism and imperialism in ways for which there are no parallels in Hintze. Politically, Hintze remained rooted in the era of classical foreign policy in the European great-power system. His scholarly work, however, is, together with Weber's and Troeltsch's, the ripest fruit of *a transformation of German historicism into historical sociology*. Of the approaches depicted here, this is probably the only one that we can make productive use of today.

Conclusion

We have reached the end of our exploration of Michael Mann's thesis about the existence of a repressed militarist tradition in sociology. For our study it has been necessary to enter into a number of discourses some of which have become very alien to us today. Some readers may have wondered along the way whether all this effort was really necessary in order to rebut a claim about the history of scholarship that was only asserted in passing and whose systematic importance for historical sociology is uncertain. But we were concerned in our investigation neither with a gigantic quibble, nor with an examination of Michael Mann's admirable work. Mann's thesis was a welcome occasion for contextualizing currents of thought that may be able to serve as points of departure for a sociology in which there will be no tendency to neglect war and violence. Such a contextualizing process may be useful over and above the immediate occasion. No doubt, Mann is right to point out that in canonizing their works and granting them the status of classics of sociology, for a long time we were only able to appropriate authors like Max Weber and Georg Simmel in a fragmentary manner, leaving various murky historical depths out of account. For Simmel this statement holds good down to the present day. In that sense Mann's thesis is itself a justified, albeit insufficiently careful, attempt at contextualization.

The findings of our study are unambiguous. We have encountered forms of an old-fashioned militarism, a number of versions of Social Darwinism, the naturalistic collective utilitarianism of Ludwig Gumplowicz, the radical liberal, anti-statist co-operative utopianism of Franz Oppenheimer, the political existentialism of Carl Schmitt as the continuation of the existential militarism of Georg Simmel, and the attempts of Otto Hintze and Max Weber to transform German historicism into historical sociology. The heterogeneous nature of these different modes of thought, both in their understanding of war and violence and in their relation to liberalism, is far too great for us to lump them together under the single heading of a non-liberal or anti-liberal 'militarist' tradition. Moreover, the enormous critical response to incipient signs of the glorification of power and of the use of force in German scholarship shows us that it is not possible to uphold the claim that there is a common trend that transcends the different tendencies. The names included in Mann's list form not a tradition, but merely a residual category. A further study would have been needed to do justice to currents of thought in other national contexts that would likewise fall into such a residual category. But it is untenable to take these heterogeneous approaches and weave them into a 'tradition' of their own that is then declared to be specifically German. In the form asserted by Mann, there is no German *Sonderweg* in the social and historical sciences.[59]

Sociology after Auschwitz
Zygmunt Bauman's Work and the Problems of German Self-Understanding

There are obvious reasons why Zygmunt Bauman's writings have been so enormously successful in Germany. Whereas his earlier publications up until 1989 had remained more or less a matter for specialists in social theory, his book *Modernity and the Holocaust*[1] struck the German debate like a bolt of lightning. Since then, most of the books of this enormously prolific writer have been translated; reviews have appeared not only in scholarly periodicals, but also in daily and weekly newspapers; and interviews with Professor Bauman have become the focus of debate in many intellectual circles. Zygmunt Bauman has become a major reference-point for the revitalization of social theory as well as for the reformulation of German self-understanding after the events of 1989.

Zygmunt Bauman's book on the Holocaust is one of the very few truly sociological attempts to interpret this most horrible fact of modern history. It is sociological in so far as it does not reduce the bureaucratic genocide to the psychological predispositions of the perpetrators or to the historical particularities of Germany. But at the same time, it differs from the more or less implicit assumptions of mainstream sociological theory by strictly rejecting every attempt to interpret the Holocaust as a deviation from the otherwise progressive course of modernization. According to Bauman, the Holocaust must not be declared a particular event in the history of German–Jewish relations, nor a passing disturbance of, or a retreat from, modernity. On the contrary, we can only understand the Holocaust if we recognize its thoroughly modern character, and we can only come to an appropriate understanding of modernity if we develop it from our understanding of the Holocaust. Bauman's book can be classified as one of the decisive texts of a *sociology after Auschwitz*.

In order to understand the highly emotional reactions in Germany towards Bauman's way of thinking, one has to bear in mind the dominant interpretation of the origins of Nazism in Germany: the so-called *Sonderweg* thesis, that is, the assumption that from a certain point onwards, German history took a special path that deviated from 'normal' Western processes of modernization. This assumption was already common in Germany in the late nineteenth and early twentieth centuries, but at that time it had a positive connotation: 'One was proud to have a strong statist tradition, a powerful and efficient civil service, a long history of reform from above – instead of revolution, *laissez faire*, and party government.'[2] Whereas this interpretation disappeared for the most part after 1918, it reappeared after 1945, but this time it was seen in a completely different light. This version of the *Sonderweg* thesis seems to go back to Thorstein Veblen's writings on Germany during the First World War and came to Germany via the works of Talcott Parsons and Ralf Dahrendorf. According to this view, Germany was considered a 'belated nation' (Helmuth Plessner), a strong state, highly successful with respect to industrialization, but behind the times as far as a democratic political culture was concerned. This view influenced large parts of liberal and leftist historiography in Germany and became one of the cornerstones of self-understanding for those intellectuals who emphasized the Westernization of West Germany after 1945 as the ultimate break with an age-old harmful tradition. Whoever doubted this interpretation quickly became labelled conservative, nationalist or reactionary.

In Zygmunt Bauman's interpretation, however, the *Sonderweg* thesis is not only avoided, but directly repudiated. When interviewers press him on this point, he concedes that the Prussian tradition of efficient bureaucracy was an important factor – but it is absolutely clear that what he means by this is not a lack of modernity in the sense of the vestiges of absolutism, but that this tradition played a sort of leading role in a general modern trend towards bureaucratization.[3] During the 1980s doubts about the validity of the *Sonderweg* thesis were growing steadily and came from all quarters, not only from conservative ones. Was the German bourgeoisie in fact particularly weak compared to major Western societies, or did the thesis imply an uncritical and idealized view of those societies? Had the Nazis been supported by the remnants of pre-industrial classes, or do we have to consider the Nazi movement as an innovative and modernizing force? Perhaps we have to distinguish several different modernization processes like bureaucratization, secularization, democratization and capitalist industrialization, and to abandon the belief that they were necessarily interconnected.[4]

The situation became even more dramatic when the so-called *Historikerstreit* [Historians' Dispute] was launched in 1986 with a vehement attack by Jürgen Habermas on Ernst Nolte's interpretation of the connections between Nazism and Bolshevism.[5] With all the eloquence and moral fervour at his command, Habermas attacked Nolte's views not only as factually incorrect, but also as a symptom of the revival of ideologies that aimed at denying the incomparable criminality of the Nazi regime and the true history of its origins. Again, one does not have to delineate the main positions in this extremely aggressive dispute – in which, by the way, sociology played practically no role at all – to understand what it meant to Germans when a Jewish sociologist from Poland or Britain was heard to say that the Holocaust is not absolutely incomparable and not to be explained exclusively in terms of the peculiarities of German history. Those who were unwilling to take such a voice seriously had no choice but to ignore it because in Bauman's case it was not possible to explain his ideas as the product of an ideological intention to absolve the German nation of guilt and responsibility.

What happened to Zygmunt Bauman in this respect is very similar to the reactions to Hannah Arendt's book on Adolf Eichmann.[6] There are clear similarities between the two books anyway. What is more intriguing, however, is the degree to which the whole second part of Arendt's book on totalitarianism has consistently been ignored both in the German debates and worldwide.[7] Almost all references to her book concentrate on those parts where she writes about communism or anti-Semitism; there is almost total silence about her claim that racism and bureaucratic domination over foreign peoples are intimately intertwined with the history of modern colonialism and imperialism. Like Bauman today, Arendt thus derived crucial traits of the Nazi regime from the history of modernity – not from a German *Sonderweg* or, as Marxists used to, from the character of capitalism. Whereas Arendt's position seems to have remained completely unassimilable for decades, Zygmunt Bauman's book encountered the strong interest, above all, of the younger generation of intellectuals in Germany. They all display clear sympathy with the general thrust of his argument, even when they criticize particular elements in it.

The most frequent criticism is that Bauman does not analyse the decision-making processes leading to the so-called Final Solution and that he does not describe the cumulative radicalization of the Nazi regime in this respect. Another related objection is that it was not bureaucracy as such that produced moral indifference but an erosion of the institutional embeddedness of modern bureaucracies. These points can be countered to some extent, of course, if we recognize that it was Bauman's explicit intention to understand not so much the history and the precise origins of the Holocaust as the goal that the Nazi leadership had in mind. From my own standpoint, it is problematic to overstate the bureaucratic character of this genocide. As the recent historiography of the Second World War has forcefully demonstrated,[8] we should not neglect the role of the regular forces of the German Army (*Wehrmacht*) in the persecution and murder of Jews and others; nor should we forget the role of spontaneous and individual violence in the everyday life of the concentration camps. Wolfgang Sofsky, a sociologist who has written an excellent book on the camps, speaks of 'absolute violence'.[9] A full picture of the Holocaust will have to integrate all these phenomena.

Bauman's Holocaust book leads to conclusions that necessitate a radical re-evaluation of our age. Bauman pursues this goal by elaborating a 'sociology of postmodernity'. There can be no doubt that he has provided one of the most convincing contributions to this diffuse field of postmodernity debates – and again, one of the few truly sociological contributions, whereas other authors, such as Lyotard or Foucault, suffer from serious deficiencies in this respect or can be understood as denying the importance of a sociological approach altogether. This part of Bauman's work also fulfilled a particular need in Germany, not only, as everywhere, to understand postmodernity, but also to come to grips with the situation of Germany after reunification, when communism had to be interpreted in the light of its collapse and its consequences, and when violence towards immigrants and the Balkan wars suddenly destroyed hopes for a more peaceful future.

At this point one has to return to the intellectual background to Bauman's reception in Germany. We can clearly discern two types of thinking that served as a foil for understanding Bauman. One is Horkheimer and Adorno's *Dialectic of Enlightenment*,[10] the other is Norbert Elias's theory of the civilizing process.[11] The authors of these works are all Germans; they all had to spend considerable parts of their lives as émigrés, and their intellectual influence is by no means restricted to Germany. In the first case, the similarities are obvious, and Bauman himself has admitted them, but many reviewers detect differences nevertheless. Whereas in their book Horkheimer and Adorno assume a linear increase in the domination of instrumental reason that, at the point of its completion and triumph, completely reveals its character, Bauman has a view that is more open to the internal contradictions of this process, less linear and more willing to allow for an alternative to the further growth in the domination of instrumental rationality today.

The second case, that of Norbert Elias, is more intricate, since his theory and the interpretations of it are deeply ambiguous on the point that is of most interest to us here. His classical early work on the civilizing process had asserted a linear process of the monopolization of violence and of the increase of affectual control in the structure of personality. However, his later work allows for a very different interpretation since it moves in the direction of a reflexivity of the civilizing process, the replacement of mere inner compulsion by responsibility and reflexivity.[12]

In addition to Horkheimer/Adorno and Elias, mention must be made of the enormous importance of Ulrich Beck's book on the 'risk society' for the German sociological debates of the last decade.[13] This is because there is a certain parallel here to the existence of two competing ways of interpreting Elias. In spite of the gloomy light Beck casts on the risks of modern technologies, he is a deeply optimistic thinker whose gaze is always directed towards the light at the end of the tunnel, that is, the rediscovery of democracy and the new understanding of politics under the influence of these enormous risks.

Now it is not very easy to situate Bauman in this terrain. Is he more of an optimistic or more of a pessimistic thinker? When we read what he has to say about postmodernity, we may be seduced into characterizing him as an optimist. But when we study his analysis of modernity, we may actually be shocked by the extent to which he describes it as a narrative of terror. There is a problem here that clearly comes to the surface when Bauman, for instance, in his contribution to a German conference on 'Modernity and Barbarism', reduces the civilizing process to a mere redistribution of violence, not its (possible) negation.[14] Legitimate violence, he says explicitly, is also violence, and as soon as we recognize this we lose all our illusions about the possible disappearance of violence. Here I (together with others) disagree, first of all because such a statement can never be falsified empirically. If we put it like that, we exclude the possibility of a peaceful culture *a priori*, not by empirical study. Second, such a position, by evading all arguments about legitimacy, opens up a space for philosophical and political decisionism. If legitimate violence is also violence, merely disguised by subjectively plausible ideologies of legitimation, then the whole sphere of discourse about legitimation is neglected or missed out.[15]

If one analyses modernity in the light of the twentieth century's major wars, one can safely say that it was not the Holocaust, but the First World War that struck the first major blow at all optimistic and linear theories of progress.[16] The period between the World Wars was certainly not dominated by optimistic views on modernization, if we think of it in terms of liberal-democratic progress. It is true that Bolshevism and Fascism articulated a particular view of progress and activism, but precisely by leaving out crucial features of the liberal and democratic philosophies of history. In order to paint something like a fully rounded picture here, we have to reconstruct the Enlightenment dreams of a modernity free of violence; the role of defensive modernization, for example for Prussian history after 1806; the constitutive role of the war for the victory of the Bolshevik revolution; the emergence of Fascism from the spirit of war; the role of civil wars in the emergence of modernity; and the impact of war and civil war on the essence of modernity.[17]

One can draw three conclusions from the argument barely sketched here. First, one may wonder whether Zygmunt Bauman should not emphasize more than he did in his masterly book on the Holocaust that it took place *during the war*. One would like to know how he interprets the causal relationship between military and genocidal strategies and their interconnections. Second, this history destroys *all* assumptions of linearity, whether they be optimistic or pessimistic, and this not only with respect to the modernization of societies but also to the modernization of war itself. We have learnt during recent years that the path to the possibility of nuclear war was not a one-way street but that there can be – alongside nuclear wars – conventional wars and civil wars in which spontaneous violence plays a major role.

And the third conclusion is perhaps the most far-reaching one. If we consider the interaction between the so-called military revolution of the sixteenth century and the process of modern state-formation, we end up relativizing the centrality of the modernization of the state within the process of modernization in general. We may ask whether, for example, England, which is often taken as the prototypical country of modernization, really went through such a process at the level of the state, or whether it was rather spared the pressures to develop an overpowering state apparatus by the advantages of its economic and geographical situation.[18] Could it not be the case that there were types of modernization that were less state-centred, maybe even orientated towards alternative principles such as the strong self-government of citizens at all levels of their polity?

Can, for example, the history of the North American colonies and the United States of America truly be covered by Bauman's ingenious metaphor of the 'gardening state'? Can the intellectual importance of pragmatist philosophy and the Chicago School of empirical social research really be grasped in terms of 'instrumental reason'?[19] To a surprising degree, Zygmunt Bauman is clearly a Continental thinker with respect to these questions. This is the point at which several of his critics in Germany have entered the debate when they complain that Bauman does not pay sufficient attention to democratic alternatives *within* modernity, that is, *before* postmodernity. For example, they criticize his analysis of Jewish emancipation and assimilation in Germany as one-sided,[20] and they object to his complete failure to show any interest in Romantic counter-tendencies to the Enlightenment. These include elements from various schools of modern thought from *Lebensphilosophie* to pragmatism and all sorts of subcultures and countercultures, even Nazi ideology, which many scholars have traced back more directly to Romanticism than to the Enlightenment. The heritage of American social thought and, perhaps more surprisingly, of an author like Martin Buber, who today inspires Shmuel Eisenstadt's quest for alternative modernities or Amitai Etzioni's attempt to form a communitarian movement – these approaches are conspicuously absent from Zygmunt Bauman's work.

A last point: Zygmunt Bauman and the postmodernity debate. As one German reviewer aptly put it, it is in large part through Bauman's work that this debate, which had lost its rationale, was turned into something serious, with a profound moral dimension and existential implications.[21] Still, it may be that Bauman gives too much credit to the postmodern talk of the violence caused by clear concepts. This idea, which originated with Henri Bergson, if I am not mistaken, entered Adorno's thinking via a dubious German philosopher named Ludwig Klages, and it plays a major role in postmodern thought. It seems to me to confuse the attitude of classification without regard to the classified with attempts at a subtle hermeneutic articulation of all particularities in language. This conflation has contributed to the widespread loss of clarity in the postmodernity debates. If 'anything goes', some authors seem to assume that they can disregard all standards of logical rigour and linguistic precision. One German reviewer wrote that to call something ambiguous is an absolutely unambiguous statement.[22] And Zygmunt Bauman's own writing style undoubtedly is very, very far removed from the mere assembly of arbitrary associations we find in a postmodernist writer like Jean Baudrillard; on the contrary, it has all the flavour of good old European rhetoric.

Bauman's work certainly does not avoid ethical questions in a playful spirit, but is a serious quest for a postmodern ethics. This, however, takes the form of a partially aporetic endeavour. Zygmunt Bauman describes our age as an age of complete uncertainty, or rather as an age of an unavoidable consciousness of uncertainty. And his quest for ethics in such an age leads him to Emmanuel Levinas's philosophy of the Other as a 'groundless ground' for moral impulses. He leads us from society as a 'factory of morality' to the 'pre-societal sources of morality'. But this characterization of our age is not fully convincing. Can we not see much certainty around, and do we really have to interpret this as the certainty of those who simply have not found out about the loss of metaphysical grounding? This is what a person interviewed by the Bellah group said: 'Why is integrity important and lying bad? I don't know. I don't know. It just is. It's just so basic. I don't want to be bothered with challenging that. It's part of me. I don't know where it came from, but it's very important.'[23] In more abstract terms, one could say that many people today experience the loss of a language to articulate their moral intuitions, not the loss of these intuitions themselves. Bauman is right when he assumes that people feel the more unable to stick to their identities, the more they have previously had the opportunity to choose their identity freely. But this, of course, does not mean that we prefer identities imposed upon us; rather, we have to form them not by choice, but by a process that William James, in his wonderful book *The Varieties of Religious Experience*, described as self-surrender.[24] The German term is *Ergriffensein*, that is, being deeply moved by, overcome by, seized by a force that makes us into the selves we aspire to be. For me, Levinas's description of our being affected by the Other is a special case of this experience – an experience that we find in acts of individual love or compassion, in religion and collective ecstasy.[25]

This argument is closer to communitarianism than Zygmunt Bauman is, but it is certainly one of the weak points of the communitarians that they attempt to revitalize values without telling us how our commitment to values comes about. This, however, should not lead us to the conclusion that we have to separate the formation of selves into an ethical space from the social structures of human life. Intersubjectivity and the self are not constant givens, but are always broken up by spontaneous impulses and the experiences of 'alterity' that, again and again, have to be reintegrated into the structures of intersubjectivity and the self.[26] Such an approach in ethics, clearly developed by George Herbert Mead, is the result of the same cultural traditions emphasized above when alternative versions of modernity were mentioned.[27]

10
War and the Risk Society

Debate with the contributions of Ulrich Beck, the theorist of the 'risk society' and of 'reflexive modernization', is never a thankful task. His diagnostic sensitivity to the age, the refreshing effects of his often all too bold, but always ingenious assertions, his wit and the ever-present implicit encouragement trigger considerable sympathy. On the other hand, his writings contain a number of astonishing logical inconsistencies; there is sometimes a complete absence of scholarly references; his love of paradox is all too evident; noteworthy, too, is his sense of pathos about an epochal rupture in our time. In particular, the prophetic gesture with which Beck presents his work has its own allure, but should alert the reader to the need for caution.

When Beck's book *Risk Society* appeared in 1986,[1] it could be said that the professional social sciences had made a sensational return to the public arena. In the preceding years it had become increasingly unusual for sociology to muster the courage and ability for a diagnosis of contemporary society. As far as the crucial topics were concerned – we need only think of the themes of the 'environment' and 'peace' – the discipline seldom aspired to make its voice heard among the general public. Caught between the discussion of postmodernism and the diagnosis of the approaching nuclear state, the contributions of the professional social sciences appeared rather feeble. Ulrich Beck, however, was unique (and not just in German sociology[2]) because he had the courage to produce subjective syntheses of a multiplicity of empirical writings on an extremely diverse range of problem areas. Instead of embarking on the labour of reflecting upon the methodological and theoretical difficulties of these different problem areas, he energetically organized his extensive material into three strands of argument whose connections with each other remained quite loose. But this fact probably made the reception of his book easier. To summarize his diagnosis briefly, Beck argued that our contemporary world must be understood in terms of the concept of a 'risk society'. By this he meant a society whose old battle-lines have been rendered obsolete by the overwhelming threat of new large-scale dangers produced by industrial society, of which Chernobyl is an instance. Simultaneously, society is said to be experiencing a rapid shift to a new 'process of individualization' in which social milieus stemming from old distinctions between estates and cultures based on class vanish and are not replaced, making way instead for socially isolated individual biographies. Lastly, under the influence of a 'reflexive modernization', the relations between politics and science lose all clear-cut boundaries, and are being redrawn in ways that contain completely new possibilities and dangers.

As early as the mid-1980s, it was very striking to see how powerfully Beck stressed the notion of a break in historical continuities so as to give a clearer shape to his analyses. The price of such a presentation is mainly a historical two-dimensionality in the depiction of an earlier age, or an age said to be approaching its end. Beck's judgement is very quick and sweeping when he proclaims the obsolete nature of class society and the nation-state. The function of the education system in allocating status not only is diminished, in his view, but has vanished altogether. Conversely, his retrospective account of the unity and the cohesiveness of the working-class milieu is untenably exaggerated. He has sensitive antennae for current trends, such as the growth of home-working with computers, but instead of simply noting them as trends, he generalizes them without any sense of proportion or any awareness of opposing tendencies. At many points particular elements of national importance are declared to be fundamental features of an approaching world epoch, without any attempt to make international comparisons. This is mainly achieved by a rhetorical sleight of hand. The concept of the 'risk society', which had been introduced in an *ad hoc* manner in order to describe specific phenomena, is tacitly treated as if it were a theoretical concept from which well-founded conclusions could be drawn. The theoretical definition of what constitutes the 'risk society' and the question of how far we can go in speaking of an epochal change is confusingly accompanied by a mere listing of current phenomena.

After the events of 1989, which many contemporaries in fact experienced as a historical rupture, Beck intensified his rhetoric along these lines. Yet in his diagnosis before 1989 he had maintained a striking silence on questions of foreign policy and also, incidentally, of military risks. In his book *The Reinvention of Politics*[3] all the usual structural categories of politics and society are dismissed as ludicrously *passé*. Beck goes so far as to proclaim that the whole of sociology must be invented anew.[4] He now believes that all the typical features of Western democratic capitalism are caught up in a process of dissolution. He denies outright the existence of a functioning security system in Europe. His preoccupation with 'globalization' makes his rhetoric about the disappearance of all the things we have taken for granted resonate with increasing pathos.[5] We may legitimately ask how long and how often this gesture will continue to grip the attention of the reading public.

In the present context, however, we are not concerned with the difficult task of distinguishing between rhetoric and substance in Beck's writings.[6] Instead, we shall confine ourselves to the narrower field of the sociology of war and violence so as to examine the usefulness of Beck's contributions to the diagnosis of the 'risk society' and his understanding of 'modernity'.

I

The conceptual field of 'modernity' is absolutely central to Beck's thinking. Beck uses the term 'modernization' frequently, but without ever making its meaning unambiguously clear. The industrial society we are leaving behind is referred to as a 'restricted modernity'. But, according to Beck, modernity also constantly brings counter-modern tendencies to the fore. The present trend towards a revival of nationalism in Europe is an example of this counter-modernization in his eyes. But even the fact that technological progress is dependent upon the imperatives of a profit-making economy is something he classifies as counter-modern. He attempts to grasp the essence of the epochal shift with the concept of 'reflexive modernization', a concept that increasingly comes to be his general term for what he analyses as the main tendencies of the present: fabricated insecurity, globalization and individualization.

What is the nature of my difficulty with these terms? Perhaps it will be simplest if I start with Beck's use of the term 'restricted modernity'. By this he means that industrial society was always dependent upon the cultural resources of values and social bonds that were not identical with the maxims of individualist utility calculation. He frequently refers to these other values as those of a 'feudal, corporative society'. In that sense, then, industrial society really would be a restricted modernity; its other half would belong to a feudal social order. However, Beck hastens to add that 'the feudal side is not a relic of the past, but the *foundation* and *product* of industrial society'.[7] So what he has in mind is not a matter of feeding upon resources from the pre-industrial age during the development of industrial society, but the new formation of values and social bonds in the course of its history. But in that case these values and bonds are not alien to industrial society, and if that is so, why should we speak of a restricted modernity? We could only do that if a complete modernity were available to us. But what would such a modernity look like? Should we think of it as a society without values and bonds that transcend the logic of economic management? We should start by asking whether Beck himself believes that such a social order is even conceivable. His statements on the obsolescence of the family lead us to the conclusion that his answer would be in the affirmative. In that case a true and complete modernization would be a society of total individualization in Beck's sense. But such a society cannot possibly be a positive model for us; even for Beck it would represent a nightmare vision. In actual fact Beck regards the progressive process of individualization as one of the factors triggering the processes running counter to modernization. But this idea, too, becomes unclear because of the lack of clarity in his concept of modernity. Initially, he uses the concept of counter-modernity with negative connotations. This is the case wherever he attacks the artificial naturalness, the 'simulated substantiality' (Habermas) of counter-modernity. But if the perfected modernity as described above is a nightmare vision, then there must also be a counter-modernity that we can evaluate positively. In that event, it is not possible to dismiss every newly arising social bond in the name of modernism. Beck vacillates between a diagnosis of conflict between modernity and counter-modernity and a diagnosis of conflict between different kinds of modernity. He really has to make up his mind. Either he has to reserve the concept of modernity for a society whose values are guided by universalist principles – in that event not all value commitments and social bonds would be subsumed under the concepts of 'corporative societies' or 'counter-modernity', but only those that break with such universalist principles; such a concept of modernity would have a positive normative meaning, but could not be used empirically to describe every development of individualization and globalization. Alternatively, Beck would have to describe the trends just referred to as modernization; but, in that case, measured by value criteria, and particularly by universalist criteria, modernity would turn out to be a highly ambivalent business. Beck cannot have it both ways. He cannot both describe developments he disapproves of as 'counter-modernization' and at the same time advance a theory that in practice rules out a complete 'modernization'.

However – and this is how I imagine that Beck would reply – this is to ignore his key concept of 'reflexive modernization'. On this point I find it unfortunate that Beck, in a kind of play on words, should have conflated reflex and reflection. Every reaction to ongoing modernization is undoubtedly a reflex; but only the discursive interrogation of the organizing principles of society can be said to involve reflection upon it. Even if it is true that reflecting on a topic is one of the many possible responses to it, the distinction remains important. The claim that there is reflection in the concept of 'reflexive modernization' is one I find very attractive. The idea resembles what Michael Walzer calls 'the art of separation' (and what I have attempted to define as the 'democratization of differentiation').[8] But Beck's vision is influenced by his assumption of an epochal rupture. It is not the case that reflection upon the need to rein in the central dynamics of modern societies has only just begun. Following this logic, is it not true that the welfare state of the twentieth century and indeed every national economic policy of the nineteenth century, together with the entire project of socialism, must belong to 'reflexive modernization'?[9]

The theory of reflexive modernization makes too many, rather than too few, concessions to the normal theory of modernization, because it has only declared the latter to be historically obsolete and invalid since the spread of the damaging ecological consequences of industrial economies, without really questioning it radically at its core. It must be asked, however, whether modernization theory *ever* truly did justice to the problems of war and violence in the modern era.[10]

II

In order to test Beck's own answer to this question I would like to turn to his talk about 'a militarily restricted democracy', the relevant theorem in *The Reinvention of Politics*. Thus, if we are to lend credence to Beck, not only was industrial society just a restricted modernity; democracy, too, was truncated. Its other half was represented by the military with its command structures and the nation-state with its stereotypes of the enemy and its exclusions. 'The military is to democracy as fire is to water.'[11] This idea is easy to understand. The difference between the military and a democratic principle of organization is evident to everyone. But it immediately again prompts the question whether this argument is sufficiently strong on its own. Who is to say that societies are wont to have no more than one principle of organization? Beck provides no justification for such an assumption. The position becomes even more confusing when he goes on to say in this context: 'Along with popular rule, democracy created the popular army, along with universal suffrage, it also created universal conscription, and along with the national, it created and incited the nationalist enthusiasm for fighting and killing in war.'[12] So now the opposite seems to be the case. It looks as if democracy is the cause of the intensification of war. To be sure, Beck qualifies this: 'One can say that the military was democratized only in the sense that it was *generalized*. The democratically legitimated state arrogated to itself the right to call *all* citizens to arms – by force, if necessary.'[13] But once again there was no need to use the same concept for the ideal of democracy and the inclusion of the entire population in the sphere of war. And above all, the historical claims, which are undoubtedly a central element of the link between modernity and violence, are dubious. A few remarks will have to suffice here.[14]

The idea that universal conscription is 'the legitimate child of democracy' (Theodor Heuss) is widespread, particularly in Germany. But there are a number of factors that should give us pause. When conscription was introduced in Prussia in 1814, there was certainly no democracy at that time. Conscription survived throughout the whole of Prussian and German history, which had precious little of democracy about it, until in 1919 at the beginning of the first German democracy, the Scheidemann government offered to abolish it as a concession to the victorious powers of the First World War. It was reintroduced in 1935 by Adolf Hitler. Under the Empire, conscripts were actually denied the right to vote. For the call-up, attempts were made to leave out the politicized town youth. Furthermore, in the nineteenth century universal conscription was more of a Prussian and German peculiarity than the international rule. In particular, the great democracies had no conscription. Not until the First World War did Great Britain and the USA introduce it, and they always intended to dismantle it again in peacetime. But does not universal military service date back to the French Revolution and old ideas of the 'republican' tradition of political thinking? In a certain sense, undoubtedly; but we should not forget that even the French Revolution only regarded it as an emergency measure and that republican ideas about militias and citizens in arms stood in opposition to the standing armies maintained by the monarchs. Thus an imaginative leap is required to turn democracy into the starting-point for universal military service.

But to deny that such a link exists is not the same thing as asserting that all military defence is incompatible with democracy in principle. All functionally differentiated societies have a number of different principles of organization. This fact robs Beck's rhetorical topos of a 'restricted democracy' of much of its force.

III

Apart from these brief and evidently problematic statements about the relations between democracy and the armed forces, there are few traces in Beck's writings of a sociological analysis of war. In his contribution to the conference on 'Modernity and Barbarism', he brings in his thesis about individualism and his assumptions about the loss of tradition in a (reflexive) modernity in order to analyse new dangers like creating new images of the enemy and ways of resisting them.[15] In the public debates about the war in Kosovo, Beck repeatedly intervened with contributions that drew attention to the novelty of the defence of human rights as justification for conducting a war.[16] But he has never constructed a bridge between the basic components of his theory of the risk society and the sociology of war.

For this reason it is legitimate to ask what such a link might look like. One obvious question is to ask how the major 'risk-society' risks might alter the conduct of war in industrial societies. As is well known, Beck stresses the fact that the new threats differ in a number of respects from the typical risks in industrial societies. These new risks are, like the old ones, socially constituted and not natural dangers. But, according to Beck, it is not possible to set limits to them, whether spatial, temporal or social; the established rules of ascription and responsibility break down in their case; the damage they cause is mainly irreversible; the dangers that threaten can never be forestalled, only minimized. In fact other authors than Beck have drawn their own conclusions from the theory of the risk society about how to analyse the 'fitness for war' of modern societies.[17] If we follow their analysis, we see right away that the industrialization of war that is typical of industrial societies has made huge strides. This holds good for the considerable increase in destructive power of so-called conventional weapons and weapon-systems through constant ' "improvements" in terms of range, speed, precision and penetration',[18] so that today even a conventional war would leave a trail of destruction far in excess of the destruction caused in the Second World War. We can say that these risks have not entered the public consciousness to the same degree as the threat of nuclear war. Furthermore, the vulnerability of modern societies to the disruption of, say, energy supplies or communication networks has also increased considerably. In both these cases – and with the exception of nuclear war – we can still speak of quantitative increases rather than a new qualitative dimension. But the consequences of war for the already existing risk potential of modern societies really do seem to point in the direction of an epochal shift. Once again the tendency has been to focus on the risks of nuclear war for global climate change, and these have been widely discussed under the heading of the 'nuclear winter'. In contrast, the consequences of conventional warfare (or, as one has to add, terrorism) for risk societies have been given only scant attention.

> Think, for example, of the numerous civilian 'industrial bombs' that are being stockpiled in the shape of nuclear power stations, chemical plants, oil refineries, toxic waste dumps or nuclear reprocessing centres in every industrialized society. Risks to such facilities as the result of collateral damage in wartime would be practically unavoidable. But even in peace-time, as a number of incidents has shown (Seveso, Bhopal, Sandoz/Basel or Chernobyl), industrial risk societies live permanently on the edge of self-destruction.[19]

The empirical analysis here is persuasive, but the conclusion the author arrives at is surprising and implausible. It is that military violence and modern society are increasingly incompatible with each other.

> This civil–military incompatibility is ... the result of two opposing developmental processes both of which are ultimately the products of industrialization. Only by linking and contrasting the declining 'struc-tural fitness for war' of advanced societies, on the one hand, and the increasing 'ultimate destructive capacity' of the armed forces, on the other, does the incompatibility gap between the civil and military spheres open up.[20]

According to this analysis, this process has long been under way, but with the invention of nuclear weapons and their inclusion in the arsenal of the competing powers it has reached its point of no return and has made steady progress ever since.

What is surprising about this prognosis at first sight is that it com-pletely ignores the possibility of the political and military participants reacting to this 'incompatibility'. If a nuclear war cannot be waged, strategists will surely direct their thoughts to viable alternatives in conventional warfare. If, in the conditions obtaining in risk societies, particular forms of conventional warfare threaten to affect one's own side, or even to render uninhabitable the territory that the two sides are fighting for, other forms will be given priority. This is not to assert that military planners will always calculate the risks of their own strategy correctly in fact, or even that they might be able to do so in principle. But every prognosis becomes misleadingly deterministic if it fails to take into account the possible reactions of the participants to the predicted developments and the modifications to which such reactions might lead. But the thesis is implausible above all because it succumbs to a kind of functionalist fallacy. This occurs when the demonstration of possible dysfunctionalities is treated as the empirical prognosis of a particular development that avoids such dysfunctionalities. If we take the thesis of civil–military incompatibility in 'risk societies' as a moral appeal to avoid risk, that will undoubtedly earn our respect. But if we take it as a prognosis that in these conditions wars will become increasingly unlikely, then this is nothing more than an unsupported inference.

Such a way of thinking simply revives under present-day conditions the assertion that industrial society is essentially peaceable in nature.[21] This assertion came to grief spectacularly in the First World War, at the latest, in the light of the industrialization of the conduct of the war. Needless to say, it would be wrong to hold Ulrich Beck responsible for inferences that others have drawn from his theory. But we should keep in mind that notwithstanding the passion with which he defends the notion of an epochal shift – or perhaps because of it – he retains assumptions of classical modernization theory to an astonishing degree in his writings without questioning them. Thus the neglect of war and violence in his theory of 'reflexive modernization' is no less marked than in conventional modernization theory.

11

War the Teacher?

The Gulf War of 1991 has left deep marks in the intellectual landscape – however quickly the public may have lost interest in it. In Germany, the debates that accompanied it left the intellectual camp in even greater disarray than the one created by the discussions about reunification that preceded it. Such disarray can be creative because it compels all the participants to clarify apparently self-evident truths and to produce new arguments. To be sure, this presupposes that people will bring care and stamina to their reflection upon historical events. It is curious that during the war many philosophers – from Robert Spaemann to Karl-Otto Apel – felt impelled to take a public stand from the lofty vantage-point of moral philosophy. But with the passage of time – which alone allows us properly to assess the validity of earlier pronouncements, since the course of the war, its conclusion and consequences provide us with a wealth of material with which to review judgements about the participants, their motives and means – there has been only silence. In contrast, the social scientists said little during the Gulf War. A charitable explanation might ascribe this to their tendency laboriously to collect rather more facts than the philosophers and to trust less when making judgements to the internal consistency of a line of argument. But an objection to this interpretation lies in the fact that silence about the problems of war and peace is something of a bad tradition in sociology. Now we have an ambitious attempt on the part of a respected social scientist not simply to state his views on the Gulf War, but also to place them in a larger theoretical and political context. Presented in popular form, Karl Otto Hondrich's essay *War the Teacher*[1] can hope to be widely read. Should we wish him this success?

Hondrich's book-length essay had been preceded at the time of the Gulf War by an essay in *Der Spiegel* with the same title. The aim of his argument had remained pretty obscure. Only two points became clear at the time. On the one hand, there was Hondrich's interpretation of the cause of the war, which he saw in the clash between the 'pre-modern predilection for violence' of Islamic culture and the 'culturally constituted pacifism of the West'. On the other hand, there was the political inference that only a new *Pax Americana et Europaea* could guarantee peace and that the West was 'condemned to dominance'. This text did not achieve any significant resonance. However, the appearance of the longer version in book form was given an enthusiastic welcome by the *Frankfurter Allgemeine Zeitung*. Its reviewer called Hondrich's book 'fascinating', and he found himself reminded of Max Weber's 'cold passion' by the way in which the war was analysed and not just morally condemned. So this considerably raises our expectations of Hondrich's book.

Hondrich's central idea consists in the fact that he interprets the Gulf War, and wars in general, within the framework of a sociological learning theory. Admittedly, this learning theory is always just hinted at and hardly ever explained. Collectives, so the theory goes, learn through wars. The peaceful nature of the Germans since 1945, which is so striking in the light of their militarist traditions, is a typical product of such a learning process about war; in this case it is the product of the shattering defeat of 1945. Now, the Gulf War has a new lesson ready for the Germans in particular. This is the 'insight' – in Hondrich's positive formulation – 'that an aggressor must be opposed, with force if need be'.[2] The educational aim for the German 'model pupils of peaceableness'[3] is different from what it was after 1945. They should not indeed instantly adopt a positive view of war, but they should understand that peace is not an absolute value. On the contrary, experience teaches that even today limited wars are certainly possible, that Germany can become involved in such a war, and that this might indeed be perfectly justifiable. Thus far, all this sounds more like a statement of Hondrich's political position than a sociological theory. But this is not how he wishes to be understood. He does indeed argue politically against the German opposition parties and their 'lamentable lack of sensitivity to new political processes in general and to foreign policy in particular',[4] and his polemic is directed above all against the moralistic views of pacifists and the peace movement. But he does not lay claim to any alternative moral or political standpoint of his own. He argues instead in favour of a 'sociological alienation from the moral view of war'.[5] What escapes the moralists is revealed to him by the sociological gaze. This reveals – in the words of one chapter heading – the 'meaning of war'. It is true, he maintains, that war mostly has no meaning for individuals, but it has a meaning for the collective. The fact is, he claims, that war is a great teacher because it tears collective ideas away from the feelings in which they are anchored and thus breaks down barriers to learning. It forces collectives out of their natural inertia and makes them learn even against their will. 'Only in this way, and not through intellectual discourse or detached negotiation, do they [collective ideas] become changed in a profound way for many people simultaneously.'[6] Thus neither pacifists and members of the peace movement nor all those who rely on discourse and argument in a learning theory will be able to share Hondrich's insight. But if we do accompany him along his path, and if our scrutiny of the place of war in the history of the world is as free from illusions as his, then what awaits us at the end of the road is not despair at so much havoc and suffering, but comfort. For what emerges from the history of modern warfare is 'a kind of unplanned syllabus for which no author exists'.[7]

> Over-ambitious interests are forced to retreat in war; over-narrow, self-centred values must give way to universally acceptable ones, such as self-determination and equal rights; the despotism of individual states is shaken off by war, to be replaced by the accepted dominance of an expanding group of superior societies. The particularizing of interests, the universalizing of values, the acceptance of dominance: once the global society has absorbed these lessons of war, it ceases to need war.[8]

Thus if only we look at the world without illusions we shall see that in history the good ends up winning and peace triumphs, if everyone learns these lessons. This is why the chapters in which Hondrich treats the individual components of the unplanned curriculum in greater detail are supplemented by a conciliatory conclusion in which a process of learning without war is at least discussed. However, the precondition of peace for him is the generally accepted and willingly exercised dominance of the Western powers – and this leads the book to the conclusion that is already familiar to us from the article in Der Spiegel: 'Whoever refuses to face up to conflict and risk, whoever refuses to accept the reality of dominance, will seek peace in vain.'[9]

Hondrich must know what he is doing. It is well known that scratching at a taboo is not without risk. Moreover, to do so with the same old-fashioned concepts that are so familiar to us from the chauvinistic professorial journalism of the First World War is at the very least ill advised. To lay claim to the aura of science for his own views presupposes a trust in the reliability of the theory that underpins them. But it is precisely here that doubts are appropriate.

These begin with Hondrich's use of the term 'learning'. It is systematically ambiguous. Throughout the entire book it remains unclear whether Hondrich regards every change of ideas as 'learning' or only those changes that take place in pursuit of an educational aim, that is to say, that actually produce more knowledge, better understanding, something that of course presupposes a yardstick for the evaluation of the changes. At the only point where Hondrich defines his concept of learning more or less clearly,[10] he explicitly distinguishes it from mere change; learning must result from experience and have a meaning, namely 'to secure the survival of the learning system in the long run in an uncertain environment'.[11] With this definition he rather grandly ignores sociology's familiar difficulties with clearly defining what stability and survival mean with regard to social phenomena. More seriously, however, he fails to maintain consistency in his use of his own definition. Thus he talks about the fact that it is possible to learn what is false or merely adventitious.[12] In general, he never explains what gives him the right to declare that specific changes are in fact the genuine products of learning. It is perfectly conceivable, for example, that the reactions of the peace movement to the Gulf War could be interpreted as the product of a successful learning process. When Hondrich maintains[13] that learning is better than refusing to learn, he is tacitly using the concept in a value-laden way. It would be absurd to suppose that every change of mind is better than every decision to stick with one's previous ideas. Thus Hondrich's concept of learning suffers in the first place from the fact that the normative criterion it inevitably contains is nowhere defined. This means that there are no controls at all on the scope for applying his learning theory.

The kernel of Hondrich's theory of learning is the emphasis he places on the anchoring of collective ideas in the emotions and – if a learning process is going to take place at all – the need to uproot these ideas and replace them with new ones also anchored in the emotions. And he believes that this process cannot be carried out simply through the non-violent compulsion of superior arguments. 'Moods are the elixir of social learning, not arguments. The latter can be adduced almost at will.'[14] Here, then, we have the same ambiguity that characterizes Hondrich's concept of learning. He does indeed wish to speak of learning and curricula, but not of the force of arguments. But if arguments can be adduced at will, how can we justify the claim that a change is valuable and that it amounts to a valid insight?

Despite this inconsistency, Hondrich's emphasis on the anchoring of collective ideas in the emotions deserves attention. This idea, however, is not new to sociology. Its classical form is to be found in Émile Durkheim, who studied the affective anchoring of cognitive contents above all in the self-transcending experience of religious rituals and their modern equivalents. Today this idea is also familiar from the sociology of social movements. What is striking about Hondrich's argument is that he relates an idea that originally included a multiplicity of collective experiences exclusively to the experience of war. He emphasizes that learning in war is characterized by the common existential experience of many individuals, and that these experiences are the basis of 'associations and cohesivenesses that would not exist without war'.[15] In Durkheim the thesis about the affective dimension of fundamental changes in ideas was quite unconnected with war. This connection is to be found in Simmel, but only in his more extravagant journalistic writing about the experience of war – and Hondrich will surely not seriously want to regard these writings as Simmel's sociological legacy. But even Simmel did not assert, as Hondrich does, that it is above all war that makes possible learning processes that are rooted in the emotions. Hondrich neither asks whether in fact the war experience of soldiers and the civilian population possesses the character of an ecstatic communal experience, nor does he relate his learning theory to internal social conflicts and struggles. If learning processes are based on the presuppositions he attributes to them, why does Hondrich call only war a teacher and not civil war, terrorism, general strike or revolution? The affinity of his theory about learning to Sorel's myth of violence is unmistakable, but even here Hondrich is not consistent. The very same lessons he expects to be learnt from war he ignores in the domestic social sphere.

The ambiguity of his 'learning' concept and the tailoring of his theory of learning to war are the premises of Hondrich's strangely optimistic evolutionist view. It is this that leads to his talk of an 'unplanned curriculum'. But here too his argument is frivolous and anything but watertight. Has he really tested whether wars lead to the results he claims? What evidence does Hondrich have for his claim that in the way wars end superior force coincides with universalistic values? Admittedly, this can be said of the victory of the Western democracies over Hitler's Germany, but might it not have turned out otherwise? Did it also hold good for the countries that fell under Soviet sway after 1945? Do defeats always bequeath insight into the value of peaceableness, or can they not lead the vanquished to seek their revenge – on the model of the Versailles Treaty? Are wars incapable of reinforcing militarism in the victor nations? Did the USA learn from its victory in the Gulf War that it should reduce its dependence on oil, or did it 'learn' that the situation favours a unipolar world order with the USA as the leading power? Hondrich's interpretation of the end of the Gulf War is unbearably euphemistic. Whereas in the *Spiegel* essay he had predicted the inevitable fall of Saddam Hussein, he now finds that his survival in office offers the best chance of a learning process leading to a democracy. The American strategy in the wake of the Gulf War of perpetuating Saddam's rule rather than risk destabilizing the region, even though this meant dashing the hopes of the Kurds, is interpreted by Hondrich as 'sparing the enemy . . . to an extent that went far beyond what the culture of war imposes on the belligerent parties, as far as the commonly accepted rules and humanitarian considerations are concerned'.[16] There is no trace here of a serious examination of the question of whether the Gulf War really did exact only the minimum number of casualties – as would be required for a just war according to the traditional view – and whether a war was really necessary to bring about the result achieved.

Admittedly, Hondrich did introduce a caveat into his understanding of evolution. 'Universalist values are produced by wars. Nevertheless, they do not owe their triumph to military force and victories, but to the fact that they are capable of generalization.'[17] However, this connection between the concept of value and the history of wars is itself completely obscure. On the one hand, we might well ask why it is not the universalist values that might succumb in a war. On the other hand, it is not unknown for highly particular interests simply to use universalist justifications for their own purposes. Not that this objection holds any terrors for Hondrich. 'Of course such interests exist! If they did not they would have to be invented. Where else would the struggle for values derive its impetus? And even more importantly, what else would curb it?'[18] But the situation is not as simple as that. To be sure, it must be admitted that in the rough and tumble of reality it is not possible to make a clear distinction between the assertion of values and the pursuit of interests. But the problem becomes virulent if values are only laid claim to when it benefits your own interests, but are ignored or even violated if it is in your interest to do so. The cause of universalist values can be harmed by the combination of legitimizing their use in some instances and a disavowing in others. Hypocrisy is not the road to moral education.

Our scrutiny of Hondrich's underlying theory shows that it is much too soft and ill-defined to enable it to bear the weight of the propositions he wishes to justify with its help. This is not the consequence of a failure to elaborate it sufficiently, something that would certainly have been inappropriate in his book. Hondrich's theory of learning needs this lack of clarity in order to cloak his *ad hoc* assertions in the mantle of greater profundity. It really is astounding to see how casually he deals with both empirical and theoretical matters throughout. When he discusses theories of peace in chapter 1 he not only ignores Marxist theories and early sociological ideas about the peaceable nature of industrial society, he also fails to comment on Kant's republican views, which then suddenly put in an appearance later on.[19] The factual claims interspersed in the text are frequently skewed and superficial. We are told that the Gulf War was the first war that the USA had not conducted in order to spread democracy. Has Hondrich taken a close look at all the instances of military intervention in Latin America? He even dignifies the Vietnam war[20] by reviving the claim that it was a struggle 'for the liberation of nations from foreign domination and internal repression'. Germany and Japan, he maintains, 'have been absolved from every military effort since 1945'[21] – even a sociologist should perhaps take the trouble to glance occasionally at the annual budgetary allocation for the armed forces! In war every side strives for 'the most intimate and most realistic knowledge'[22] of the opposing side – perhaps a glance at propaganda and the origins of our images of the enemy would be helpful. The hostile picture of an intolerant Islam appears in Hondrich in the seemingly neutral contrast between two abstract types of culture.[23] And – a grotesque detail in passing – a statement is attributed to the classical sociologist Simmel in 1922, at which date he had been dead for years.

All of this is only worth mentioning because it is symptomatic of a botched book. The extent of Hondrich's ignorance of peace research is incredible. There is scarcely a trace of either theoretical or empirical knowledge of the causes or consequences of war. The only lessons of war to appear are those that suit the author's book. Needless to say, Hondrich is no warmonger. His text is, if anything, tentative; it is full of qualifications and of attempts to ward off criticism in advance. If we take the book as a piece of sociology, it is simply slapdash and bad. I would not make any great fuss about that. But as a contribution to the formation of public opinion the book is ill considered and irresponsible. I see this – aside from its faults of execution – in three aspects. First, a book that proclaims with scientific mien that war has a meaning cuts off the laborious discourse that is attempting to establish whether a war is meaningful or not. Second, Hondrich adopts not just a scientific manner, but also the manner of *realpolitik*. This immediately relegates the question of avoiding wars to the preoccupation of dreamers.

In Germany more than anywhere the tradition of selling adventurist war objectives as '*realpolitik*' ought surely not to be forgotten. And finally, the book devalues the last elements of a universalist justification of the Gulf War when Hondrich explicitly envisages the approaching 'world state' not in reinforcing the authority of the United Nations, but in the simple dominance of the Western powers. If this is the contribution of the discipline of sociology to the process of intellectually digesting the Gulf War, it would have been better for the discipline and the reputation of its author if he had remained silent.

12
Action Theory and the Dynamics of Violence

In recent decades, whenever a wave of collective violence has swept over one of the advanced Western nations, public attention has always turned urgently to the search for an explanation. From one day to the next, the media quickly cobble together a whole battery of interpretations of every conceivable kind. Scholars who have the benefit of having devoted themselves to such matters over a long period of time are hauled out of the tranquillity of their studies or university offices, where they were dying of despair from the public lack of interest, and are passed round from radio interview to Protestant Academy and TV talk show. The government sets up committees of experts who for the most part produce lengthy reports in several fat volumes years after the spectacular events, reports that no one wants to buy or read and that gather dust on the shelves until a new wave of violence once again triggers a public panic.

We may distinguish between two principal types of explanation among those put forward by sociologists. The first type focuses on the socio-structural characteristics of the perpetrators. As a rule, it regards violent acts as rational actions that go beyond the bounds of legality and certainly of what is morally acceptable – one has to think here of actions of the disadvantaged or excluded, who protest against their disadvantaging or exclusion by using force against their oppressors or against scapegoats and who attract the attention of the public by their shocking deeds. The very experts who have long called for the elimination of social evils and injustices and have warned about their incalculable consequences feel confirmed by the outbreaks of violence and exploit the undoubtedly regrettable opportunity to set themselves up as the advocates of the perpetrators and, while distancing themselves from the acts of violence, to defend the latent element of protest in those acts.

The second type is concerned not with rational decisions and interests, but with values and norms. It sees the origins of acts of violence chiefly in the presence or absence of certain values. I would like to make a distinction between two sub-types here. In the one case, a culture of violence is held responsible, that is to say, long historical traditions of warlike orientation or the habituation to an engrained measure of violence. This includes such things as attempts to privilege male gender roles or the long-standing acceptance of military traditions as important components of explanations, as well as the classical theory of anomie in criminal sociology, which emphasizes the discrepancy between values and the opportunities for putting them into practice. We could also include studies in which the cultural peculiarities of the victims play the decisive role as opposed to those of the perpetrators. More frequently, however, we find studies that put the blame for a new wave of violence on a change or a loss of values. Ideas about the associated causal links are very varied. Some authors think in terms of the weakening of the authorities responsible for keeping violence in check; others point to a climate of general permissiveness or to false models derived from the presentation of violence in the media. Yet others emphasize the absence of motivating ideals and the violence that springs from the resulting vacuum. With this type it is of course important also to look at the cause of the change in values, in order to lend some plausibility to the explanation. Here the spectrum goes all the way from left to right, from the emphasis on individualization and cultural erosion arising from the subjection of all life processes to the market under capitalism, to complaints about the undermining of values by the expressive individualism of the student movement and a consumerist youth culture. In this case, too, the demands that experts have been making for years are at long last able to gain the ear of the public; what these experts call for ranges from the taming of capitalist modernization to an end to permissiveness, from a reinforcement of the powers of the authorities to the need to use education to transmit moral values.

Whether either explanation is right can of course only be established by empirical evidence in particular situations. Normally, this is attended by considerable difficulties. Thus in the case of the violence against foreigners in Germany in recent years, almost all the structural sociological explanations that have been put forward have been discredited,[1] even though they seemed so illuminating at the outset. Those who have been arrested as offenders or participants turned out for the most part not to be the young unemployed or children from so-called broken homes. Young people with apprenticeships or other trainee posts are frequently more markedly hostile to foreigners than those without them. Similarly, the logic of capitalism can only be used to explain East German events if these are attributed to the sudden introduction of a new economic system. But against this is the fact that even before the collapse of the GDR there was a definite potential for youth violence there. An explanation in terms of the familiar pattern of the 'authoritarian character' seems plausible when applied to the East Germans, but this is far less relevant to the old Federal Republic. Here, on the contrary, we find the permissiveness thesis far more frequently, although there does not appear to be a very clear link between the circles from which the young people involved come and the subcultures and milieus that had adopted the attitudes of expressive individualism. Cultural critics in the USA encounter similar problems when they attempt to explain ghetto criminality in terms of the moral failings of the student movement. Thus the confidence with which explanations of both types are put forward is frequently not based on sound empirical evidence.

In what follows, however, I am concerned with a different point. Needless to say, neither of these explanatory types is a universal key – but nor are they *a priori* misguided. It is just as legitimate to inquire into structural social causes and interests as into prevailing values or the loss of direction. But both types of explanation share a common defect. This is that they are relatively silent on the question of the timing of an outbreak of violence and of its internal dynamics, as well as the extent of its spread, the very factors that enable a single incident to form part of a wave. In both types of explanation structural tensions, whether social or cultural, are regarded as primary; it is assumed that they must mutate into collective action at a specific point, and that the point in time to be explained is that very point. The internal course of the outburst of violence is then held to be secondary. However, this supposition is by no means self-evident. It is wrong for us to misinterpret the dissatisfaction with social evils or negative attitudes towards particular categories of one's fellow-citizens as a kind of preparatory stage to turning towards violence. For many people there are many possible consequences of dissatisfaction or prejudice, but violence is not one of them, and, conversely, many acts of violence are notable for an indiscriminate attitude in their choice of victims. At the very least, then, it may be profitable to attempt to explain the phenomena of collective and spontaneous violence by taking a closer look primarily at the dynamics at work in the origins and further development of the violent acts themselves. I have in mind here both the *interpersonal* dynamics at work in the process of escalation and the *intrapersonal* dynamics at work in the consequences of the experience of violence for one's own actions. In my view, the predominance of both of the types of explanation that I have mentioned is not a coincidence, but derives from a kind of compulsive way of thinking that in general shapes and constrains the way in which social scientists deal with human action, and that has to be overcome if we are to make progress in explaining violent phenomena.

Essentially, for over a century now the theory of action has oscillated between two poles. At one end, from the times of early political economy and the moral philosophy of utilitarianism, there has been a type of thinking that conceives of human action in terms of a growth in subjective or objective utility, as the consistent pursuit of a clearly envisaged goal with the aid of whatever technically appropriate and economically viable means are available. This way of thinking has found its clearest expression in the model of *homo oeconomicus* that governs economics, but also goes far beyond that, and is influential for example in psychology, too. By contrast, ever since the end of the nineteenth century, sociology has acquired its identity by defining itself in contrast to economics and psychology. It resists the tendency of both disciplines either to reduce collective experiences to individual phenomena, or to regard them as mere aggregates of individual phenomena. Accordingly, on the question of human action, it places the moral constitution of individual preferences and the value-related and normative character of human actions in the foreground. From Émile Durkheim in 1893, via Talcott Parsons in 1937, to Amitai Etzioni in 1988, there have been profound efforts to demonstrate the superiority of the norm-based, cultural model over that of *homo oeconomicus*.

My concern here is to show that we can add a third model to the two predominant models of rational and normatively orientated action in studies of violence. For this third model the idea that commends itself is that of the *creative* nature of human action.[2] Just as the normativist model is superior to the merely 'rational model', since it makes clear that an emphasis on rationality is a normative orientation as well, so, too, is the creative model superior to the normativist model, because it leads to the examination of two questions that would otherwise remain unresolved. The first is the question of how norms and values are to be applied to specific situations, and the second is the question of how values that guide our actions can arise in the first place. If it is not possible to deduce how values should be applied in particular situations, but, instead, particular situations call for independent creative specifications of these values, and if a commitment to specific values does not arise through intention, but only through powerful, affective experiences, then a space opens up in which there is scope for this third model of creative action.

In contrast to the theories that are predicated on rational action, this theory does not produce a counter-model of the non-rational; it does not start by imposing an evaluative framework upon the actual multiplicity of action phenomena. Even in a type of thought that does not perceive the *homo oeconomicus* to be everywhere at work, a form of action that rationalizes ends, values and consequences remains the ideal. In such a mode of thought, acts of violence *must* be classified either as rational actions or as irrational deviations on the basis of a set of values adhered to fanatically, an affect-led loss of control or an inherited tendency to violence. All of this may be readily comprehensible, particularly from a moral point of view, but analytically it is uninformative and has the further drawback that acts of violence have to be comprehended in the same categories as the creative achievements of humankind. Measured by the yardstick of a means–ends rationality, the differences between violence and creativity disappear.

It is not my intention here to cast any doubt on the empirical usefulness of models of rational action for the analyses of specific social phenomena. What is being questioned is simply and solely the claim that, because of its utility, it is possible to extend this model of rational action, with its many assumptions, to ever new fields of application without a thorough-going examination of those inherent premises. This is why it is important to analyse *the intentional character of human action, the specific corporeal dimensions and the original social nature of the human capacity for action.*[3] Thus we are concerned here with three dimensions: the dynamics of *setting* aims; the dialectics of body control and body release; and the yearning for revitalization in the individual or collective experience of self-transcendence. All three dimensions are indispensable for the understanding of a multiplicity of individual actions, and even more so for an appropriate reconstruction of the dynamic processes of collective action.[4]

In the analysis of such processes it is particularly easy to recognize the inappropriateness of the rational model and the normativist model. The rational model only has a chance either where individuals are able to calculate the benefits to themselves over against collective action, like the 'free rider', such as a non-unionized worker who nevertheless benefits from wage agreements negotiated by the union, or where collective action is viewed by 'organizational entrepreneurs' from the standpoint of the rational mobilization of resources. In the normativist model spontaneous processes of non-institutionalized action are initially not catered for at all. It is typical that the most famous attempt to formulate a theory of collective action along these lines (that of Neil Smelser) is based on the economic process of a step-by-step accretion of value.[5] But the economic model is based on a process in which every earlier stage has to be viewed, at least in retrospect, as a means to a future end. For the dynamics of non-institutionalized action such a teleological scheme is inappropriate. In such cases, the situational definitions and the norms that arise in the course of the process, and even the ultimate goals of the process together with the choice of means, are unclear for the most part and unknown to the participants; they are only clarified by the process itself. Smelser also builds social control into his model of collective action as a particular phase. But this renders invisible the element of struggle in the interaction between collective outburst and social control, because social control is not conceived as a countervailing force whose structure obeys its own laws and which itself becomes active on the basis of 'theories' of its own about outbreaks of collective action. Instead of taking a teleological model as our guide, we should rather focus our attention on processes that cannot be deduced from pre-existing psychic dispositions or social problems, but where the participants gradually develop into what they represent for a social movement that may only just be emerging. It is collective action itself that defines the problems it relates to; it generates motives and identities, shapes new social relations and communities, gives rise to profound changes in identity (conversion and regeneration), produces affectively cathected symbols and leaves behind symbolic attachments capable of structuring biographies.[6]

With these critical comments I have already listed the desiderata for a more appropriate analysis. These desiderata seem to me to have been most satisfactorily fulfilled in studies of collective action carried out from an approach influenced by symbolic interactionism. Examples are Ralph Turner's work on race riots in America[7] and the Trier studies on attacks on foreigners in Germany.[8] But in recent years there have been other moves in this direction. In research on terrorism in the Federal Republic of Germany in the 1970s, for example, Friedhelm Neidhardt, Fritz Sack and Susanne Karstedt-Henke had already begun thinking about the autonomous dynamics of violent processes.[9] Several decades ago, in his famous work *Crowds and Power*, Elias Canetti, as an outsider latching on to work on mass psychology, had already developed some difficult, often idiosyncratic, ideas on such matters as the internal logic of 'the pack' [*die Meute*]. It is no accident that in recent years these ideas have been increasingly taken up again by sociologists.[10] And even rationalist approaches have in a certain sense developed in parallel through the more accurate decoding of the threshold values that have to be overcome before there is an outburst of violence, and by paying greater heed to the internal heterogeneity of masses and the graduated process of escalation as a result of the sinking 'costs' of participation where there are a growing number of expected participants. For example, their explanation of the course taken by the Monday demonstrations in Leipzig in 1989 is successful in my view.[11] But of course the Leipzig Monday demonstrations were not violent outbreaks and they contained clear, albeit for the most part negatively defined, goals. They did not in the least correspond to what American researchers have called 'issueless riots'.[12]

The Trier studies offer analyses not only of the escalation processes internal to the movements involved, but also of the interactions between activists and their opponents, the state institutions, the media and counter-movements. Thus attention can focus upon the interplay between asylum seekers and the general population, the reaction of political elites and changes in the terms of the public debate, the behaviour of the police, whose withdrawal can lead 'to a euphoric sense of power and an intoxicating and stimulating experience of anarchy or anomie',[13] and the interaction between the mass media and the wave of violence. Since in about 90 per cent of the relevant cases we are dealing with group offences, the majority of which are committed spontaneously, this approach is particularly appropriate. A wave of violence that starts in this way can of course lead to the formation of new structures, particularly if it is successful. These new structures can survive over long periods and can lead to the establishment of organizations with co-ordination and planning.

Above all, research on Federal German terrorism of the 1970s has shown very clearly how what begins as spontaneous breaches of taboos on violence, together with the reactions of the state to them, can lead to a spiral of events from which no one can break out merely by an act of will. For the state, violent actions can be the trigger for profound restructurings of the security apparatus and the source of additional legitimacy; an 'internal enemy' with all its dichotomizing effects offers itself up as an opponent to be combated. On the terrorist side, there is also a completely new situation that is due to the formation of a new organizational nucleus. As has been shown, for example, by Peter Waldmann with reference to Northern Ireland and the Basque country,[14] this organization calls for its own material infrastructure and its own ideological system of justification. The effect of this is that new material and status interests are attached to acts of violence, and the return to stable, peaceful conditions can only be threatening for these interests. Topical examples can be seen in the wake of the Balkan conflicts. This is the climate in which the freeloading beneficiaries of violence carry on their apolitical activities. We should not forget that it is not just the process of escalation towards violence that possesses its own dynamics that cannot be reduced to the intentions of the parties to the conflict, but the same is true of violence itself. Violence has a tendency to perpetuate itself, which, like an autonomous process, seems to condemn all the participants to impotence. As Schiller says, 'This is the curse of the evil deed, that, procreating further, it must needs continue to give birth to evil.' Every serious effort to change quasi-institutionalized violent conditions cannot limit itself to such factors as insight and means–ends rationality, or morality and values; it must also pay heed to the conditions and the phases of waves of violence.

I shall attempt to illustrate these rather abstract reflections with reference to the American research into ghetto riots. For that it is necessary to look at the preconditions for the emergence and growth of such violence. For our present purposes we can ignore pre-existing social or cultural tensions, and also patterns of inequality and their consequences, which of course in practice almost always form part of the background of spontaneous, non-institutionalized outbreaks of collective violence. We can list five kinds of preconditions that must be present if a wave of violence is to occur.[15]

First, for the most part, there will scarcely be any live, active communication between the opposing groups – the potential group of activists and the potential victims. Either such links were always absent or else they were paralysed by prior events.

In the second place, however, it is not just the immediate relations between the opposing groups that matter, but also their relation to the institutions and the state monopoly of the means of violence. Thus, in the American race riots of recent decades the wave of violence was often preceded by acts of violence on the part of the police and alleged or real acts of racial discrimination on the part of the justice system. In the absence of the aura of strength *and* impartiality, government authorities are unable to assuage or channel conflicts.

A further important precondition – the third – is concerned with the absence of a more broadly based social movement in which feelings of injustice and attempts at rectification might find an outlet. Of course, there are also social movements that consciously build acts of violence into their strategy in order to achieve their own goals, or – independently of their goals – to weld the members of the group together by means of a shared, intoxicating experience of violence. It is true of all social movements, however, that they have to calculate the costs of their use of violence in terms of government repression, the violence of their opponents and internal dissension. For this reason they mainly attempt to suppress every sign of spontaneous or short-term violence in their own long-term interests. An organized movement simultaneously both disciplines and motivates its members. In contrast to the racial disturbances of the sixties, the Los Angeles riots of 1992 should not be seen in the context of a reform-led civil rights movement. They erupted without being influenced by, or without having any impact on, such a movement. Their brutality towards persons was significantly greater than in the earlier period.

As the fourth condition we may mention changes in values and norms of a kind that promotes violence. When social groups are alienated from one another, when they have ceased to trust the available mechanisms for conflict resolution and there is no social movement to organize discontent, this will lead to changes in the interpretation of norms relating to violence. Such changes need not in themselves act as the trigger for acts of violence, but they can prepare the ground for the approval of them, if recourse is had to violence by individual activists.

Fifth and last, it is typically not individuals – at least in the case of the race riots – but pre-existing groups inclined towards violence, gangs, for example, who seize the initiative and then draw others into the violent events. The situation is quite different from what is assumed by ideas of the unstructured masses. The ghettoes actually contain a multiplicity of overlapping social networks that serve as a pool from which people can be mobilized, and in many of these, because of the change in norms, violence towards the police or whites is often felt to be legitimate and has even become ritualized as such. The tradition of symbolic interactionism is originally concerned with the emergence of norms and groups in its analysis. In taking into consideration this evidence of the social structuring of the 'masses', this tradition also takes account of other approaches, above all the resource-mobilization school. Thus in his analysis of the different stages of escalation, Ralph Turner is very willing to acknowledge explanations of a rational choice type to explain a gradual process of escalation. In particular, he lays stress on a test phase that precedes the actual outbreak of a wave of violent actions. If such 'tests' end with a negative result, for example because of a police presence or insufficient support for the perpetrators of violence, they do not for the most part even figure in the history of race riots or of social movements; they remain classified as 'pre-political' and do not attract any notice beyond the regional level.

Not only the *inter*personal dynamics, but the *intra*personal dynamics, too, constitute an important field for research. Here, the difficulty for empirical research in establishing causal connections between the traumas of childhood and adult behaviour is familiar enough. Only psychoanalysis has had the confidence to believe it could achieve much in this field. More easily accessible – though still difficult enough – is the link between the traumas of violence and changes in identity in adult life. We are in a position to make somewhat more substantial statements here, thanks to the extensive American research into the effects of the war in Vietnam, and, in particular, into the after-effects of the experience of violence during the war upon the actions of the veterans after it. Such research, too, need not necessarily be conducted according to behaviourist ideas about the extent to which people become habituated to violence. Instead, it is possible to pursue ideas about identity formation that derive from the same tradition of symbolic interactionism as the productive studies on the dynamics of the escalation of interpersonal interactions. These ideas may be suggestive of a new interpretation of the ways in which the experience of violence can have its effect on the formation of identity.[16] This interpretation, too, will then point to an understanding of human action that goes beyond rationalist and normativist models.[17]

Notes

Introduction

1 Herbert Butterfield, *The Whig Interpretation of History*, London, 1931.
2 Ibid., p. 30.
3 Ibid., p. 23.
4 This book contains no chapter on 1961, the year the Wall was built. It does, however, contain a discussion of the preceding, painful phase in which the division of Germany took place (see chapter 4 'After the War: Democracy and Anti-Communism in Berlin after 1945', pp. 85ff). Harold Hurwitz, the author of the study discussed there, was one of the closest associates of Brandt and Bahr.
5 Martin Sabrow, 'Hinterrücks zusammengebrochen', in the *Frankfurter Allgemeine Zeitung*, 20.11.1998, p. 46.
6 Hans Joas and Helmut Steiner (eds), *Machtpolitischer Realismus und pazifistische Utopie. Krieg und Frieden in der Geschichte der Sozialwissenschaften*, Frankfurt am Main, 1989. My own contribution to this volume ('Die Klassiker der Soziologie und der Erste Weltkrieg', pp. 179–210) represents a first and very preliminary version of chapter 3 (pp. 55ff) in the present volume.
7 Klaus von Beyme, 'Selbstgleichschaltung. Warum es in der DDR keine Politologie gegeben hat', in Bernd Giesen and Claus Leggewie (eds), *Experiment Vereinigung. Ein sozialer Großversuch*, Berlin 1991, pp. 123–32, here p. 124.
8 On this question see chapter 5 in this volume, pp. 95ff. This text refers to a volume in which these explanations are reviewed and contrasted with each other: Hans Joas and Martin Kohli (eds), *Der Zusammenbruch der DDR. Soziologische Analysen*, Frankfurt am Main, 1993. For a comprehensive study of this topic, see Charles S. Maier, *Dissolution. The Crisis of Communism and the End of East Germany*, Princeton, 1999.

9   See especially chapter 12, pp. 187ff.
10 Ekkehart Krippendorff, *Staat und Krieg. Die historische Logik politischer Unvernunft*, Frankfurt am Main, 1985.
11 For example, by Herfried Münkler, 'Staat, Krieg und Frieden. Die verwechselte Wechselbeziehung. Eine Auseinandersetzung mit Ekkehart Krippendorff', in Reiner Steinweg (ed.), *Kriegsursachen*, Frankfurt am Main, 1987, pp. 135–44. See also my review in *Soziologische Revue* 11 (1988), pp. 450–2.
12 Karl Otto Hondrich, *Lehrmeister Krieg*, Reinbek, 1992.
13 See chapter 11, pp. 180ff, below. Hondrich reacted to my polemic in K.O. Hondrich, 'Krieg – und unser progressiver Theorie-Alltag', in *Kölner Zeitschrift für Soziologie und Sozialpsychologie* 44 (1992), pp. 544–8.
14 Hans Magnus Enzensberger, *Civil War* (1993), London, 1994; a critical view of this book can be found in Axel Honneth, 'Universalismus als politische Falle?', in *Merkur* 546/7 (1994), pp. 867–83.
15 See chapter 6, pp. 111ff, which bases itself on the sociological research on US soldiers in Vietnam.
16 Chapter 9, pp. 163ff, is based on the writings of Zygmunt Bauman and is concerned exclusively with the 'bureaucratic' side of the Holocaust. There is as yet no study that integrates this with spontaneous violence that can be ascribed to particular individuals.
17 Some comments on the specific preconditions of sociological work in Berlin can be found at the beginning of chapter 4, pp. 85ff.
18 See on this point my comments in Hans Joas, 'Decline of Community? Comparative Observations on Germany and the United States' (1995), in Josef Janning, Charles A. Kupchan and Dirk Rumberg (eds), *Civic Engagement in the Atlantic Community*, Gütersloh, 1999, pp. 55–66.
19 See chapter 2, pp. 43ff. This text provoked a reply from one of the most important modernization theorists, namely Edward Tiryakian, 'War: The Covered Side of Modernity'. A further critique appeared by Ian Roxborough, 'The Persistence of War as a Sociological Problem', both in *International Sociology* 14 (1999), pp. 473–90 and 491–500; this issue also contained my reply, 'For Fear of New Horrors', pp. 501–3.
20 See chapter 10, pp. 171ff. Ulrich Beck replied to an earlier version of this chapter in Ulrich Beck, 'Erwiderungen', in *Mittelweg* 36, no. 3 (1994), pp. 37–42.
21 Hans Joas, *The Creativity of Action* (1992), Cambridge, 1996.
22 Ibid., especially pp. 246ff.
23 Ibid., p. 250.
24 However, this omission is to be made good in a forthcoming study.
25 An essential contribution to this process of historical qualification of modernization theory and an excellent survey of the major attempts to modify it in the writings of Shmuel Eisenstadt, Michael Mann, Alain Touraine and Johann Arnason has now been provided by Wolfgang Knöbl, *Spielräume der Modernisierung. Das Ende der Eindeutigkeit*, Weilerswist, 2001.
26 For an overview of the critical objections to differentiation theory, see Joas, *The Creativity of Action*, pp. 223ff. There I contrast this theory with other

approaches that I call 'constitution theories' and their merits. It is also worth mentioning that – with some exceptions – the relevant military sociology contains but few initiatives in the direction of such historically based constitution theories. An exception is Hans Speier, *Social Order and the Risks of War. Papers in Political Psychology*, Cambridge, Mass., 1969, and especially pp. 223–319.

27 For a magisterial critique of these ideas, see Bernard Yack, *The Fetishism of Modernities. Epochal Self-Consciousness in Contemporary Social and Political Thought*, Notre Dame, Ind., 1997.

28 Max Miller and Hans-Georg Soeffner's Introduction to Miller and Soeffner (eds), *Modernität und Barbarei. Soziologische Zeitdiagnose am Ende des 20. Jahrhunderts*, Frankfurt am Main, 1996, pp. 12–27, here especially p. 14.

29 Ibid., p. 17. This typology could be expanded to include the revaluation of violence, from a weariness with rationality and modernity, to a positive counter-concept in the mythologies of violence of people like Georges Sorel and Benito Mussolini, and to include further a more precise distinction between the different variants of the ideas of violence and barbarism as specifically modern phenomena. See on this point the interesting discussion in Christoph Liell, 'Gewalt: diskursive Konstruktion und soziale Praxis', Soziologische Diplomarbeit, Freie Universität Berlin, 1997.

30 Shmuel Eisenstadt, 'Barbarism and Modernity', in *Society* 33 (1996), pp. 31–9, here especially pp. 35 and 39.

31 See on this point my critique of the concepts used by Beck in chapter 10, esp. pp. 173ff, as well as the excellent comments by Ralf Dahrendorf, based on his profound knowledge of Western societies, 'Widersprüche der Modernität', in Miller and Soeffner (eds), *Modernität und Barbarei*, pp. 194–204.

32 Thomas Nipperdey, *Deutsche Geschichte 1866–1918*, vol. 1, Munich, 1990, p. 595.

33 An exemplary case is to be found in Stefan Meineke, 'Friedrich Meinecke und der "Krieg der Geister"', in Wolfgang Mommsen (ed.), *Kultur und Krieg. Die Rolle der Intellektuellen, Künstler und Schriftsteller im Ersten Weltkrieg*, Munich, 1996, pp. 97–118, especially p. 114.

34 Georg Simmel, *Der Krieg und die geistigen Entscheidungen*, Munich, 1917. See also my interpretation in Hans Joas, *The Genesis of Values* (1997), Cambridge, 2000, pp. 74ff.

35 Max Scheler, 'Der Genius des Krieges und der deutsche Krieg' (1915), in Scheler, *Gesammelte Werke*, vol. 4, *Politisch-Pädagogische Schriften*, Bern, 1982, pp. 7–251; Ernst Jünger, *Der Kampf als inneres Erlebnis*, Berlin, 1925.

36 As I do in chapter 3 in this volume. See there n. 22 (pp. 206–7), with the reference to Arnold Zweig.

37 On Mussolini, see below, pp. 50ff; on Carl Schmitt, see pp. 38ff.

38 Roger Caillois, *Man and the Sacred* (1939), Urbana, Ill., 2001, especially the appendix, and also his *Bellone ou la pente de la guerre*, Brussels, 1963.

39 Denis Hollier (ed.), *Le Collège de Sociologie*, Paris, 1979. See also my comments in Hans Joas, 'Die Soziologie und das Heilige. Schlüsseltexte der Religionssoziologie', in *Merkur* 53, no. 605/6 (1999), pp. 990–8.

40   George Herbert Mead: 'The Psychology of Punitive Justice', in *The American Journal of Sociology* XXIII (1917–18), pp. 577–602, also in Mead, *Selected Writings*, ed. Andrew Reck, Indianapolis, 1964, pp. 212–39; 'The Psychological Bases of Internationalism', in *Survey* XXIII (1914–15), pp. 604–7; and also 'National-Mindedness and International-Mindedness' (1929), in Mead, *Selected Writings*, pp. 355–70. With this comment I revert in a sense to the starting-point of my interests, as described above, in a social psychology of democracy and its implications for the securing of peace.

41   See n. 34 above.

42   See chapter 6, pp. 111ff.

43   Axel Honneth, *The Struggle for Recognition: The Moral Grammar of Social Conflicts* (1992), Cambridge, 1996.

44   A critique of the concealed teleology in Honneth's theory can also be found in Jeffrey Alexander and Maria Pia Lara, 'The Struggle for Recognition', in *New Left Review* 220 (1996), pp. 126–36.

45   A comprehensive account of the origins of this connection, though one that has attracted almost no attention outside Italy, is given in Massimo Mori's book *La ragione delle armi. Guerra e conflitto nella filosofia classica tedesca (1770–1830)*, Milan, 1984. A brief version of this book can be found in Mori, 'Krieg und Frieden in der klassischen deutschen Philosophie', in Joas and Steiner (eds), *Machtpolitischer Realismus und pazifistische Utopie*, pp. 49–91.

46   Carl Schmitt, *Die Wendung zum diskriminierenden Kriegsbegriff* (1938), Berlin, 1988, pp. 1f.

47   Cora Stephan, *Das Handwerk des Krieges*, Berlin, 1998. For my view of these ideas of Schmitt's, see chapter 1, pp. 38ff.

48   Jürgen Habermas, 'Kant's Idea of Perpetual Peace: At Two Hundred Years' Historical Remove', in Habermas, *The Inclusion of the Other. Studies in Political Theory* (1996), Cambridge, 1998, pp. 165–201, here p. 193.

49   Knud Krakau, *Missionsbewußtsein und Völkerrechtsdoktrin in den Vereinigten Staaten von Amerika*, Frankfurt am Main/Berlin, 1967.

50   Classically in John Stuart Mill, 'A Few Words on Non-Intervention' (1859), in Mill, *Essays on Politics and Culture*, ed. Gertrude Himmelfarb, Garden City, NY, 1963, pp. 368–84. For an overview, see Michael W. Doyle, *Ways of War and Peace. Realism, Liberalism, and Socialism*, New York, 1997, esp. pp. 389ff.

51   Mill, 'A Few Words on Non-Intervention', p. 383.

52   Jürgen Habermas, 'Bestialität und Humanität. Ein Krieg an der Grenze zwischen Recht und Moral', in *Die Zeit*, 29.4.1999, pp. 1 and 6f. My view is to be found in Hans Joas, 'Wann darf der Westen eingreifen?', in *die tageszeitung (taz)*, 13.7.1999, p. 12. I make use here of some of the statements in that article.

53   In more recent studies, I have attempted to expand my theory of the 'genesis of values' in the direction of an understanding of unavoidable conflicts of values. See Hans Joas, 'Combining Value Pluralism with Moral Universalism. Isaiah Berlin and Beyond', in *The Responsive Community* 9 (1999), pp. 17–29; and also 'Die Sakralität der Person und die Politik der

Würde (Über Avishai Margalit)', in *Deutsche Zeitschrift für Philosophie* 47 (1999), pp. 325–33.

54 Most convincingly in my view by Dieter and Eva Senghaas, 'Si vis pacem, para pacem', in *Leviathan* 20 (1992), pp. 230–47; see also Dieter Senghaas, 'Peace Theory and the Restructuring of Europe', in *Alternatives* 16 (1991), pp. 353–66.

Chapter 1   The Dream of a Modernity without Violence

This chapter first appeared in *Sinn und Form* 46, no. 2 (1994), pp. 309–18.

1 These towns witnessed racially motivated attacks on foreigners in 1992–3. [*Trans.*]

2 Albert J. Reiss, Jr. and Jeffrey A. Roth (eds), *Understanding and Preventing Violence*, Washington, DC, 1993; for a critical view, see the review symposium in *Contemporary Sociology* 22 (1993), pp. 344–50, and the editors' introduction: 'Gewalt in den USA. Deutsche und amerikanische Perspektiven', in Hans Joas and Wolfgang Knöbl (eds), *Gewalt in den USA*, Frankfurt am Main, 1994, pp. 7–18.

3 Albert Hirschman, *The Passions and the Interests. Political Arguments for Capitalism before Its Triumph*, Princeton, 1977, pp. 56ff.

4 See on this point chapter 8 in this volume, pp. 141ff.

5 For the documentation and interpretation of these intellectual developments, Kurt von Raumer's book continues to be useful: Kurt von Raumer (ed.), *Ewiger Friede, Friedensrufe und Friedenspläne seit der Renaissance*, Freiburg/Munich, 1953.

6 Wolfgang Mommsen, 'Außenpolitik und öffentliche Meinung im Wilhelminischen Deutschland 1897–1914', in Mommsen, *Der autoritäre Nationalstaat. Verfassung, Gesellschaft und Kultur des deutschen Kaiserreiches*, Frankfurt am Main, 1990, pp. 358–79.

7 An excellent contribution on this point is the little book by Michael Howard, *War and the Liberal Conscience*, New Brunswick, NJ, 1978.

8 The documentation on this point can be found in Anita and Walter Dietze (eds), *Ewiger Friede? Dokumente einer deutschen Diskussion um 1800*, Leipzig/Weimar, 1989.

9 Joseph Görres, 'Der allgemeine Frieden, ein Ideal' (1798), in Zwi Batscha and Richard Saage (eds), *Friedensutopien*, Frankfurt am Main, 1979, pp. 111–76, here p. 168.

10 Carl Schmitt, Review (1926) of Friedrich Meinecke, *Die Idee der Staatsräson in der neueren Geschichte*, Munich/Berlin, 1924, reprinted in Carl Schmitt, *Positionen und Begriffe im Kampf mit Weimar–Genf–Versailles*, Berlin, 1940 (2nd edn, 1988), pp. 45–52, here p. 50. See also further texts in this volume of Schmitt's collected essays.

11 Carl Schmitt, *Die Wendung zum diskriminierenden Kriegsbegriff* (1938), Berlin, 1988.

12 On this point, see Knud Krakau, *Missionsbewußtsein und Völkerrechtsdoktrin in den Vereinigten Staaten von Amerika*, Frankfurt am Main/Berlin, 1967.

13   Dieter Senghaas, 'Frieden als Zivilisierungsprojekt', in Senghaas (ed.), *Den Frieden denken. Si vis pacem, para pacem*, Frankfurt am Main, 1995, pp. 196–223.

14   Georges Sorel, *Reflections on Violence* (1914), Cambridge, 1999; Frantz Fanon, *The Wretched of the Earth* (1961), London, 1965; Richard Slotkin, *Regeneration through Violence. The Mythology of the American Frontier, 1600–1860*, Middletown, Conn., 1973; Richard Slotkin, *The Fatal Environment. The Myth of the Frontier in the Age of Industrialization, 1800–1890*, New York, 1985.

15   On this point, see chapter 12 in this volume, pp. 187ff.

Chapter 2   The Modernity of War

This chapter was first published in *Leviathan* 24 (1996), pp. 13–27. I am grateful to Johannes Berger, Wolfgang Knöbl and Wolfgang Vortkamp for their helpful comments. [The present text is a revised version of a translation that appeared in *International Sociology* 14 (1999), pp. 457–72. *Trans.*]

1   See chapter 5 in this volume, pp. 95ff. An original attempt to capture the ups and downs of modernization theory in terms of rhetoric and general world-views has been made by Jeffrey Alexander, 'Modern, Anti, Post and Neo: How Intellectuals Have Coded, Narrated, and Explained the "New World of Our Time"', in Alexander, *Fin de Siècle Social Theory*, London, 1995, pp. 6–64.

2   Wolfgang Zapf, 'Modernisierung und Modernisierungstheorien', in Zapf (ed.), *Die Modernisierung moderner Gesellschaften. Verhandlungen des 25. Deutschen Soziologentags* (1990), Frankfurt am Main, 1991, pp. 23–39; Ulrich Beck, 'Der Konflikt der zwei Modernen', in ibid., pp. 40–53. My view of Beck's theory can be found in chapter 10 in this volume, pp. 171ff.

3   Immanuel Wallerstein, 'Modernization: *Requiescat in Pace*', in Wallerstein, *The Capitalist World-Economy*, New York, 1979, pp. 132–7; Edward Tiryakian, 'Modernization: *Exhumetur in Pace* (Rethinking Macrosociology in the 1990s)', in *International Sociology* 6 (1991), pp. 165–80.

4   For an overview, see Helmut Thome, 'Gesellschaftliche Modernisierung und Kriminalität. Zum Stand der sozialhistorischen Kriminalitäts-forschung', in *Zeitschrift für Soziologie* 21 (1992), pp. 212–28.

5   Norbert Elias, *The Civilizing Process*, Oxford, 1976. I am well aware of the fact that, contrary to my strong emphasis on the linearity in Elias's assumptions about an increasing complexity of social relations and an increasing control of the emotions, there are interpretations that focus on the international constellations and their contingency in Elias's work and thus view his work as close to the goals pursued in this chapter. See, for example, Artur Bogner, 'Die Theorie des Zivilisationsprozesses als Modernisierungstheorie', in Helmuth Kuzmics and Ingo Mörth (eds), *Der unendliche Prozeß der Zivilisation. Zur Kultursoziologie der Moderne nach Norbert Elias*, Frankfurt am Main, 1991, pp. 33–58; see also some

of the writings of Johann Arnason. This is not the place to attempt to integrate the two views.

6   See chapter 1 in this volume, esp. pp. 29ff.

7   See chapter 3 in this volume, pp. 55ff.

8   Thorstein Veblen: *Imperial Germany and the Industrial Revolution* (1915), New Brunswick, NJ, 1990; and *The Nature of Peace and the Terms of Its Perpetuation*, New York, 1917. For Veblen's image of Germany, see Colin Loader and Rick Tilman, 'Thorstein Veblen's Analysis of German Intellectualism', in *American Journal of Economics and Sociology* 54 (1995), pp. 339–55.

9   A similar argument has been advanced by Randall Collins, 'German-Bashing and the Theory of Democratic Modernization', in his book *Macrohistory. Essays in Sociology of the Long Run*, Stanford, 1999, pp. 152–76; see also Wolfgang Knöbl's commentary on Collins, *Zeitschrift für Soziologie* 24 (1995), pp. 465–8, and a very balanced account of the discussion on the German *Sonderweg* in Jürgen Kocka, 'German History before Hitler. The Debate about the German "*Sonderweg*"', *Journal of Contemporary History* 23 (1988), pp. 3–16. See also his essay 'Asymmetrical Historical Comparison. The Case of the German *Sonderweg*', in *History and Theory* 38 (1999), pp. 40–50. Equally important, and of direct relevance to Veblen, are the qualifying remarks by Thomas Nipperdey, *Deutsche Geschichte 1866–1918*, vol. 2, Munich, 1992, pp. 902f and *passim*.

10 Cyril E. Black, *The Dynamics of Modernization*, New York, 1966.

11 Reinhard Bendix: 'Tradition and Modernity Reconsidered', in *Comparative Studies in Society and History* 9 (1966/7), pp. 292–346 (on historical foundations in general); 'Modernisierung in internationaler Perspektive', in Wolfgang Zapf (ed.), *Theorien des sozialen Wandels*, Cologne, 1970. pp. 505–12 (on the relationship between pioneers and latecomers of modernization); and *Kings or People. Power and the Mandate to Rule*, 2 vols, Berkeley, 1978 (on his own approach to historical sociology).

12 Hans-Ulrich Wehler classifies German history between 1789 and 1815 under the heading 'Defensive Modernization'. See Hans-Ulrich Wehler, *Deutsche Gesellschaftsgeschichte*, vol. 1, Munich, 1987, pp. 343ff.

13 Theda Skocpol, *States and Social Revolutions. A Comparative Analysis of France, Russia and China*, Cambridge, 1979; Barrington Moore, Jr, *Social Origins of Dictatorship and Democracy. Lord and Peasant in the Making of the Modern World*, London, 1967.

14 This point has been strongly argued by Randall Collins, 'Imperialism and Legitimacy. Weber's Theory of Politics', in Collins, *Weberian Sociological Theory*, Cambridge, 1986, pp. 145–66.

15 Enrico Corradini speaks explicitly of the 'modernità della guerra' in his article 'La guerra' in the periodical *Il Regno* 1, no. 4 (1904), pp. 2–4; quoted here from the reprint in Delia Castelnuovo Frigessi (ed.), *La cultura italiana del '900 attraverso le reviste ('Leonardo', 'Hermes', 'Il Regno')*, vol. 2, Turin, 1960, pp. 482–5, here p. 483.

16 See Ernst Nolte, *Three Faces of Fascism: Action Française, Italian Fascism, National Socialism* (1963), New York, 1966; Zeev Sternhell, *The Birth of*

Fascist Ideology. From Cultural Rebellion to Political Revolution, Princeton, 1994.

17 Werner Sombart, *Krieg und Kapitalismus*, Munich/Leipzig, 1913; Max Weber, *General Economic History* (1923), New York, 1927, see especially pp. 308f.

18 Michael Mann, *The Sources of Social Power*, 2 vols, Cambridge, 1986 and 1993; John Hall, *Powers and Liberties. The Causes and Consequences of the Rise of the West*, London, 1985/Berkeley, 1986; Anthony Giddens, *The Nation-State and Violence*, Cambridge, 1985. An excellent overview of these developments has been provided by Wolfgang Knöbl, 'Nationalstaat und Gesellschaftstheorie', in *Zeitschrift für Soziologie* 22 (1993), pp. 221–35. For illuminating critical evaluations of Giddens, see Christopher Dandeker, 'The Nation-State and the Modern World System', and John Breuilly, 'The Nation-State and Violence: A Critique of Giddens', both in Jon Clark, Celia Modgil and Sohan Modgil (eds), *Anthony Giddens. Consensus and Controversy*, London, 1990, pp. 257–69 and pp. 271–88. In German sociology, Friedrich Tenbruck has long been preoccupied with an overcoming of the nation-state perspective within a conservative framework. See, for example, Friedrich Tenbruck, 'Gesellschaftsgeschichte oder Weltgeschichte?', in *Kölner Zeitschrift für Soziologie und Sozialpsychologie* 3 (1989), pp. 417–39.

19 This idea obviously stems from the historian Otto Hintze, who remains shamefully neglected in German sociology, despite his closeness to the discipline. See, for instance, his classic essay, 'Military Organization and the Organization of the State' (1906), in *The Historical Essays of Otto Hintze*, ed. Felix Gilbert, New York, 1975, pp. 178–215. The geopolitical tendencies in Hintze's arguments have been convincingly qualified by Wolfgang Reinhard, 'Staat und Heer in England im Zeitalter der Revolutionen', in Johannes Kunisch (ed.), *Staatsverfassung und Heeresverfassung in der europäischen Geschichte der frühen Neuzeit*, Berlin, 1986, pp. 173–212. Hintze's argument has been taken up and reformulated in a sociologically acceptable form by Brian M. Downing, 'Constitutionalism, Warfare and Political Change in Early Modern Europe', in *Theory and Society* 17 (1988), pp. 7–56 and in greater detail in his book *The Military Revolution and Political Change. Origins of Democracy and Autocracy in Early Modern Europe*, Princeton, 1992. On Hintze, see also chapter 8 of this book, pp. 157ff.

20 On Michael Roberts's concept of a 'military revolution', see especially Geoffrey Parker, *The Military Revolution. Military Innovation and the Rise of the West, 1500–1800*, Cambridge, 1988; Bruce Porter, *War and the Rise of the State. The Military Foundations of Modern Politics*, New York, 1994, see especially pp. 63ff. The work of Charles Tilly is of crucial importance for the sociological analysis of these questions. See his essay 'Reflections on the History of European State Making', in Tilly, *The Formation of National States in Western Europe*, Princeton, 1975, pp. 3–83, and his book *Coercion, Capital, and European States 990–1990*, Oxford, 1990.

21 Stephen Toulmin, *Cosmopolis. The Hidden Agenda of Modernity*, New York, 1990.

22   Parallel to my own studies on war, Wolfgang Knöbl has worked on the legitimate use of force within states. See Wolfgang Knöbl, *Polizei und Herrschaft im Modernisierungsprozeß. Staatsbildung und 'innere Sicherheit' in Preußen, England und Amerika 1700–1914*, Frankfurt am Main, 1998.

23   For a critique of the assumptions of differentiation theory in modernization theory, see chapter 4.3 of my book *The Creativity of Action* (1992; Cambridge, 1996) and the literature there. Still eminently worth reading in this context is Hans–Ulrich Wehler, *Modernisierungstheorie und Geschichte*, Göttingen, 1975.

24   The forecasts about China's future are a case in point. While modernization theory would entail optimistic forecasts about an inevitable democratization, the approach taken here includes radically different scenarios. Will China's regional military dominance force the successful East Asian trading nations increasingly to militarize themselves? Will democratization threaten the unity of the Chinese state? See Kay Möller, 'Muß man vor China Angst haben?', in *Süddeutsche Zeitung*, 19.5.1995, p. 9; Nicholas D. Kristof, 'The Real Chinese Threat', in *The New York Times Magazine*, 27.8.1995, pp. 50–2; and on modernization theory in China, Bettina Gransow, 'Chinesische Modernisierung und kultureller Eigensinn', in *Zeitschrift für Soziologie* 24 (1993), pp. 183–95.

Chapter 3   Ideologies of War

This chapter is the significantly enlarged and revised version of my contribution to a symposium organized by Wolfgang Mommsen at the Historisches Kolleg in Munich in 1993.

1   Emil Lederer, 'Zur Soziologie des Weltkriegs', in *Archiv für Sozialwissenschaft und Sozialpolitik* 39 (1915), pp. 357–84, reprinted in Lederer, *Kapitalismus, Klassenstruktur und Probleme der Demokratie in Deutschland 1910–1940*, Göttingen, 1979, pp. 119–44, here p. 137.

2   See on this point, Sven Papcke, 'Dienst am Sieg. Die Sozialwissenschaften im Ersten Weltkrieg', in Papcke, *Vernunft und Chaos*, Frankfurt am Main, 1985, pp. 125–42; Dirk Käsler, *Die frühe deutsche Soziologie 1909–1934 und ihre Entstehungsmilieus. Eine wissenschaftssoziologische Untersuchung*, Opladen, 1984.

3   Johann Plenge, *1789 und 1914. Die symbolischen Jahre in der Geschichte des politischen Geistes*, Berlin, 1916. On Plenge, see Axel Schildt, 'Ein konservativer Prophet moderner nationaler Integration. Biographische Skizze des streitbaren Soziologen Johann Plenge (1874–1963)', in *Vierteljahreshefte für Zeitgeschichte* 35 (1987), pp. 523–70.

4   Werner Sombart: *Krieg und Kapitalismus*, Munich/Leipzig, 1913; and *Händler und Helden. Patriotische Besinnungen*, Munich, 1915. I accept the criticism of Friedrich Lenger – in his contribution 'Werner Sombart as Propagandist of a German War' ['Werner Sombart als Propagandist eines deutschen Krieges'], in Wolfgang Mommsen (ed.), *Kultur und Krieg. Die Rolle der Intellektuellen, Künstler und Schriftsteller im Ersten Weltkrieg*,

Munich, 1966, p. 66, n. 8 – that in my earlier writings I was in error about a break in Sombart's thought, in so far as even in the prewar period Sombart had published writings in which Germany figured as salvation from commercialism. See also Lenger's book *Werner Sombart 1863–1941. Eine Biographie*, Munich, 1994, especially pp. 245ff.

5   Sombart, *Krieg und Kapitalismus*, p. 14.
6   Max Weber, *General Economic History* (1923), New York, 1927, pp. 308f.
7   John Nef, *War and Human Progress*, Cambridge, Mass., 1952.
8   J.M. Winter, 'The Economic and Social History of War', in J.M. Winter (ed.), *War and Economic Development. Essays in Memory of David Joslin*, Cambridge, 1975, pp. 1–10.
9   John Hall, 'War and the Rise of the West', in Colin Creighton and Martin Shaw (eds), *The Sociology of War and Peace*, London, 1987, pp. 37–53.
10 Sombart, *Krieg und Kapitalismus*, p. v.
11 Klaus Schwabe, *Wissenschaft und Kriegsmoral. Die deutschen Hochschullehrer und die politischen Grundfragen des Ersten Weltkriegs*, Göttingen, 1965, p. 29.
12 Sombart, *Händler und Helden*, p. 47.
13 Ibid., p. 55.
14 Ibid., p. 65.
15 Ibid., p. 64.
16 Max Weber, *Political Writings*, ed. Peter Lassman and Ronald Speirs, Cambridge, 1994, pp. 1–28.
17 Ibid., pp. 14–15.
18 Ibid., p. 159.
19 Ibid., p. 269.
20 Günther Roth has shown that Weber's concept of an 'ethics of responsibility' flows directly from the concepts of power politics and *realpolitik*, with the aim of bestowing an ethical dimension even on these key concepts of the age. In practice, this conceptual strategy enables Weber to rule out any attitude to capitalism and the World War other than one of an ethics of conviction. Günther Roth, 'Max Weber's Ethics and the Peace Movement Today', in *Theory and Society* 13 (1984), pp. 491–511.
21 Georg Simmel, *Der Krieg und die geistigen Entscheidungen*, Munich, 1917, p. 58.
22 Arnold Zweig's novel *Young Woman of 1914* (1931), New York, 1932, contains a bitter passage aimed at the kind of aestheticizing justification of war represented by Simmel, with its emphasis on the intensity of experience

> A great mass of the German people, the educated classes more especially, the readers of newspapers, the professors and their satellites, the female intellectuals, doctors, judges, teachers, authors, bankers, industrialists and great landowners, both men and women, all these had long since ceased to live in the war as it really was. Those who lived in the real war were the survivors of the dead, the women-folk of men on service, the working men and women in the factories who were expected to work their utmost on very short rations. But the

others all lived for the coming world dominance of the ideals of
Germany, by which they meant the control of mineral deposits,
Channel ports, Russian provinces, Turkish concessions and oil as far
as Persia. The purpose of the war as they conceived it was to be read
in many places: much had been written about the exalted and
historic mission of Germany, the new Rome, the Gothic race, the
modern Imperium, and how 'our time had come'. For them our boys
in grey did not die screaming for their mothers, but uncomplaining,
dignified and grave; they fell in decorative poses with their young,
heroic, leaders at their head. For these men at home and their
pastoral carers all that counted now was the unperishable memory
of the slain and the pose they had adopted for their grandchildren.
Cheap actors, they bore their own troubles without a murmur, they
gave up their sons alive, feasting on the magnitude of their sacrifice
that would cast a sombre glory on times to come: the mighty destiny
of a mighty race. (pp. 375–6)

The extravagance of Simmel's views reaches its pinnacle in pleas that he
made public on a number of occasions (for example, in Georg Simmel,
'Die Umwertung der Werte. Ein Wort an die Wohlhabenden', in the
Frankfurter Zeitung of 5.3.1915, morning edition, p. 2), in which he appealed
to the rich not to switch to cheap foods during the war lest they threaten
the supplies of the poor, but to consume almost nothing but luxury goods.
Needless to say, the idea of distributing lobster and artichokes to the poor
never occurred to people in the circles in which he moved.

23   Max Scheler, 'Der Genius des Krieges und der deutsche Krieg', in Scheler,
     Gesammelte Werke, vol. 4, *Politisch-Pädagogische Schriften*, Bern, 1982, pp.
     7–251, here pp. 11f.
24   Leopold von Wiese, *Politische Briefe über den Weltkrieg. Zwölf Skizzen*,
     Munich/Leipzig, 1914.
25   Roberto Michels: ' "Razze" e "Nazioni" nella Guerra Attuale', in *Nuova
     Antologia* (1914), pp. 220–8; and 'Die wirtschaftlichen Wirkungen des
     Völkerkrieges auf Italien in den ersten Monaten', in *Archiv für Sozialwis-
     senschaft und Sozialpolitik* 40 (1915), pp. 592–619.
26   Ferdinand Tönnies, *Der englische Staat und der deutsche Staat*, Berlin, 1917.
27   Émile Boutroux, *L'Allemagne et la guerre*, Paris, 1915, here p. 29.
28   Henri Bergson, *La signification de la guerre*, Paris, 1915, here p. 34.
29   Interestingly, Georg Simmel himself responded to the news of Bergson's
     utterances on the war: Georg Simmel, 'Bergson und der deutsche
     "Zynismus" ', in *Internationale Monatsschrift für Kunst, Wissenschaft und
     Technik* 9 (1914), pp. 197–200. In contrast to Gerhart Hauptmann's naïve
     polemics, he had the greatness of mind to describe Bergson, despite their
     political differences, as 'the most powerful intellect of the present genera-
     tion of philosophers'. Simmel's intellectual debt to Bergson is palpable, as
     is his gratitude for Bergson's efforts to publicize his writings in France.
     However, he has no argument with which to oppose Bergson, other than
     the notion that the German conduct of the war cannot be called cynical

because the cynicism of the prewar period had been eliminated by the experience of war.

30 Wolf Lepenies, *Between Literature and Science. The Rise of Sociology* (1985), Cambridge, 1988, p. 78.

31 Émile Durkheim, *Qui a voulu la guerre? Les origines de la guerre d'après les documents diplomatiques*, Paris, 1915. [Appeared in English as *Who Wanted War? The Origin of the War According to Diplomatic Documents*, Paris, 1915.]

32 Émile Durkheim, *'Germany Above All'. The German Mentality and the War*, Paris, 1915.

33 Émile Durkheim, *The Division of Labor in Society* (1893), New York, 1984, p. 194.

34 Ibid., p. 195.

35 Émile Durkheim, *Professional Ethics and Civic Morals* (1950), London, 1957.

36 See Werner Gephart, 'Die französische Soziologie und der Erste Weltkrieg. Spannungen in Émile Durkheims Deutung des Großen Krieges', in Mommsen (ed.), *Kultur und Krieg*, pp. 49–63. Also on France, Martha Hanna, *The Mobilization of Intellect. French Scholars and Writers during the Great War*, Cambridge, Mass., 1996.

37 See, for example, William J. Barber, 'British and American Economists and Attempts to Comprehend the Nature of War, 1919–20', in *Economics and National Security – A History of Their Interaction*, Annual Supplement to *History of Political Economy* 23 (1991), pp. 61–86. For the reaction of the sole professor of sociology in Britain, L.T. Hobhouse, see Stefan Collini, *Liberalism and Sociology. L.T. Hobhouse and Political Argument in England 1880–1914*, Cambridge, 1979, pp. 245ff.

38 Benedetto Croce, *Opera omnia*, series 4, vol. III, *L'Italia da 1914 al 1919. Pagine sulla guerra*, Naples, 1919; Bern, 1928. For an overview of the Italian situation, see David D. Roberts, 'Croce and Beyond. Italian Intellectuals and the First World War', in *International History Review* 3 (1981), pp. 201–35. A study of the situation in Russia and particularly the writings of Pitirim Sorokin would also be important. For the moment see Leonid Ionin and Alla Cernych, 'Krieg und Frieden in der frühen russischen Soziologie', in Hans Joas and Helmut Steiner (eds), *Machtpolitischer Realismus und pazifistische Utopie*, Frankfurt am Main, 1989, pp. 117–52.

39 Knud Krakau, 'American Foreign Relations: A National Style?', in *Diplomatic History* 8 (1984), pp. 253–72.

40 Carol Gruber, *Mars and Minerva. World War I and the Use of the Higher Learning in America*, Baton Rouge, La, 1975.

41 Albion Small, 'Germany and American Opinion. Professor Albion Small to Professor Georg Simmel', in *Sociological Review* 7 (1914), pp. 106–11.

42 Franklin Giddings, *The Responsible State. A Re-examination of Fundamental Political Doctrines in the Light of the War and the Menace of Anarchism*, Boston, 1918.

43 Josiah Royce, *The Hope for the Great Community*, New York, 1916.

44 George Santayana, *Character and Opinion in the United States: with Reminiscences of William James and Josiah Royce and Academic Life in America*, London, 1920, pp. 123–6.

45 George Santayana, *Egotism in German Philosophy*, in Santayana, *Works*, vol. VI, New York, 1936, pp. 145–249.
46 Ibid., p. 147.
47 John Dewey: 'The Tragedy of the German Soul' (1916), in Dewey, *Middle Works*, vol. 10, Carbondale, Ill., 1980, pp. 305–9; and *German Philosophy and Politics*, New York, 1915.
48 Christopher Lasch, '*The New Republic* and the War: "An Unanalysable Feeling"', in Lasch, *The New Radicalism in America (1889–1963)*, New York, 1965, pp. 181–224.
49 An admirable account can be found in Robert Westbrook, *John Dewey and American Democracy*, Ithaca, NY, 1991, pp. 195–227.
50 John Dewey, 'Progress', in Dewey, *Character and Events*, vol. 2, New York, 1929, pp. 820–30, here p. 820.
51 George Herbert Mead, 'National-Mindedness and International-Mindedness' (1929), in Mead, *Selected Writings*, ed. Andrew Reck, Indianapolis, 1964, pp. 355–70, here p. 367.
52 Thorstein Veblen, *The Nature of Peace and the Terms of Its Perpetuation*, New York, 1917. For a critique of Veblen, see Mead's review of the book in *Journal of Political Economy* 26 (1918), pp. 752–62. While fundamentally agreeing with Veblen, he attempts to loosen up his rigid views by means of his own social psychology.

Raymond Aron ('War and Industrial Society', in Leon Bramson and George W. Goethals (eds), *War: Studies from Psychology, Sociology and Anthropology*, New York, 1968, pp. 359–402) is probably the first to have noticed a certain similarity between Veblen's theory and Schumpeter's theory of imperialism (Joseph Schumpeter, *Imperialism and Social Classes*, New York, 1951). Schumpeter's major study, which was first published in 1919, can certainly be interpreted in part as a sociological response to the World War. For Schumpeter, as for Veblen, imperialism, which he defines as 'the objectless disposition on the part of a state to unlimited forcible expansion' (p. 77), is an 'atavism' in the present. In the age of capitalism, imperialism is said no longer to have any soil in which to breed; it is simply a vestige of absolutism surviving in social and individual psychic structures. There is no doubt that with his proof of the pacifist nature of capitalism and of Britain as its mother country, Schumpeter takes up ideas of the utilitarian liberal tradition. Schumpeter explains the threat of war in the present as arising from export monopolism, which, however, is not – as the socialists imagined – a necessary consequence of the development of capitalism. It follows that universal free trade will make possible peaceful relations between capitalist states. This idea, which is of great significance for our own world since the end of the Second World War, cannot be discussed adequately here. It is a consequence not of the sociological theory of the peaceful character of industrial society, but of the economic theory of the pacifying effects of free trade. I must add, however, that Aron seems to me to overstate the similarities between Veblen and Schumpeter in one respect: this is that he does not make clear that Veblen's theory follows from a political theory about the peaceful effects of republicanism, and that, unlike Schumpeter's theory, it therefore contains elements that are critical of a capitalist market economy. One should add that both Veblen and Schumpeter fail to appreciate the nature of modern nationalism or patriotism when they interpret it as a dynastic or feudal relic (Veblen, *The Nature of Peace*, pp. 31ff; Schumpeter, *Imperialism and Social Classes*, pp. 128f).

53   Joseph Dorfman, *Thorstein Veblen and His America*, New York, 1961, p. 382.
54   Thorstein Veblen, *Imperial Germany and the Industrial Revolution* (1915), New Brunswick, NJ, 1990. It would be necessary, of course, to clarify the relationship between Veblen's war writings and his sociological works. An excellent study of this has now become available: Gunnar Schmidt, 'Die konstruierte Moderne. Thorstein Veblen und der Erste Weltkrieg', in *Leviathan* 28 (2000), pp. 39–68.
55   Bernd Faulenbach, *Ideologie des deutschen Wegs. Die deutsche Geschichte in der Historiographie zwischen Kaiserreich und Nationalsozialismus*, Munich, 1980. This careful study contains nothing about the American debate.
56   For example, Ralf Dahrendorf, *Society and Democracy in Germany* (1965), London, 1968.
57   Scheler, 'Der Genius des Krieges und der deutsche Krieg', p. 9.
58   Modris Eksteins, *Rites of Spring. The Great War and the Birth of the Modern Age*, New York, 1990; H. Stuart Hughes, *Consciousness and Society. The Reconstruction of European Social Thought 1890–1930*, New York, 1977; Roland Stromberg, *Redemption by War. The Intellectuals and 1914*, Lawrence, Kan., 1982.
59   Lederer, 'Zur Soziologie des Weltkrieges', in Lederer, *Kapitalismus*, pp. 121f.
60   Ibid., p. 130. In my account I do not wish to affirm the truth of his assertions, but only the style of his arguments.
61   Ibid., p. 141.
62   Ibid., p. 143.
63   Dieter Senghaas, *Friedensprojekt Europa*, Frankfurt am Main, 1992. See also chapter 1 in this volume, pp. 29ff.

Chapter 4   After the War

This chapter was first published in *Die Neue Gesellschaft/Frankfurter Hefte* 38, no. 12 (1991), pp. 1135–9.
1   Harold Hurwitz, *Demokratie und Antikommunismus in Berlin nach 1945*, 5 vols, Cologne 1983 (vol. 1); 1984 (vols 2 and 3); 1990 (vol. 4 in two parts); 1997 (vol. 5).

- Vol. 1: *Die politische Kultur der Bevölkerung und der Neubeginn konservativer Politik*.
- Vol. 2: *Autoritäre Tradierung und Demokratiepotential in der sozialdemokratischen Arbeiterbewegung* (with Klaus Sühl).
- Vol. 3: *Die Eintracht der Siegermächte und die Orientierungsnot der Deutschen*.

- Vol. 4: *Die Anfänge des Widerstandes*, Part 1: *Führungsanspruch und Isolation der Sozialdemokraten*; Part 2: *Zwischen Selbsttäuschung und Zivilcourage: der Fusionskampf*.
- Vol. 5: *Die Stalinisierung der SED. Zum Verlust von Freiräumen und sozialdemokratischer Identität in den Vorständen 1946–1949*.

2 See Harold Hurwitz's highly readable autobiographical article, 'Mein Leben in Berlin', *Leviathan* 27 (1999), pp. 264–79.
3 Hurwitz, vol. 2, p. 280.
4 Vol. 1, p. 8.
5 Vol. 3, p. 10.
6 Ibid., pp. 78ff.

Chapter 5 After the Cold War

This chapter was written together with Martin Kohli. It served originally as the introduction to Hans Joas and Martin Kohli (eds), *Der Zusammenbruch der DDR. Soziologische Analysen*, Frankfurt am Main, 1993. It has been slightly revised and abridged for the present volume. I have not included a discussion of the extensive recent literature since the emphasis of the argument here lies on the typology of explanations in sociology and for this no modification seemed necessary.

1 Jürgen Habermas, *Die nachholende Revolution*, Frankfurt am Main, 1990.
2 Ehrhard Neubert, *Die protestantische Revolution*, Berlin, 1991.
3 Klaus von Beyme, 'Selbstgleichschaltung. Warum es in der DDR keine Politologie gegeben hat', in Bernd Giesen and Claus Leggewie (eds), *Experiment Vereinigung. Ein sozialer Großversuch*, Berlin, 1991, pp. 123–32.
4 Rolf Reißig, 'Das Scheitern der DDR und des realsozialistischen Systems. Einige Ursachen und Folgen', in Joas and Kohli (eds), *Der Zusammenbruch der DDR*, pp. 49–69.
5 Claus Offe, 'Wohlstand, Nation, Republik. Aspekte des deutschen Sonderwegs vom Sozialismus zum Kapitalismus', in ibid., pp. 282–301.
6 Randall Collins: 'The Future Decline of the Russian Empire', in Collins, *Weberian Sociological Theory*, Cambridge, 1986, pp. 186–209; and 'The Geopolitical Basis of Revolution. The Prediction of the Soviet Collapse', in Collins, *Macrohistory. Essays in Sociology of the Long Run*, Stanford, 1999, pp. 37–68.
7 Hans-Joachim Maaz, *Der Gefühlsstau. Ein Psychogramm der DDR*, Berlin, 1990.
8 Reißig, 'Das Scheitern der DDR und des realsozialistischen Systems', see n. 4.
9 See Sigrid Meuschel, *Legitimation und Parteiherrschaft in der DDR*, Frankfurt am Main, 1991.
10 Heinz Bude, 'Das Ende einer tragischen Gesellschaft', in Joas and Kohli (eds), *Der Zusammenbruch der DDR*, pp. 267–81.

11   Detlef Pollack, 'Religion und gesellschaftlicher Wandel. Zur Rolle der evangelischen Kirche im Prozeß des gesellschaftlichen Umbruchs', in ibid., pp. 246–66.

12   See Jürgen Kocka, 'Revolution und Nation 1989. Zur historischen Einordnung der gegenwärtigen Ereignisse', in *Tel Aviver Jahrbuch für deutsche Geschichte* 19 (1990), pp. 471–99.

13   Offe, 'Wohlstand, Nation, Republik'. See n. 5.

14   Jan Wielgohs and Marianne Schulz, 'Von der "friedlichen Revolution" in die politische Normalität. Entwicklungsetappen der ostdeutschen Bürgerbewegung', in Joas and Kohli (eds), *Der Zusammenbruch der DDR*, pp. 222–45.

15   Karl-Dieter Opp, 'Spontaneous Revolutions. The Case of East Germany in 1989', in Heinz D. Kurz (ed.), *United Germany and the New Europe*, Cheltenham, 1993, pp. 11–30.

16   Wolfgang Zapf, 'Die DDR 1989/1990 – Zusammenbruch einer Sozialstruktur?', in Joas and Kohli (eds), *Der Zusammenbruch der DDR*, pp. 29–48.

17   Gert-Joachim Glaeßner, 'Am Ende des Staatssozialismus – Zu den Ursachen des Umbruchs in der DDR', in ibid., pp. 70–92.

18   Rainer Weinert, 'Massenorganisationen in mono-organisationalen Gesellschaften. Über den strukturellen Restaurationszwang des Freien Deutschen Gewerkschaftsbundes im Zuge des Zusammenbruchs der DDR', in ibid., pp. 125–50.

19   Manfred Lötsch, 'Der Sozialismus – eine Stände- oder Klassengesellschaft?', in ibid., pp. 115–24.

20   Sigrid Meuschel, 'Revolution in der DDR. Versuch einer sozialwissenschaftlichen Interpretation', in ibid., pp. 93–114.

21   Artur Meier, 'Abschied von der sozialistischen Ständegesellschaft', in *Aus Politik und Zeitgeschichte* (Supplement to the weekly *Das Parlament*), B 16–17/90 (13.4.1990), pp. 3–14.

22   An interesting contribution to the question of the modernity of so-called 'actually existing socialist' societies is to be found in Ilja Srubar, 'War der reale Sozialismus modern? Versuch einer strukturellen Bestimmung', in *Kölner Zeitschrift für Soziologie und Sozialpsychologie* 43 (1991), pp. 415–32.

23   Heiner Ganßmann, 'Die nichtbeabsichtigten Folgen einer Wirtschaftsplanung. DDR-Zusammenbruch, Planungsparadox und Demokratie', in Joas and Kohli (eds), *Der Zusammenbruch der DDR*, pp. 172–93.

24   See Collins, 'The Future Decline of the Russian Empire'. See n. 6.

25   A similar point can be made with regard to the cultural system, and especially the realm of science. There was only a positional authority derived from the political hierarchy and legitimated by it, that is to say, by the responsibility 'entrusted' to it for the welfare of society as a whole. It was no longer necessary to give rational reasons for orders. A striking example can be found in a story of Jürgen Kuczynski, the Nestor of the GDR social sciences, in his account of a conversation with Honecker about a question of science policy. Kuczynski reports that he had objected to a decision taken by Honecker, but withdrew it with a statement whose gist was as follows: 'I am responsible for the development of the social sciences, and

you, Erich, are responsible for the security of socialism. The security of socialism is more important than the development of the social sciences, and so you are in the right.'

26 Immanuel Wallerstein, '1968, Revolution in the World-System. Thesis and Queries', in *Theory and Society* 18 (1989), pp. 431–49.

27 See the opening address by Wolfgang Zapf at the 25th Congress of the German Sociological Association in Frankfurt am Main in 1990: 'Modernisierung und Modernisierungstheorien', in Zapf (ed.), *Die Modernisierung moderner Gesellschaften. Verhandlungen des 25. Deutschen Soziologentags* (1990), Frankfurt am Main, 1991, pp. 23–39. See also Dieter Senghaas, 'Jenseits des Nebels der Zukunft. Europas ordnungspolitische Option', in Senghaas (ed.), *Europa 2000. Ein Friedensplan*, Frankfurt am Main, 1990, pp. 57–77; and also Edward Tiryakian, 'Modernization: *Exhumetur in Pace* (Rethinking Macrosociology in the 1990s)', in *International Sociology* 6 (1991), pp. 165–80. For a critical view, see Klaus Müller, ' "Modernizing" Eastern Europe. Theoretical Problems and Political Dilemmas' in *Archives Européennes de Sociologie* 32 (1992), pp. 109–50.

28 Hans Joas, *The Creativity of Action* (1992), Cambridge, 1996, especially pp. 223ff, as well as the Introduction, pp. 1ff and chapter 2, pp. 43ff in the present volume.

29 *How* considerable is often overlooked in the West German discussions – in the absence of a comparative perspective. See Martin Kohli, 'Institutionalisierung und Individualisierung der Erwerbsbiographie. Aktuelle Veränderungstendenzen und ihre Folgen', in Ditmar Brock, Hans Rudolf Leu, Christine Preiss and Hans-Rolf Vetter (eds), *Subjektivität im technischen und sozialen Wandel*, Munich, 1989, pp. 249–78. Thus, for example, the assertion that a total employment figure at the level of the former GDR was not possible in a Western economy was refuted by a comparison with Sweden. Of course, such an employment policy cannot simply be taken over at will and is unlikely to be available for adoption in German conditions.

30 In the old Federal Republic, the element of competition between the two German systems was effective in stimulating many fundamental social innovations, not least in the development of the welfare state (such as Adenauer's great pension reform of 1957).

Chapter 6   Sprayed and Betrayed

This chapter first appeared in Hans Joas and Wolfgang Knöbl (eds), *Gewalt in den USA*, Frankfurt am Main, 1994, pp. 300–13.

The text that follows is not to be understood as a strict research report on the extensive sociological research on the topic, but rather as a study that has singled out a small number of representative points on the inter-related topics of the experience of violence and the tendency to resort to it, the transformation of identity and feelings of self-betrayal.

For a strictly scientific overview the following can be recommended: Ellen Frey-Wouters and Robert S. Laufer, *Legacy of a War. The American Soldier in Vietnam*, Armonk, NY, 1986; and for a brief survey of the literature, see John Modell and Timothy Haggerty, 'The Social Impact of War', *Annual Review of Sociology* 17 (1991), pp. 205–24.

1   On this theme, see D. Michael Shafer, 'The Vietnam-Era Draft: Who Went, Who Didn't and Why It Matters', in Shafer (ed.), *The Legacy. The Vietnam War in the American Imagination*, Boston, 1990, pp. 57–79. For a comprehensive survey of the fate of the Vietnam generation, see Lawrence M. Baskir and William A. Strauss, *Chance and Circumstance. The Draft, the War and the Vietnam Generation*, New York, 1978.

2   On this point, see Keith Walker, *A Piece of My Heart. 26 Women in Vietnam*, Novato, Calif., 1985; Stephen J. Dienstfrey, 'Women Veterans' Exposure to Combat', in *Armed Forces and Society* 14 (1988), pp. 549–58.

3   Charles Moskos, 'The American Combat Soldier in Vietnam', in *Journal of Social Issues* 31 (1985), pp. 25–38.

4   See D. Michael Shafer, 'The Vietnam Combat Experience: The Human Legacy', in Shafer, *The Legacy*, pp. 80–103.

5   On what follows, see John Keegan, *The Face of Battle*, Harmondsworth, 1978.

6   Guy Chapman, *A Passionate Prodigality*, London, 1965, quoted by Keegan, *The Face of Battle*, p. 48.

7   Chaim F. Shatan, 'The Grief of Soldiers. Vietnam Combat Veterans' Self-Help Movement', in *American Journal of Ortho-Psychiatry* 43 (1973), pp. 640–53.

8   Robert S. Laufer, M.S. Gallops and Ellen Frey-Wouters, 'War Stress and Trauma: The Vietnam Veteran Experience', in *Journal of Health and Social Behaviour* 25 (1984), pp. 65–85. This essay contains an explicit revision of previous studies by the authors.

9   There is an excellent overview in Dane Archer and Rosemary Gartner, 'Violent Acts and Violent Times. The Effect of Wars on Postwar Homicide Rates', in Archer and Gartner, *Violence and Crime in a Cross-National Perspective*, New Haven, Conn., 1984, pp. 63–97.

10   Best of all by Ghislaine Boulanger, 'Violence and Vietnam Veterans', in Boulanger and Charles Kadushin (eds), *The Vietnam Veteran Redefined. Fact and Fiction*, Hillsdale, NJ, 1986, pp. 79–90.

11   See Keegan, *The Face of Battle*, p. 334.

12   Of great interest regarding the German case, see Bernd Ulrich, 'Nerven und Krieg. Skizzierung einer Beziehung', in Bedrich Löwenstein (ed.), *Geschichte und Psychologie. Annäherungsversuche*, Pfaffenweiler, 1992, pp. 163–92.

13   The most gripping account is probably that of Robert Jay Lifton, *Home From the War. Vietnam Veterans: Neither Victims Nor Executioners*, New York, 1973. However, see also Shatan, 'The Grief of Soldiers (n. 7) and also – without reference to rap groups – Herbert Hendin and Ann Pollinger Haas, *Wounds of the War. The Psychological Aftermath of Combat in Vietnam*, New York, 1984; Arthur Egendorf, *Healing from the War. Trauma and Transformation after Vietnam*, Boston, 1986.

14 Wilbur J. Scott, 'Competing Paradigms in the Assessment of Latent Disorders. The Case of Agent Orange', in *Social Problems* 35 (1988), pp. 145–61.
15 See Tadeusz Rózewicz, 'Neue philosophische Schule', in Tadeusz Rózewicz, *In der schönsten Stadt der Welt*, Berlin, 1971, pp. 47–68.

Chapter 7   Between Power Politics and Pacifist Utopia

This chapter was translated by Jeremy Gaines and Doris Jones and first published as 'Between Power Politics and Pacifist Utopia: Peace and War in Sociological Theory', in *Current Sociology* 39 (1991), copyright © International Sociological Association 1991. The translation has been revised for inclusion in this volume, and is reprinted by permission of Sage Publications Ltd. The original first appeared in Hans Peter Dreitzel and Horst Stenger (eds), *Ungewollte Selbstzerstörung*, Frankfurt am Main, 1990, pp. 135–59.

1 Václav Havel, 'Words on Words', *The New York Review of Books*, 18 January (1990), pp. 5–8.
2 In the case of Great Britain this has been studied empirically by David Marsland, *Neglect and Betrayal. War and Violence in Modern Sociology*, London, 1985. He devalues his investigation, however, by his extremely polemical tone and tendentious political judgements. A summary of the state of affairs in the US is available in Lester B. Kurtz, 'War and Peace on the Sociological Agenda', in Terence C. Halliday and Morris Janowitz (eds), *Sociology and Its Publics. The Forms and Fates of Disciplinary Organization*, Chicago, 1992, pp. 61–98. Lester Kurtz has drawn the logical conclusion from his own diagnosis and instigated a comprehensive encyclopedia: Lester B. Kurtz (ed.), *Encyclopedia of Violence, Peace and Conflict*, 3 vols, San Diego, Calif., 1999.
3 Alain Touraine, *Return of the Actor. Social Theory in Postindustrial Society* (1984), Minneapolis, 1988, pp. 32ff; Anthony Giddens, *The Nation-State and Violence*, Cambridge, 1985.
4 See chapter 8 in this volume, pp. 141ff.
5 For an overview of the early approaches to thinking about peace, see James Turner Johnson, *The Quest for Peace. Three Moral Traditions in Western Cultural History*, Princeton, 1987.
6 On the German discussion around 1800, the most important contributions are to be found in Anita and Walter Dietze (eds), *Ewiger Friede? Dokumente einer deutschen Diskussion um 1800*, Leipzig/Weimar, 1989.
7 A pioneering work from this point of view is the study by Massimo Mori, 'Krieg und Frieden in der klassischen deutschen Philosophie', in Hans Joas and Helmut Steiner (eds), *Machtpolitischer Realismus und pazifistische Utopie. Krieg und Frieden in der Geschichte der Sozialwissenschaften*, Frankfurt am Main, 1989, pp. 49–91. This is a summary of his comprehensive study *La ragione delle armi. Guerra e conflitto nella filosofia classica tedesca (1770–1830)*, Milan, 1984.

8   For an overview, see Michael Howard, *War and the Liberal Conscience*, New Brunswick, NJ, 1978.
9   See Dieter Klein, *Chancen für einen friedensfähigen Kapitalismus*, Berlin, 1988.
10 See Horst Duhnke, *Die KPD von 1933 bis 1945*, Cologne, 1972.
11 On this question, see the detailed account in chapter 3 in this volume, pp. 55ff and the relevant references; the following summary is based on that chapter.
12 See Raymond Aron, *Peace and War* (1962), London, 1966; C. Wright Mills, *The Causes of World War Three*, New York, 1958.
13 On postwar developments, see Martin Shaw, 'Ideen über Krieg und Militarisierung in der Gesellschaftstheorie des späten zwanzigsten Jahrhunderts', in Hans Joas and Helmut Steiner (eds), *Machtpolitischer Realismus und pazifistische Utopie. Krieg und Frieden in der Geschichte der Sozialwissenschaften*, Frankfurt am Main, 1989, pp. 283–308.
14 This thesis has been advanced by Zsuzsa Hegedus to counter the condemnation of the peace movement by the majority of French intellectuals. See Zsuzsa Hegedus, 'Social Movements and Social Change in Self-Creative Society', in *International Sociology* 4 (1989), pp. 19–34.
15 Amitai Etzioni, *The Active Society*, New York, 1968; Anthony Giddens, *The Constitution of Society*, Cambridge, 1989; Cornelius Castoriadis, *The Imaginary Institution of Society*, Cambridge, 1987; Alain Touraine, *The Voice and the Eye* (1978), Cambridge, 1981; Roberto Mangabeira Unger, *Politics*, 3 vols, Cambridge, 1987. For a more detailed discussion, see my own book, *The Creativity of Action* (1992), Cambridge, 1996, especially part IV.
16 Michael Mann, *The Sources of Social Power*, vol. 1, Cambridge, 1986.

Chapter 8   Is There a Militarist Tradition in Sociology?

1   Michael Mann, *States, War and Capitalism*, Oxford, 1988. His chief work is *The Sources of Social Power*, 2 vols, Cambridge, 1986 and 1993.
2   In Mann, *States, War and Capitalism*, pp. 146–65, and especially pp. 146–9.
3   Ibid., pp. 2 and 126.
4   Ibid., p. 148.
5   Donald N. Levine, *Visions of the Sociological Tradition*, Chicago, 1995. See also my discussion of this book, 'A Postdisciplinary History of Disciplines', *European Journal of Social Theory* 2 (1999), pp. 109–22.
6   See chapter 3 in this volume, pp. 55ff.
7   For an overview, see Hansjoachim Koch, *Der Sozialdarwinismus. Seine Genese und sein Einfluß auf das imperialistische Denken*, Munich, 1973.
8   On what follows, see Pitirim Sorokin, 'Sociological Interpretation of the "Struggle for Existence" and the Sociology of War', in Sorokin, *Contemporary Sociological Theories*, New York, 1928, pp. 309–56. This contains numerous further references to the Italian, French, British, American and Russian literature, which amounts to an impressive documentation of the international scope of this discussion. In contrast, Max Scheler argued that Social Darwinism was related to utilitarianism and was therefore alien to

German thought. See Max Scheler, 'Der Genius des Krieges und der Deutsche Krieg' (1915), in Scheler, *Gesammelte Werke*, vol. 4, *Politisch-Pädagogische Schriften*, Bern, 1982, pp. 7–251, and especially p. 16.

9   Ludwig Gumplowicz: *Der Rassenkampf* (1883), Innsbruck, 1926; *Outlines of Sociology* (1885), New Brunswick, NJ, 1980; and *Die soziologische Staatsidee* (1892), Innsbruck, 1902. Outstanding in the secondary literature is Gerald Mozetic, 'Ein unzeitgemäßer Soziologe: Ludwig Gumplowicz', in *Kölner Zeitschrift für Soziologie und Sozialpsychologie* 37 (1985), pp. 621–47.

10   Mozetic, 'Ein unzeitgemäßer Soziologe', p. 624.

11   Otto Hintze, Review of Gumplowicz, *Soziologie und Politik* and *Die soziologische Staatsidee*, in *Schmollers Jahrbuch* 21 (1897), pp. 715f. The quotation is on p. 716.

12   Otto Hintze, 'Soziologische und geschichtliche Staatsauffassung. Zu Franz Oppenheimers System der Soziologie' (1929), in Hintze, *Soziologie und Geschichte. Gesammelte Abhandlungen*, vol. 2, Göttingen 1964 (2nd edn), pp. 239–305, here p. 240.

13   Ibid.

14   On Ratzenhofer and Gumplowicz, see John Torrance, 'The Emergence of Sociology in Austria 1885–1935', in *Archives Européennes de Sociologie* 17 (1976), pp. 185–219, especially pp. 185ff.

15   Émile Durkheim, 'La sociologie selon Gumplowicz' (1885), in Durkheim, *Textes*, vol. 1, Paris, 1975, pp. 344–54.

16   On the connections here, see Dieter Haselbach, 'Die Staatstheorie von L. Gumplowicz und ihre Weiterentwicklung bei Franz Oppenheimer und Alexander Rüstow', in *Österreichische Zeitschrift für Soziologie* 15 (1990), pp. 84–99.

17   Hintze, 'Soziologische und geschichtliche Staatsauffassung', p. 242. Hintze's other discussion of Oppenheimer is entitled 'Probleme einer europäischen Sozial- und Wirtschaftsgeschichte'. This appeared first in 1930 and is also reprinted in Hintze, *Soziologie und Geschichte*, vol. 2, pp. 306–12.

18   Franz Oppenheimer: *The State* (1907), New York, 1975; and *System der Soziologie*, Jena, 1922–6.

19   Hintze, 'Soziologische und geschichtliche Staatsauffassung', p. 243.

20   Ibid., p. 293.

21   Ibid., p. 274.

22   Alexander Rüstow, *Ortsbestimmung der Gegenwart*, 3 vols, Zurich, 1950ff. On Rüstow, see also Haselbach, 'Die Staatstheorie von L. Gumplowicz und ihre Weiterentwicklung bei Franz Oppenheimer und Alexander Rüstow' (n. 16), pp. 91–5.

23   In contrast to the sparse literature on Gumplowicz and Oppenheimer, commentaries on Schmitt are so voluminous that I cannot claim to offer a complete overview. Of particular importance for the present argument is the older book by Christian Graf von Krockow, *Die Entscheidung. Eine Untersuchung über Ernst Jünger, Carl Schmitt, Martin Heidegger* (1958), Frankfurt am Main, 1990.

24   Carl Schmitt, *The Concept of the Political* (1932), New Brunswick, NJ, 1976.

25   Ibid., p. 22.
26   Ibid.
27   Ibid., p. 26.
28   Ibid., p. 33.
29   Ibid., p. 35.
30   Ibid.
31   Ibid., p. 38.
32   Ibid., p. 72.
33   Ibid., p. 67.
34   Ibid., p. 49. It should be noted that I have no wish to deny the sociologi-
      cal advantages of this approach. On this point, see above, chapter 1, pp.
      29ff.
35   Schmitt, *The Concept of the Political*, p. 49.
36   Ibid., p. 33.
37   In the German edition: Carl Schmitt, *Der Begriff des Politischen* (1932), Berlin,
      1963, p. 14. He refers to Otto Brunner, *Land und Herrschaft. Grundfragen der
      territorialen Verfassungsgeschichte Österreichs* (1939), Vienna, 1990, p. 2.
38   Schmitt, *The Concept of the Political*, p. 77.
39   Ibid., p. 45, n. 19. He is referring to Emil Lederer, 'Zur Soziologie
      der Weltkriegs', in *Archiv für Sozialwissenschaft und Sozialpolitik* 39 (1915),
      pp. 357–84 and especially pp. 373f; reprinted in Lederer, *Kapitalismus,
      Klassenstruktur und Probleme der Demokratie in Deutschland 1910–1940*,
      Göttingen, 1979, pp. 119–44, especially p. 137.
40   On the exceptional nature of Lederer's text, see chapter 3 in this volume,
      pp. 78ff.
41   Otto Hintze, Review of Carl Schmitt, *Verfassungslehre* (Munich, 1928), in
      Historische Zeitschrift 139 (1929), pp. 562–8.
42   The first to do this was probably Herbert Marcuse, 'The Struggle against
      Liberalism in a Totalitarian View of the State' (1934), in Marcuse, *Negations*,
      Harmondsworth, 1968, pp. 3–42, especially pp. 30–1. The following
      interpretation is influenced by Michael Großheim's essay, 'Politischer
      Existentialismus', in Günter Meuter and Henrique Ricardo Otten (eds),
      Der Aufstand gegen die Bürger. Antibürgerliches Denken im 20. Jahrhundert,
      Würzburg, 1999, pp. 127–63.
43   Helmut Kuhn, Review of C. Schmitt, *Der Begriff des Politischen*, in *Kant-
      Studien* 38 (1933), pp. 190–6, I am indebted to Großheim for drawing my
      attention to this text.
44   Georg Simmel, *Der Krieg und die geistigen Entscheidungen*, Munich, 1917,
      especially pp. 20f. On Simmel's 'absolute situation', see my discussion in
      Hans Joas, *The Genesis of Values* (1997), Cambridge, 2000, pp. 74f.
45   In what follows I shall concentrate on Hintze and mention Weber only in
      passing. One reason for this is that others have already made the crucial
      statements about Weber; another is that he is treated in greater detail
      elsewhere in this book (see chapter 3, pp. 61ff). A pioneering study of
      Weber has been provided by Wolfgang Mommsen, *Max Weber and German
      Politics 1890–1920*, Chicago, 1984.
46   Jürgen Kocka, 'Otto Hintze', in Hans-Ulrich Wehler (ed.), *Deutsche
      Historiker*, vol. 3, Göttingen, 1973, pp. 41–64. Further important interpre-

tations of Hintze's life work include: Gerhard Oestreich, 'Otto Hintzes Stellung zur Politikwissenschaft und Soziologie', in Otto Hintze, *Soziologie und Geschichte*, vol. 2, pp. 7*–67*; Felix Gilbert, 'Introduction', in *The Historical Essays of Otto Hintze*, ed. Gilbert, New York, 1975, pp. 3–30; Dietrich Gerhard, 'Otto Hintze: His Work and His Significance in Historiography', in *Central European History* 3 (1970), pp. 17–48 (reprinted in Gerhard, *Gesammelte Aufsätze*, Göttingen, 1977, pp. 268–95); as well as the collection of essays of Otto Büsch and Michael Erbe (eds), *Otto Hintze und die moderne Geschichtswissenschaft*, Berlin, 1983. This volume also contains an account by Winfried Schulze of Hintze's reception of sociology and the reception (or non-reception) of Hintze's work by sociology, pp. 134–49.

47 Kocka, 'Otto Hintze', p. 41.
48 This passage comes from his critique of Oppenheimer, in *Soziologie und Geschichte*, vol. 2, p. 285.
49 Otto Hintze, 'Roschers politische Entwicklungstheorie' (1897), in ibid., pp. 3–45, here pp. 19f.
50 To cite the concise account of German historicism in Herbert Schnädelbach, *Philosophy in Germany 1831–1933*, Cambridge, 1984, pp. 42ff, here p. 46. On this tradition in general, see Georg G. Iggers, *The German Conception of History. The National Tradition of Historical Thought from Herder to the Present*, Middletown, Conn., 1968. However, Iggers's interpretation is, in my view, too strongly influenced by the thesis of the German *Sonderweg*. See also Gerhard, 'Otto Hintze: His Work and His Significance in Historiography', p. 291, n. 34.
51 Otto Hintze, Review of Oswald Spengler, *Der Staat* etc., in *Zeitschrift für die gesamte Staatswissenschaft* 79 (1925), pp. 541–7, here p. 546.
52 Ibid., p. 541.
53 Hintze, *Soziologie und Geschichte*, vol. 2, p. 286.
54 Jürgen Kocka, 'Otto Hintze, Max Weber und das Problem der Bürokratie', in Büsch and Erbe (eds), *Otto Hintze und die moderne Geschichtswissenschaft*, pp. 150–88.
55 Otto Hintze, 'Max Webers Soziologie' (1926), in Hintze, *Soziologie und Geschichte*, vol. 2, pp. 135–47.
56 Ibid., p. 142.
57 As Kocka maintains, see 'Otto Hintze, Max Weber und das Problem der Bürokratie', especially p. 177.
58 Ibid., p. 167.
59 This assertion does not of course rule out the possibility of admitting the reality of the specific features of Germany, for example in its ideologizing of the First World War, and giving a more precise account of them.

Chapter 9   Sociology after Auschwitz

This text contains the slightly revised version of an address that I gave in honour of Zygmunt Bauman on 22 March 1996 at the invitation of the University of Leeds. I should like to thank Wolfgang Engler, Thomas Neumann and Frank Sieren for some useful suggestions. My title echoes a formulation of

Harald Welzer: see his article ' "Verweilen beim Grauen". Bücher über den Holocaust', in *Merkur* 48 (1994), pp. 67–72, here, p. 67. The English-language original of my text can be found in *Theory, Culture and Society* 15 (1998), pp. 47–55. The same issue of the journal contains a further examination of the reception of Bauman's work in Germany: Ian Varcoe, 'Identity and the Limits of Comparison', in ibid., pp. 57–72.

1   Zygmunt Bauman, *Modernity and the Holocaust*, Cambridge, 1989.

2   Jürgen Kocka, 'German History before Hitler. The Debate about the German *Sonderweg*', *Journal of Contemporary History* 23 (1988), pp. 3–16, here p. 3.

3   Helga Hirsch, 'Der Holocaust ist nicht einmalig. Gespräch mit dem polnischen Soziologen Zygmunt Bauman', in *Die Zeit*, 23.4.1993, p. 68.

4   Randall Collins, 'German-Bashing and the Theory of Democratic Modernization', in Collins, *Macrohistory. Essays in Sociology of the Long Run*, Stanford, 1999, pp. 152–76.

5   Rudolf Augstein et al. (eds), *Historikerstreit. Die Dokumentation der Kontroverse um die Einzigartigkeit der nationalsozialistischen Judenvernichtung*, Munich, 1987; Charles S. Maier, *The Unmasterable Past. History, Holocaust and German National Identity*, Cambridge, Mass., 1988.

6   Hannah Arendt, *Eichmann in Jerusalem. A Report on the Banality of Evil*, London, 1963.

7   Hannah Arendt, *The Origins of Totalitarianism*, London, 1967.

8   I wrote this text *before* the publication of Daniel Goldhagen's book *Hitler's Willing Executioners. Ordinary Germans and the Holocaust*, New York, 1996. This is not the place to discuss the arguments of that book and its profound differences from Zygmunt Bauman's work.

9   Wolfgang Sofsky, *The Order of Terror. The Concentration Camp* (1993), Princeton, 1997.

10   Max Horkheimer and Theodor W. Adorno, *Dialectic of Enlightenment* (1944), New York, 1972.

11   Norbert Elias, *The Civilizing Process* (1939), Oxford, 1978.

12   Wolfgang Engler, *Die ungewollte Moderne. Ost–West-Passagen*, Frankfurt am Main, 1995, pp. 113–43.

13   Ulrich Beck, *Risk Society. Towards a New Modernity* (1986), London, 1992.

14   Zygmunt Bauman, 'Gewalt – modern und postmodern', in Max Miller and Hans-Georg Soeffner (eds), *Modernität und Barbarei. Soziologische Zeitdiagnose am Ende des 20. Jahrhunderts*, Frankfurt am Main, 1996, pp. 36–67, here p. 39.

15   Gertrud Nunner-Winkler, 'Gewalt – ein Spezifikum der Moderne?', in ibid., pp. 81–95.

16   See chapter 3 in this volume, pp. 55ff.

17   See chapter 2 in this volume, pp. 43ff.

18   Otto Hintze, 'Military Organization and the Organization of the State' (1906), in *The Historical Essays of Otto Hintze*, ed. Felix Gilbert, New York, 1975, pp. 178–215; Brian Downing, 'Constitutionalism, Warfare and Political Change in Early Modern Europe', in *Theory and Society* 17 (1988), pp. 7–56.

19 On this point, see Hans Joas, *Pragmatism and Social Theory* (1992), Chicago, 1993.

20 Ernst Köhler, 'Fragen an Zygmunt Bauman', in *Kommune* 8 (1994), pp. 54–8.

21 Heinz Bude, 'Gewalt durch Verfahren. Zygmunt Bauman über die Modernität des Bösen', in *Frankfurter Allgemeine Zeitung*, 8.12.1992, p. 17.

22 Sighard Neckel, 'Gefährliche Fremdheit. Notizen zu Zygmunt Bauman', in *Ästhetik und Kommunikation* 23, no. 85/6 (1994), pp. 45–9.

23 Robert Bellah, Richard Madsen, William M. Sullivan, Ann Swidler and Steven M. Tipton, *Habits of the Heart. Individualism and Commitment in American Life*, Berkeley, 1985, p. 7.

24 William James, *The Varieties of Religious Experience*, New York, 1902.

25 I have developed these ideas further in Hans Joas, *The Genesis of Values* (1997), Cambridge, 2000.

26 Richard Bernstein, *The New Constellation. The Ethical-Political Horizons of Modernity/Postmodernity*, Cambridge, Mass., 1993, pp. 67ff.

27 The talk on which this paper is based ended with the following personal remark:

> I started this talk by saying that it is a great honour for me to talk to you, Professor Zygmunt Bauman, today and to contribute to this celebration of your work. To say this was not a mere formality on my part. Indeed it was a pleasure to articulate in public how fruitful reading your books has been for my own way of thinking. But more than that, you will understand better why I consider this occasion a particular honour when I tell you that I am the son of a German Nazi who did not renounce his convictions even after 1945 and who retained them for the most part right up to his death in the late 1950s. I am a member of the postwar generation, but my whole development has been profoundly influenced by the fact that I felt deeply irritated and repelled by his entire world-view from early on in my life.
>
> Today, as a social theorist and a specialist on North America, I am speaking on British soil to you, a Jewish, Polish colleague, and I have even found the courage to point out to you some of the merits of the intellectual and cultural traditions of America. There is a deep irony of fate in this; there is also some reason for historical optimism, and, for me personally, a feeling of gratitude and honour.

Chapter 10   War and the Risk Society

1 Ulrich Beck, *Risk Society. Towards a New Modernity* (1986), London, 1992. See Hans Joas, 'Das Risiko der Gegenwartsdiagnose', in *Soziologische Revue* 11 (1988), pp. 1–6. I have made use of some passages in this review for the present article, as well as of my criticism of Beck in Hans Joas, 'Modernität

und Krieg', in Max Miller und Hans-Georg Soeffner (eds), *Modernität und Barbarei. Soziologische Zeitdiagnose am Ende des 20. Jahrhunderts*, Frankfurt am Main, 1996, pp. 344–53.

2   This can be seen from the overwhelmingly positive reception of Beck's book in the sociology of Anthony Giddens.

3   Ulrich Beck, *The Reinvention of Politics. Rethinking Modernity in the Global Social Order* (1993), Cambridge, 1997.

4   Ibid., p. 3.

5   Ulrich Beck, *What is Globalization?* (1997), Cambridge, 2000.

6   For an attempt at a rhetorical interpretation, see also Jeffrey Alexander and Philip Smith, 'Social Science and Salvation. Risk Society as Mythical Discourse', in *Zeitschrift für Soziologie* 25 (1996), pp. 251–62.

7   Beck, *Risk Society*, p. 108.

8   Michael Walzer, 'Liberalism and the Art of Separation', in *Political Theory* 12 (1984), pp. 315–30; Hans Joas, 'The Democratization of Differentiation. On the Creativity of Collective Action', in Jeffrey Alexander and Piotr Sztompka (eds), *Rethinking Progress*, Boston, 1990, pp. 181–201, and *The Creativity of Action* (1992), Chicago, 1996, pp. 223ff.

9   Johann Arnason, *Nation and Modernity*, Reykjavik Lectures. Aarhus, 1996, pp. 29ff. Similarly, see Bernard Yack, *The Fetishism of Modernities. Epochal Self-Consciousness in Contemporary Social and Political Thought*, Notre Dame, Ind., 1997, pp. 137ff.

10 See especially chapter 2 in this volume, pp. 43ff. There is also a (fierce) critique of the theory of reflexive modernity in Jeffrey Alexander, 'Critical Reflections on "Reflexive Modernization"', in *Theory, Culture and Society* (1996), pp. 133–8.

11 Beck, *The Reinvention of Politics*, p. 78. Beck's ideas about 'militarily restricted democracy' are to be found first in Ulrich Beck, 'Der feindlose Staat. Militär und Demokratie nach dem Kalten Krieg', in *Die Zeit*, 23.10.1992, pp. 65f.

12 Beck, *The Reinvention of Politics*, p. 77.

13 Ibid., p. 77.

14 On these observations, see the following contributions from the German debates on universal military service: Manfred Messerschmidt, 'Der Staatsbürger muß sich über die Uniform legitimieren. Die allgemeine Wehrpflicht wirkte bis 1945 vor allem als Katalysator gesellschaftlicher Militarisierung', in *Frankfurter Rundschau*, 31.8.1993, p. 16; Wolfram Wette, 'Kein Kind der Demokratie', in *Die Zeit*, 19.2.1993, p. 5; Martin Kutz, 'Nachschub für das Menschenschlachthaus. Wehrpflicht und Dienstpflicht im industrialisierten Krieg', *Führungsakademie der Bundeswehr, Fachgruppe Sozialwissenschaften. Beiträge zur Lehre und Forschung* 3/93. An illuminating and sophisticated view of the American situation is to be found in Manfred Berg, 'War and Voting Rights in American History', in David K. Adams and Cornelis A. van Minnen (eds), *Reflections on American Exceptionalism*, Keele, 1994, pp. 188–225.

15 Ulrich Beck, 'Wie aus Nachbarn Juden werden. Zur politischen Konstruktion des Fremden in der reflexiven Moderne', in Miller and Soeffner (eds), *Modernität und Barbarei*, pp. 318–43.

16 For example, Ulrich Beck, 'Der militärische Pazifismus. Über den postna-
    tionalen Krieg', in *Süddeutsche Zeitung*, 19.4.1999, pp. 15–17.
17 In particular Wolfgang R. Vogt; see, for example, 'Militär und Risiko-
    gesellschaft. Tendenzen "struktureller Unvereinbarkeit" zwischen be-
    waffneter Friedenssicherung und industriellem Zivilisationsprozeß', in
    Sicherheit und Frieden 4 (1989), pp. 198–205.
18 Ibid., p. 199.
19 Ibid.
20 Ibid., p. 200.
21 See my account of Comte and Spencer in chapter 7 in this volume, pp.
    132ff.

Chapter 11   War the Teacher?

The present contribution appeared first in *Kölner Zeitschrift für Soziologie und
Sozialpsychologie* 44 (1992), pp. 538–43.

1   Karl Otto Hondrich, *Lehrmeister Krieg*, Reinbek, 1992.
2   Ibid., p. 7.
3   Ibid., p. 30.
4   Ibid., p. 31.
5   Ibid., p. 8.
6   Ibid.
7   Ibid., p. 9.
8   Ibid.
9   Ibid., p. 152.
10 Ibid., pp. 41f.
11 Ibid., p. 42.
12 Ibid., p. 65.
13 Ibid., p. 39.
14 Ibid., p. 33.
15 Ibid., p. 43.
16 Ibid., p. 74.
17 Ibid., p. 106.
18 Ibid., pp. 88f.
19 Ibid., p. 64.
20 Ibid., p. 90.
21 Ibid., p. 117.
22 Ibid., p. 58.
23 Ibid., pp. 93ff.

Chapter 12   Action Theory and the Dynamics of Violence

This chapter appeared first in Wolfgang Vogt (ed.), *Gewalt und Konflikt-
bearbeitung*, Baden-Baden, 1997, pp. 67–75.

1   Helmut Willems, 'Fremdenfeindliche Gewalt. Entwicklung, Strukturen,
    Interaktionsprozesse', in *Gruppendynamik* 23 (1992), pp. 433–48; for an

English-language publication, see Helmut Willems, 'Development, Patterns and Causes of Violence against Foreigners in Germany', in Thorbjörn Björgo (ed.), *Terrorism and Political Violence* 7 (1985), pp. 162–81.

2   Hans Joas, *The Creativity of Action* (1992), Cambridge, 1996.

3   A detailed account is to be found in ibid., pp. 148–95.

4   Ibid., pp. 290–306.

5   Neil Smelser, *Theory of Collective Behaviour*, London, 1962.

6   Ralph H. Turner and Lewis M. Killian, *Collective Behavior*, Englewood Cliffs, NJ, 1987.

7   Ralph H. Turner, 'Race Riots Past and Present. A Cultural-Collective Behavior Approach', in *Symbolic Interaction* 17 (1994), pp. 309–24.

8   For example, Willems, 'Fremdenfeindliche Gewalt'.

9   Friedhelm Neidhardt, 'Über Zufall, Eigendynamik und Institutionalisierbarkeit absurder Prozesse. Notizen am Beispiel einer terroristischen Gruppe', in Heine von Alemann and Hans-Peter Thurn (eds), *Soziologie in weltbürgerlicher Absicht. Festschrift für René König zum 75. Geburtstag*, Opladen, 1981, pp. 243–57; Fritz Sack, 'Staat, Gesellschaft und politische Gewalt. Zur "Pathologie" politischer Konflikte', in Sack and Heinz Steinert (eds), *Protest und Reaktion. Analysen zum Terrorismus*, vol. 4/2, Opladen, 1984, pp. 17–386; Susanne Karstedt-Henke, 'Theorien zur Erklärung terroristischer Bewegungen', in Erhard Blankenburg (ed.), *Politik der inneren Sicherheit*, Frankfurt am Main, 1980, pp. 169–237.

10   Elias Canetti, *Crowds and Power*, London, 1962; Wolfgang Sofsky, 'Die Meute. Zur Anthropologie der Menschenjagd', in *Neue Rundschau* 4 (1994), pp. 9–21.

11   Karl-Dieter Opp, 'Spontaneous Revolutions. The Case of East Germany in 1989', in Heinz D. Kurz (ed.), *United Germany and the New Europe*, Cheltenham, 1983, pp. 11–30.

12   Gary Marx, 'Issueless Riots', in *The Annals of the American Academy of Political and Social Sciences* 391 (1970), pp. 21–33.

13   Willems, 'Fremdenfeindliche Gewalt', p. 444.

14   Peter Waldmann, 'Gewaltsamer Separatismus. Am Beispiel der Basken, Franko-Kanadier und Nordiren', in *Kölner Zeitschrift für Soziologie und Sozialpsychologie* 37 (1985), pp. 203–29.

15   A modified version of that given by Turner, 'Race Riots Past and Present'.

16   See on this point chapter 6, pp. 111ff. There is an interesting approach to the analysis of the dynamic structure of pogroms in Werner Bergmann, 'Pogrom: eine spezifische Form kollektiver Gewalt', in *Kölner Zeitschrift für Soziologie und Sozialpsychologie* 50 (1998), pp. 644–65.

17   There are growing signs that important strands of more recent German research on violence are actually moving in this direction. See Trutz von Trotha, 'Zur Soziologie der Gewalt' and Birgitta Nedelmann, 'Gewaltsoziologie am Scheideweg', both of which appear in Trutz von Trotha (ed.), *Soziologie der Gewalt* (*Kölner Zeitschrift für Soziologie und Sozialpsychologie*, Special Issue 37), 1997, pp. 9–56 and 59–85.

Bibliography

Alexander, Jeffrey, 'Modern, Anti, Post and Neo: How Intellectuals Have Coded, Narrated, and Explained the "New World of Our Time"', in Alexander, *Fin de Siècle Social Theory*, London, 1995, pp. 6–64.

—— 'Critical Reflections on "Reflexive Modernization"', in *Theory, Culture and Society* 13 (1996), pp. 133–8.

—— and Maria Pia Lara, 'The Struggle for Recognition', in *New Left Review* 220 (1996), pp. 126–36.

—— and Philip Smith, 'Social Science and Salvation. Risk Society as Mythical Discourse', in *Zeitschrift für Soziologie* 25 (1996), pp. 251–62.

—— and Piotr Sztompka (eds), *Rethinking Progress*, Boston, 1990.

Archer, Dane and Rosemary Gartner, 'Violent Acts and Violent Times. The Effect of Wars on Postwar Homicide Rates', in Archer and Gartner, *Violence and Crime in a Cross-National Perspective*, New Haven, Conn., 1984, pp. 63–97.

Arendt, Hannah, *Eichmann in Jerusalem. A Report on the Banality of Evil*, London, 1963.

—— *The Origins of Totalitarianism*, London, 1967.

Arnason, Johann, *Nation and Modernity*, Reykjavik Lectures, Aarhus, 1996.

Aron, Raymond, *Peace and War* (1962), London, 1966.

—— 'Max Weber und die Machtpolitik', in Otto Stammer (ed.), *Max Weber und die Soziologie heute*, Tübingen, 1965, pp. 103–20.

—— 'War and Industrial Society', in Leon Bramson and George W. Goethals (eds), *War: Studies from Psychology, Sociology and Anthropology*, New York, 1968, pp. 359–402.

Ashworth, Clive and Christopher Dandeker, 'Warfare, Social Theory and West European Development', in *Sociological Review* 35 (1987), pp. 1–18.

Augstein, Rudolf, *Historikerstreit. Die Dokumentation der Kontroverse um die Einzigartigkeit der nationalsozialistischen Judenvernichtung*, Munich, 1987.

Baier, Horst, *Vom bewaffneten zum ewigen Frieden? Die Zähmung der Gewalt als Thema der Sozialphilosophie und Soziologie*, Konstanz, 1985.

Barber, William J., 'British and American Economists and Attempts to Comprehend the Nature of War, 1910–20', in *Economics and National Security – A History of Their Interaction*, Annual Supplement to the *History of Political Economy* 23 (1991), pp. 61–86.

Baskir, Lawrence M. and William A. Strauss, *Chance and Circumstance. The Draft, the War and the Vietnam Generation*, New York, 1978.

Bauman, Zygmunt, *Modernity and the Holocaust*, Cambridge, 1989.

—— 'Gewalt – modern und postmodern', in Max Miller and Hans-Georg Soeffner (eds), *Modernität und Barbarei. Soziologische Zeitdiagnose am Ende des 20. Jahrhunderts*, Frankfurt am Main, 1996, pp. 36–67.

Beck, Ulrich, *Risk Society. Towards a New Modernity* (1986), London, 1992.

—— 'Der Konflikt der zwei Modernen', in Wolfgang Zapf (ed.), *Die Modernisierung moderner Gesellschaften. Verhandlungen des 25. Deutschen Soziologentags* (1990), Frankfurt am Main, 1991, pp. 40–53.

—— 'Der feindlose Staat, Militär und Demokratie nach dem Kalten Krieg', in *Die Zeit*, 23.10.1992, pp. 65f.

—— *The Reinvention of Politics. Rethinking Modernity in the Global Social Order* (1993), Cambridge, 1997.

—— 'Erwiderungen', in *Mittelweg* 36, no. 3 (1994), pp. 37–42.

—— 'Wie aus Nachbarn Juden werden. Zur politischen Konstruktion des Fremden in der reflexiven Moderne', in Max Miller and Hans-Georg Soeffner (eds), *Modernität und Barbarei. Soziologische Zeitdiagnose am Ende des 20. Jahrhunderts*, Frankfurt am Main, 1996, pp. 318–43.

—— *What is Globalization?* (1997), Cambridge, 2000.

—— 'Der militärische Pazifismus. Über den postnationalen Krieg', in *Süddeutsche Zeitung*, 19.4.1999, pp. 15–17.

Bellah, Robert, Richard Madsen, William M. Sullivan, Ann Swidler and Steven M. Tipton, *Habits of the Heart. Individualism and Commitment in American Life*, Berkeley, 1985.

Bendix, Reinhard, 'Tradition and Modernity Reconsidered', in *Comparative Studies in Society and History* 9 (1966/7), pp. 292–346.

—— 'Modernisierung in internationaler Perspektive', in Wolfgang Zapf (ed.), *Theorien des sozialen Wandels*, Cologne, 1970, pp. 505–12.

—— *Kings or People. Power and the Mandate to Rule*, 2 vols, Berkeley, 1978.

Berg, Manfred, 'War and Voting Rights in American History', in David K. Adams and Cornelis A. van Minnen (eds), *Reflections on American Exceptionalism*, Keele, 1994, pp. 188–225.

Bergmann, Werner, 'Pogrome: eine spezifische Form kollektiver Gewalt', in *Kölner Zeitschrift für Soziologie und Sozialpsychologie* 50 (1998), pp. 644–55.

Bergson, Henri, *La signification de la guerre*, Paris, 1915.

Bernstein, Richard, *The New Constellation. The Ethical-Political Horizons of Modernity/Postmodernity*, Cambridge, Mass., 1993.

Beyme, Klaus von, 'Selbstgleichschaltung. Warum es in der DDR keine Politologie gegeben hat', in Bernd Giesen and Claus Leggewie (eds), *Experiment Vereinigung. Ein sozialer Großversuch*, Berlin, 1991, pp. 123–32.

Black, Cyril E., *The Dynamics of Modernization*, New York, 1966.

Bogner, Artur, 'Die Theorie des Zivilisationsprozesses als Modernisierungs-theorie', in Helmuth Kuzmics and Ingo Mörth (eds), *Der unendliche Prozeß der Zivilisation. Zur Kultursoziologie der Moderne nach Norbert Elias*, Frankfurt am Main, 1991, pp. 33–58.

Boulanger, Ghislaine, 'Violence and Vietnam Veterans', in Boulanger and Charles Kadushin (eds), *The Vietnam Veteran Redefined. Fact and Fiction*, Hillsdale, NJ, 1986, pp. 79–90.

Boutroux, Émile, *L'Allemagne et la guerre*, Paris, 1915.

Breuilly, John, 'The Nation-State and Violence: A critique of Giddens', in Jon Clark, Celia Modgil and Sohan Modgil (eds), *Anthony Giddens. Consensus and Controversy*, London, 1990, pp. 271–88.

Brunner, Otto, *Land und Herrschaft. Grundfragen der territorialen Verfassungs-geschichte Österreichs* (1939), Vienna, 1990.

Bude, Heinz, 'Gewalt durch Verfahren. Zygmunt Bauman über die Modernität des Bösen', in *Frankfurter Allgemeine Zeitung*, 8.12.1992, p. 17.

——'Das Ende einer tragischen Gesellschaft', in Hans Joas and Martin Kohli (eds), *Der Zusammenbruch der DDR. Soziologische Analysen*, Frankfurt am Main, 1993, pp. 267–81.

——and Martin Kohli, 'Die Normalisierung der Kritik', in Bude and Kohli, *Radikalisierte Aufklärung. Studentenbewegung und Soziologie in Berlin 1965 bis 1970*, Weinheim, 1989, pp. 17–42.

Burger, John S. and Mary Jo Deegan, 'G.H. Mead on Internationalism, Demo-cracy and War', in *Wisconsin Sociologist* 18 (1981), pp. 72–83.

Büsch, Otto and Michael Erbe (eds), *Otto Hintze und die moderne Geschichtswis-senschaft*, Berlin, 1983.

Butterfield, Herbert, *The Whig Interpretation of History*, London, 1931.

Caillois, Roger, *Man and the Sacred* (1939), Urbana, Ill., 2001.

——*Bellone ou la pente de la guerre*, Brussels, 1963.

Canetti, Elias, *Crowds and Power*, London, 1962.

Castoriadis, Cornelius, *The Imaginary Institution of Society*, Cambridge, 1987.

Chapman, Guy, *A Passionate Prodigality*, London, 1965.

Collini, Stefan, *Liberalism and Sociology. L.T. Hobhouse and Political Argument in England 1880–1914*, Cambridge, 1979.

Collins, Randall, 'The Future Decline of the Russian Empire', in Collins, *Weberian Sociological Theory*, Cambridge, 1986, pp. 186–209.

——'Imperialism and Legitimacy. Weber's Theory of Politics', in Collins, *Weberian Sociological Theory*, Cambridge, 1986, pp. 145–66.

——'The Geopolitical Basis of Revolution. The Prediction of the Soviet Collapse', in Collins, *Macrohistory. Essays in Sociology of the Long Run*, Stanford, 1999, pp. 37–68.

——'German-Bashing and the Theory of Democratic Modernization', in Collins, *Macrohistory. Essays in Sociology of the Long Run*, Stanford, 1999, pp. 152–76.

Corradini, Enrico, 'La guerra', in *Il Regno* 1, no. 4 (1904), pp. 2–4; reprinted in Delia Castelnuovo Frigessi (ed.), *La cultura italiana del '900 attraverso le reviste* (*'Leonardo', 'Hermes', 'Il Regno'*), vol. 2, Turin, 1960, pp. 482–5.

Croce, Benedetto, *Opera omnia*, series 4, vol. III, *L'Italia da 1941 al 1918. Pagine sulla guerra*, Naples, 1919; Bern, 1928.

Dahrendorf, Ralf, *Society and Democracy in Germany* (1965), London, 1968.

—— 'Widersprüche der Modernität', in Max Miller and Hans-Georg Soeffner (eds), *Modernität und Barbarei. Soziologische Zeitdiagnose am Ende des 20. Jahrhunderts*, Frankfurt am Main, 1996, pp. 194–204.

Dandeker, Christopher, 'The Nation-State and the Modern World System', in Jon Clark, Celia Modgil and Sohan Modgil (eds), *Anthony Giddens. Consensus and Controversy*, London, 1990, pp. 257–69.

Dewey, John, *German Philosophy and Politics*, New York, 1915.

—— 'The Tragedy of the German Soul' (1916), in Dewey, *Middle Works*, vol. 10, Carbondale, Ill., 1980, pp. 305–9.

—— 'Progress', in Dewey, *Character and Events*, vol. 2, New York, 1929, pp. 820–30.

Dienstfrey, Stephen J., 'Women Veterans' Exposure to Combat', in *Armed Forces and Society* 14 (1988), pp. 549–58.

Dietze, Anita and Walter Dietze (eds), *Ewiger Friede? Dokumente einer deutschen Diskussion um 1800*, Leipzig/Weimar, 1989.

Dorfman, Joseph, *Thorstein Veblen and His America*, New York, 1961.

Downing, Brian M., 'Constitutionalism, Warfare and Political Change in Early Modern Europe', in *Theory and Society* 17 (1988), pp. 7–56.

—— *The Military Revolution and Political Change. Origins of Democracy and Autocracy in Early Modern Europe*, Princeton, 1992.

Doyle, Michael W., *Ways of War and Peace. Realism, Liberalism, and Socialism*, New York, 1997.

Duhnke, Horst, *Die KPD von 1933 bis 1945*, Cologne, 1972.

Durkheim, Émile, 'La sociologie selon Gumplowicz' (1885), in Durkheim, *Textes*, vol. 1, Paris, 1975, pp. 344–54.

—— *The Division of Labor in Society* (1893), New York, 1984.

—— *'Germany above all'. The German Mentality and the War*, Paris, 1915.

—— *Who Wanted War? The Origin of the War According to Diplomatic Documents*, Paris, 1915.

—— *Professional Ethics and Civic Morals* (1950), London, 1957.

—— *Textes*, 3 vols, Paris, 1975.

Egendorf, Arthur, *Healing from the War. Trauma and Transformation after Vietnam*, Boston, 1986.

Eisenstadt, Shmuel, 'Barbarism and Modernity', in *Society* 33 (1996), pp. 31–9.

Eksteins, Modris, *Rites of Spring. The Great War and the Birth of the Modern Age*, New York, 1990.

Elias, Norbert, *The Civilizing Process* (1939), Oxford, 1978.

Engler, Wolfgang, *Die ungewollte Moderne. Ost–West-Passagen*, Frankfurt am Main, 1995.

Enzensberger, Hans Magnus, *Civil War* (1993), London, 1994.

Etzioni, Amitai, *The Active Society*, New York, 1968.

Fanon, Frantz, *The Wretched of the Earth* (1961), London, 1965.

Faulenbach, Bernd, *Ideologie des deutschen Weges. Die deutsche Geschichte in der Historiographie zwischen Kaiserreich und Nationalsozialismus*, Munich, 1980.

Frey-Wouters, Ellen and Robert S. Laufer, *Legacy of a War. The American Soldier in Vietnam*, Armonk, NY, 1986.

Ganßmann, Heiner, 'Die nichtbeabsichtigten Folgen einer Wirtschaftsplanung. DDR-Zusammenbruch, Planungsparadox und Demokratie', in Hans Joas and Martin Kohli (eds), *Der Zusammenbruch der DDR. Soziologische Analysen*, Frankfurt am Main, 1993, pp. 172–93.

Gephart, Werner, 'Die französische Soziologie und der Erste Weltkrieg. Spannungen in Émile Durkheims Deutung des Großen Krieges', in Wolfgang Mommsen (ed.), *Kultur und Krieg. Die Rolle der Intellektuellen, Künstler und Schriftsteller im Ersten Weltkrieg*, Munich, 1996, pp. 49–63.

Gerhard, Dietrich, 'Otto Hintze: His Work and His Significance in Historiography', in *Central European History* 3 (1970), pp. 17–48; reprinted in Gerhard, *Gesammelte Aufsätze*, Göttingen, 1977, pp. 268–95.

Giddens, Anthony, *The Nation-State and Violence*, Cambridge, 1985.

——*The Constitution of Society*, Cambridge, 1989.

Giddings, Franklin, *The Responsible State. A Re-examination of Fundamental Political Doctrines in the Light of the War and the Menace of Anarchism*, Boston, 1918.

Gilbert, Felix, 'Introduction', in *The Historical Essays of Otto Hintze*, ed. Gilbert, New York, 1975, pp. 3–30.

Glaeßner, Gert-Joachim, 'Am Ende des Staatssozialismus – Zu den Ursachen des Umbruchs in der DDR', in Hans Joas and Martin Kohli (eds), *Der Zusammenbruch der DDR. Soziologische Analysen*, Frankfurt am Main, 1993, pp. 70–92.

Goldhagen, Daniel Jonah, *Hitler's Willing Executioners. Ordinary Germans and the Holocaust*, New York, 1996.

Görres, Joseph, 'Der allgemeine Frieden, ein Ideal' (1798), in Zwi Batscha and Richard Saage (eds), *Friedensutopien*, Frankfurt am Main, 1979, pp. 111–76.

Gransow, Bettina, 'Chinesische Modernisierung und kultureller Eigensinn', in *Zeitschrift für Soziologie* 24 (1993), pp. 183–95.

Großheim, Michael, 'Politischer Existentialismus', in Günter Meuter and Henrique Ricardo Otten (eds), *Der Aufstand gegen die Bürger. Antibürgerliches Denken im 20. Jahrhundert*, Würzburg, 1999, pp. 127–63.

Gruber, Carol, *Mars and Minerva. World War I and the Use of the Higher Learning in America*, Baton Rouge, La, 1975.

Gumplowicz, Ludwig, *Der Rassenkampf* (1883), Innsbruck, 1926.

——*Outlines of Sociology* (1885), New Brunswick, NJ, 1980.

——*Die soziologische Staatsidee* (1892), Innsbruck, 1902.

Habermas, Jürgen, *Die nachholende Revolution*, Frankfurt am Main, 1990.

——'Kant's Idea of Perpetual Peace: At Two Hundred Years' Historical Remove', in Habermas, *The Inclusion of the Other. Studies in Political Theory* (1996), Cambridge, 1998, pp. 165–201.

——'Bestialität und Humanität. Ein Krieg an der Grenze zwischen Recht und Moral', in *Die Zeit*, 29.4.1999, pp. 1 and 6f.

Hall, John, *Powers and Liberties. The Causes and Consequences of the Rise of the West*, London, 1985/Berkeley, 1986.

——'War and the Rise of the West', in Colin Creighton and Martin Shaw (eds), *The Sociology of War and Peace*, London, 1987, pp. 37–53.

Hanna, Martha, *The Mobilization of Intellect. French Scholars and Writers during the Great War*, Cambridge, Mass., 1996.

Haselbach, Dieter, 'Die Staatstheorie von L. Gumplowicz und ihre Weiterentwicklung bei Franz Oppenheimer und Alexander Rüstow', in *Österreichische Zeitschrift für Soziologie* 15 (1990), pp. 84–99.

Havel, Václav, 'Words on Words', in *The New York Review of Books*, 18 January 1990, pp. 5–8.

Hegedus, Zsuzsa, 'Social Movements and Social Change in Self-Creative Society', in *International Sociology* 4 (1989), pp. 19–34.

Hendin, Herbert and Ann Pollinger Haas, *Wounds of the War. The Psychological Aftermath of Combat in Vietnam*, New York, 1984.

Hintze, Otto, Review of Ludwig Gumplowicz, *Soziologie und Politik* and *Die soziologische Staatsidee*, in *Schmollers Jahrbuch* 21 (1897), pp. 715–16.

—— 'Roschers politische Entwicklungstheorie' (1897), in Hintze, *Soziologie und Geschichte. Gesammelte Abhandlungen*, vol. 2, Göttingen, 1964 (2nd edn), pp. 3–45.

—— 'Military Organization and the Organization of the State' (1906), in *The Historical Essays of Otto Hintze*, ed. Felix Gilbert, New York, 1975, pp. 178–215.

—— Review of Oswald Spengler, *Der Staat* etc., in *Zeitschrift für die gesamte Staatswissenschaft* 79 (1925), pp. 541–7.

—— 'Max Webers Soziologie' (1926), in Hintze, *Soziologie und Geschichte. Gesammelte Abhandlungen*, vol. 2, Göttingen, 1964 (2nd edn), pp. 3–45.

—— Review of Carl Schmitt, *Verfassungslehre* (Munich, 1928), in *Historische Zeitschrift* 139 (1929), pp. 562–8.

—— 'Soziologische und geschichtliche Staatsauffassung. Zu Franz Oppenheimers System der Soziologie' (1929), in Hintze, *Soziologie und Geschichte. Gesammelte Abhandlungen*, vol. 2, Göttingen, 1964 (2nd edn), pp. 239–305.

—— 'Probleme einer europäischen Sozial- und Wirtschaftsgeschichte' (1930), in Hintze, *Soziologie und Geschichte. Gesammelte Abhandlungen*, vol. 2, Göttingen, 1964 (2nd edn), pp. 306–12.

—— *The Historical Essays of Otto Hintze*, ed. Felix Gilbert, New York, 1975.

Hirsch, Helga, 'Der Holocaust ist nicht einmalig. Gespräch mit dem polnischen Soziologen Zygmunt Bauman', in *Die Zeit*, 23.4.1993, p. 68.

Hirschman, Albert, *The Passions and the Interests. Political Arguments for Capitalism before Its Triumph*, Princeton, 1977.

Hollier, Denis (ed.), *Le Collège de Sociologie*, Paris, 1979.

Hondrich, Karl Otto, 'Krieg – und unser progressiver Theorie-Alltag', in *Kölner Zeitschrift für Soziologie und Sozialpsychologie* 44 (1992), pp. 544–8.

—— *Lehrmeister Krieg*, Reinbek, 1992.

Honneth, Axel, *The Struggle for Recognition. The Moral Grammar of Social Conflicts* (1992), Cambridge, 1996.

—— 'Universalismus als politische Falle?', in *Merkur* 546/7 (1994), pp. 867–83.

Horkheimer, Max and Theodor W. Adorno, *Dialectic of Enlightenment* (1944), New York, 1972.

Howard, Michael, *War and the Liberal Conscience*, New Brunswick, NJ, 1978.

Hughes, H. Stuart, *Consciousness and Society. The Reorientation of European Social Thought 1890–1930*, New York, 1977.

Hurwitz, Harold, *Demokratie und Antikommunismus in Berlin nach 1945*, 5 vols, Cologne, 1983 (vol. 1), 1984 (vols 2 and 3), 1990 (vol. 4 in two parts), 1997 (vol. 5).
Vol. 1: *Die politische Kultur der Bevölkerung und der Neubeginn konservativer Politik.*
Vol. 2: *Autoritäre Tradierung und Demokratiepotential in der sozialdemokratischen Arbeiterbewegung* (with Klaus Sühl).
Vol. 3: *Die Eintracht der Siegermächte und die Orientierungsnot der Deutschen.*
Vol. 4: *Die Anfänge des Widerstandes*, Part 1: *Führungsanspruch und Isolation der Sozialdemokraten*, Part 2: *Zwischen Selbsttäuschung und Zivilcourage: Der Fusionskampf.*
Vol. 5: *Die Stalinisierung der SED. Zum Verlust von Freiräumen und sozialdemokratischer Identität in den Vorständen 1946–1949.*
——'Mein Leben in Berlin', in *Leviathan* 27 (1999), pp. 264–79.
Iggers, Georg G., *The German Conception of History. The National Tradition of Historical Thought from Herder to the Present*, Middletown, Conn., 1968.
Ionin, Leonid and Alla Cernych, 'Krieg und Frieden in der frühen russischen Soziologie', in Hans Joas and Helmut Steiner (eds), *Machtpolitischer Realismus und pazifistische Utopie*, Frankfurt am Main, 1998, pp. 117–52.
James, William, *The Varieties of Religious Experience*, New York, 1902.
——'The Moral Equivalent of War', in James, *Memories and Studies*, New York, 1911, pp. 265–96.
Jandy, C. Edward, *Charles Horton Cooley. His Life and His Social Theory*, New York, 1942.
Janowitz, Morris, 'Introduction', in William Isaac Thomas, *On Social Organization and Social Personality*, Chicago, 1966, pp. vii–lviii.
Jerusalem, Wilhelm, *Der Krieg im Lichte der Gesellschaftslehre*, Stuttgart, 1915.
Joas, Hans, *George Herbert Mead. A Contemporary Re-examination of His Thought* (1980), Cambridge, 1985; Cambridge, Mass., 1997 (2nd edn).
——'Die politischen Ideen des amerikanischen Pragmatismus', in Iring Fetscher and Herfried Münkler (eds), *Pipers Handbuch der politischen Ideen*, vol. 5, Munich, 1987, pp. 611–20.
——'Symbolic Interactionism', in Jonathan Turner and Anthony Giddens (eds), *Social Theory Today*, Cambridge, 1987, pp. 82–115, and also in Joas, *Pragmatism and Social Theory*, Chicago, 1993, pp. 14–51.
——Review of Reiner Steinweg, *Kriegsursachen*, in *Soziologische Revue* 11 (1988), pp. 450–2.
——'Das Risiko der Gegenwartsdiagnose', in *Soziologische Revue* 11 (1988), pp. 1–6.
——'The Democratization of Differentiation. On the Creativity of Collective Action', in Jeffrey Alexander and Piotr Sztompka (eds), *Rethinking Progress*, Boston, 1990, pp. 182–201.
——*The Creativity of Action* (1992), Cambridge, 1996.
——*Pragmatism and Social Theory* (1992), Chicago, 1993.
——'Decline of Community? Comparative Observations on Germany and the United States' (1995), in Josef Janning, Charles A. Kupchan and Dirk

Rumberg (eds), *Civic Engagement in the Atlantic Community*, Gütersloh, 1999, pp. 55–66.

—— 'Modernität und Krieg', in Max Miller and Hans-Georg Soeffner (eds), *Modernität und Barbarei. Soziologische Zeitdiagnose am Ende des 20. Jahrhunderts*, Frankfurt am Main, 1996, pp. 344–53.

—— *The Genesis of Values* (1997), Cambridge, 2000.

—— 'Combining Value Pluralism with Moral Universalism. Isaiah Berlin and Beyond', in *The Responsive Community* 9 (1999), pp. 17–29.

—— 'For Fear of New Horrors. A Reply to E. Tiryakian and I. Roxborough', in *International Sociology* 14 (1999), pp. 501–3.

—— 'A Postdisciplinary History of Disciplines', in *European Journal of Social Theory* 2 (1999), pp. 109–22.

—— 'Die Sakralität der Person und die Politik der Würde (Über Avishai Margalit)', in *Deutsche Zeitschrift für Philosophie* 47 (1999), pp. 325–33.

—— 'Die Soziologie und das Heilige. Schlüsseltexte der Religionssoziologie', in *Merkur* 53, no. 605/6 (1999), pp. 990–8.

—— 'Wann darf der Westen eingreifen?', in *die tageszeitung (taz)*, 13.7.1999, p. 12.

—— and Wolfgang Knöbl, 'Gewalt in den USA. Deutsche und amerikanische Perspektiven', in Joas and Knöbl (eds), *Gewalt in den USA*, Frankfurt am Main, 1994, pp. 7–18.

—— and Martin Kohli (eds), *Der Zusammenbruch der DDR. Soziologische Analysen*, Frankfurt am Main, 1993.

—— and Helmut Steiner (eds), *Machtpolitischer Realismus und pazifistische Utopie. Krieg und Frieden in der Geschichte der Sozialwissenschaften*, Frankfurt am Main, 1989.

Johnson, James Turner, *The Quest for Peace. Three Moral Traditions in Western Cultural History*, Princeton, 1987.

Jünger, Ernst, *Der Kampf als inneres Erlebnis*, Berlin, 1925.

Karstedt-Henke, Susanne, 'Theorien zur Erklärung terroristischer Bewegungen', in Erhard Blankenburg (ed.), *Politik der inneren Sicherheit*, Frankfurt am Main, 1980, pp. 169–237.

Käsler, Dirk, *Die frühe deutsche Soziologie 1909–1934 und ihre Entstehungsmilieus. Eine wissenschaftssoziologische Untersuchung*, Opladen, 1984.

Keegan, John, *The Face of Battle*, Harmondsworth, 1978.

Klein, Dieter, *Chancen für einen friedensfähigen Kapitalismus*, Berlin, 1988.

Knöbl, Wolfgang, 'Nationalstaat und Gesellschaftstheorie', in *Zeitschrift für Soziologie* 22 (1993), pp. 221–35.

—— 'Kommentar zu Randall Collins' "German-Bashing and the Theory of Democratic Modernization"', in *Zeitschrift für Soziologie* 24 (1995), pp. 465–8.

—— *Polizei und Herrschaft im Modernisierungsprozeß. Staatsbildung und 'innere Sicherheit' in Preußen, England und Amerika 1700–1914*, Frankfurt am Main, 1998.

—— *Spielräume der Modernisierung. Das Ende der Eindeutigkeit*, Weilerswist, 2001.

Koch, Hansjoachim, *Der Sozialdarwinismus. Seine Genese und sein Einfluß auf das imperialistische Denken*, Munich, 1973.

Kocka, Jürgen, 'Otto Hintze', in Hans-Ulrich Wehler (ed.), *Deutsche Historiker*, vol. 3, Göttingen, 1973, pp. 41–64.

—— 'Otto Hintze, Max Weber und das Problem der Bürokratie', in Otto Büsch and Michael Erbe (eds), *Otto Hintze und die moderne Geschichtswissenschaft*, Berlin, 1983, pp. 150–88.

—— 'German History before Hitler. The Debate about the German *Sonderweg*', *Journal of Contemporary History* 23 (1988), pp. 3–16.

—— 'Revolution und Nation 1989. Zur historischen Einordnung der gegenwärtigen Ereignisse', in *Tel Aviver Jahrbuch für deutsche Geschichte* 19 (1990), pp. 471–99.

—— 'Asymmetrical Historical Comparison. The Case of the German "*Sonderweg*"', in *History and Theory* 38 (1999), pp. 40–50.

Köhler, Ernst, 'Fragen an Zygmunt Bauman', in *Kommune* 8 (1994), pp. 54–8.

Kohli, Martin, 'Institutionalisierung und Individualisierung der Erwerbs-biographie. Aktuelle Veränderungstendenzen und ihre Folgen', in Ditmar Brock, Hans Rudolf Leu, Christine Preiss and Hans-Rolf Vetter (eds), *Subjektivität im technischen und sozialen Wandel*, Munich, 1989, pp. 249–78.

Krakau, Knud, *Missionsbewußtsein und Völkerrechtsdoktrin in den Vereinigten Staaten von Amerika*, Frankfurt am Main/Berlin, 1967.

—— 'American Foreign Relations: A National Style?', in *Diplomatic History* 8 (1984), pp. 253–72.

Krippendorff, Ekkehart, *Staat und Krieg. Die historische Logik politischer Unvernunft*, Frankfurt am Main, 1985.

Kristof, Nicholas D., 'The Real Chinese Threat', in *The New York Times Magazine*, 27.8.1995, pp. 50–2.

Krockow, Christian Graf von, *Die Entscheidung. Eine Untersuchung über Ernst Jünger, Carl Schmitt, Martin Heidegger* (1958), Frankfurt am Main, 1990.

Kuhn, Helmut, Review of C. Schmitt, *Der Begriff des Politischen*, in *Kant-Studien* 38 (1933), pp. 190–6.

Kurtz, Lester R., 'War and Peace on the Sociological Agenda', in Terence C. Halliday and Morris Janowitz (eds), *Sociology and Its Publics. The Forms and Fates of Disciplinary Organization*, Chicago, 1992, pp. 61–98.

—— (ed.), *Encyclopedia of Violence, Peace and Conflict*, 3 vols, San Diego, Calif., 1999.

Kutz, Martin, 'Nachschub für das Menschenschlachthaus. Wehrpflicht und Dienstpflicht im industrialisierten Krieg', in *Führungsakademie der Bundeswehr, Fachgruppe Sozialwissenschaften. Beiträge zur Lehre und Forschung* 3/93.

Lasch, Christopher, '*The New Republic* and the War: "An Unanalyzable Feeling"', in Lasch, *The New Radicalism in America (1889–1963)*, New York, 1965, pp. 181–224.

Laufer, Robert S., M.S. Gallops and Ellen Frey-Wouters, 'War Stress and Trauma. The Vietnam Veteran Experience', in *Journal of Health and Social Behavior* 25 (1984), pp. 65–85.

Lederer, Emil, 'Zur Soziologie des Weltkrieges', in *Archiv für Sozialwissenschaft und Sozialpolitik* 39 (1915), pp. 357–84; reprinted in Lederer, *Kapitalismus, Klassenstruktur und Probleme der Demokratie in Deutschland 1910–1940*, Göttingen, 1979, pp. 119–44.

Lenger, Friedrich, *Werner Sombart 1863–1941. Eine Biographie*, Munich, 1994.

—— 'Werner Sombart als Propagandist eines deutschen Krieges', in Wolfgang Mommsen (ed.), *Kultur und Krieg. Die Rolle der Intellektuellen, Künstler und Schriftsteller im Ersten Weltkrieg*, Munich, 1996, pp. 65–76.

Lepenies, Wolf, *Between Literature and Science. The Rise of Sociology* (1985), Cambridge, 1988.

Levine, Donald N., *Visions of the Sociological Tradition*, Chicago, 1995.

Liell, Christoph, 'Gewalt: diskursive Konstruktion und soziale Praxis', Soziologische Diplomarbeit, Freie Universität Berlin, 1997.

Lifton, Robert Jay, *Home from the War. Vietnam Veterans: Neither Victims Nor Executioners*, New York, 1973.

Loader, Colin and Rick Tilman, 'Thorstein Veblen's Analysis of German Intellectualism', in *American Journal of Economics and Sociology* 54 (1995), pp. 339–55.

Lötsch, Manfred, 'Der Sozialismus – eine Stände- oder eine Klassengesellschaft?', in Hans Joas and Martin Kohli (eds), *Der Zusammenbruch der DDR. Soziologische Analysen*, Frankfurt am Main, 1993, pp. 115–24.

Lübbe, Hermann, 'Die philosophischen Ideen von 1914', in Lübbe, *Politische Philosophie in Deutschland. Studien zu ihrer Geschichte*, Basel, 1963, pp. 171–235.

Maaz, Hans-Joachim, *Der Gefühlsstau. Ein Psychogramm der DDR*, Berlin, 1990.

Maier, Charles, S., *The Unmasterable Past. History, Holocaust and German National Identity*, Cambridge, Mass., 1988.

—— *Dissolution. The Crisis of Communism and the End of East Germany*, Princeton, 1999.

Mann, Michael, 'War and Social Theory. Into Battle with Classes, Nations and States', in Colin Creighton and Martin Shaw (eds), *The Sociology of War and Peace*, London, 1987, pp. 54–72.

—— *States, War and Capitalism*, Oxford, 1988.

—— *The Sources of Social Power*, 2 vols, Cambridge, 1986 and 1993.

Mann, Thomas, *Reflections of a Nonpolitical Man* (1918), New York, 1983.

Marcuse, Herbert, 'The Struggle Against Liberalism in a Totalitarian View of the State' (1934), in Marcuse, *Negations*, Harmondsworth, 1968, pp. 3–42.

Marsland, David, *Neglect and Betrayal. War and Violence in Modern Sociology*, London, 1985.

Marx, Gary, 'Issueless Riots', in *The Annals of the American Academy of Political and Social Sciences* 391 (1970), pp. 21–33.

Mead, George Herbert, 'The Psychological Bases of Internationalism', in *Survey* XXXIII (1914–15), pp. 604–7.

—— 'Germany's Crisis – its Effects on Labor'; 'America's Ideals and the War'; 'Democracy's Issues in the World War'; 'War Issues to U.S. Forced by Kaiser', in *Chicago Herald*, 1917.

—— 'The Psychology of Punitive Justice', in *The American Journal of Sociology* XXIII (1917–18), pp. 577–602; reprinted in Mead, *Selected Writings*, ed. Andrew Reck, Indianapolis, 1964, pp. 212–39.

—— *The Conscientious Objector*, New York, 1918.

—— Review of Thorstein Veblen, *The Nature of Peace and the Terms of Its Perpetuation* (1917), in *Journal of Political Economy* 26 (1918), pp. 752–62.

—— 'Social Work, Standards of Living and the War', in *Proceedings of the National Conference of Social Work* 45 (1918), pp. 637–44.

—— 'National-Mindedness and International-Mindedness' (1929), in Mead, *Selected Writings*, ed. Andrew Reck, Indianapolis, 1964, pp. 355–70.

Meier, Artur, 'Abschied von der sozialistischen Ständegesellschaft', in *Aus Politik und Zeitgeschichte* (Supplement to the weekly *Das Parlament*), B 16–17/90 (13.4.1990), pp. 3–14.

Meineke, Stefan, 'Friedrich Meinecke und der "Krieg der Geister"', in Wolfgang Mommsen (ed.), *Kultur und Krieg. Die Rolle der Intellektuellen, Künstler und Schriftsteller im Ersten Weltkrieg*, Munich, 1996, pp. 97–118.

Messerschmidt, Manfred, 'Der Staatsbürger muß sich über die Uniform legitimieren. Die allgemeine Wehrpflicht wirkte bis 1945 vor allem als Katalysator gesellschaftlicher Militarisierung', in *Frankfurter Rundschau*, 31.8.1993, p. 16.

Meuschel, Sigrid, *Legitimation und Parteiherrschaft in der DDR*, Frankfurt am Main, 1991.

—— 'Revolution in der DDR. Versuch einer sozialwissenschaftlichen Interpretation', in Hans Joas and Martin Kohli (eds), *Der Zusammenbruch der DDR. Soziologische Analysen*, Frankfurt am Main, 1993, pp. 93–114.

Michels, Roberto, ' "Razze" e "Nazioni" nella Guerra Attuale', in *Nuova Antologia* (1914), pp. 220–8.

—— 'Die wirtschaftlichen Wirkungen des Völkerkrieges auf Italien in den ersten Monaten', in *Archiv für Sozialwissenschaft und Sozialpolitik* 40 (1915), pp. 592–619.

Mill, John Stuart, 'A Few Words on Non-Intervention' (1859), in Mill, *Essays on Politics and Culture*, ed. Gertrude Himmelfarb, Garden City, NY, 1963, pp. 368–84.

Miller, Max and Hans-Georg Soeffner, 'Einleitung', in Miller and Soeffner (eds), *Modernität und Barbarei. Soziologische Zeitdiagnose am Ende des 20. Jahrhunderts*, Frankfurt am Main, 1996, pp. 12–27.

—— (eds), *Modernität und Barbarei. Soziologische Zeitdiagnose am Ende des 20. Jahrhunderts*, Frankfurt am Main, 1996.

Mills, C. Wright, *The Causes of World War Three*, New York, 1958.

Modell, John and Timothy Haggerty, 'The Social Impact of War', in *Annual Review of Sociology* 17 (1991), pp. 205–24.

Möller, Kay, 'Muß man vor China Angst haben?', in *Süddeutsche Zeitung*, 19.5.1995, p. 9.

Mommsen, Wolfgang, *Max Weber and German Politics 1890–1920*, Chicago, 1984.

—— 'Außenpolitik und öffentliche Meinung im Wilhelminischen Deutschland 1897–1914', in Mommsen, *Der autoritäre Nationalstaat. Verfassung, Gesellschaft und Kultur des deutschen Kaiserreiches*, Frankfurt am Main, 1990, pp. 358–79.

—— (ed.), *Kultur und Krieg. Die Rolle der Intellektuellen, Künstler und Schriftsteller im Ersten Weltkrieg*, Munich, 1966.

Moore, Barrington, Jr, *Social Origins of Dictatorship and Democracy. Lord and Peasant in the Making of the Modern World*, London, 1967.

Mori, Massimo, *La ragione delle armi. Guerra e conflitto nella filosofia classica tedesca (1770–1830)*, Milan, 1984.

——'Krieg und Frieden in der klassischen deutschen Philosophie', in Hans Joas and Helmut Steiner (eds), *Machtpolitischer Realismus und pazifistische Utopie. Krieg und Frieden in der Geschichte der Sozialwissenschaften*, Frankfurt am Main, 1989, pp. 49–91.

Moskos, Charles, 'The American Combat Soldier in Vietnam', in *Journal of Social Issues* 31 (1985), pp. 25–38.

Mozetic, Gerald, 'Ein unzeitgemäßer Soziologe: Ludwig Gumplowicz', in *Kölner Zeitschrift für Soziologie und Sozialpsychologie* 37 (1985), pp. 621–47.

Müller, Klaus, '"Modernizing" Eastern Europe. Theoretical Problems and Political Dilemmas' in *Archives Européennes de Sociologie* 32 (1992), pp. 109–50.

Münkler, Herfried, 'Staat, Krieg und Frieden. Die verwechselte Wechselbeziehung. Eine Auseinandersetzung mit Ekkehart Krippendorff', in Reiner Steinweg (ed.), *Kriegsursachen*, Frankfurt am Main, 1987, pp. 135–44.

——*Gewalt und Ordnung. Das Bild des Krieges im politischen Denken*, Frankfurt am Main, 1992.

Neckel, Sighard, 'Gefährliche Fremdheit. Notizen zu Zygmunt Bauman', in *Ästhetik und Kommunikation* 23, no. 85/6 (1994), pp. 45–9.

Nedelmann, Birgitta, 'Gewaltsoziologie am Scheideweg', in Trutz von Trotha (ed.), *Soziologie der Gewalt* (*Kölner Zeitschrift für Soziologie und Sozialpsychologie*, Special Issue 37), 1997, pp. 59–85.

Nef, John, *War and Human Progress*, Cambridge, Mass., 1952.

Neidhardt, Friedhelm, 'Über Zufall, Eigendynamik und Institutionalisierbarkeit absurder Prozesse. Notizen am Beispiel einer terroristischen Gruppe', in Heine von Alemann and Hans-Peter Thurn (eds), *Soziologie in weltbürgerlicher Absicht. Festschrift für René König zum 75. Geburtstag*, Opladen, 1981, pp. 243–57.

Neubert, Ehrhard, *Die protestantische Revolution*, Berlin, 1991.

Nipperdey, Thomas, *Deutsche Geschichte 1866–1918*, vol. 1, Munich, 1990; vol. 2, Munich, 1992.

Nolte, Ernst, *Three Faces of Fascism: Action Française, Italian Fascism, National Socialism* (1963), New York, 1966.

Nunner-Winkler, Gertrud, 'Gewalt – ein Spezifikum der Moderne?', in Max Miller and Hans-Georg Soeffner (eds), *Modernität und Barbarei. Soziologische Zeitdiagnose am Ende des 20. Jahrhunderts*, Frankfurt am Main, 1996, pp. 81–95.

Oestreich, Gerhard, 'Otto Hintzes Stellung zur Politikwissenschaft und Soziologie', in Otto Hintze, *Soziologie und Geschichte. Gesammelte Abhandlungen*, vol. 2, Göttingen, 1964, pp. 7*–67*.

Offe, Claus, 'Wohlstand, Nation, Republik. Aspekte des deutschen Sonderwegs vom Sozialismus zum Kapitalismus', in Hans Joas and Martin Kohli (eds), *Der Zusammenbruch der DDR. Soziologische Analysen*, Frankfurt am Main, 1993, pp. 282–301.

Opp, Karl-Dieter, 'Spontaneous Revolutions. The Case of East Germany in 1989', in Heinz D. Kurz (ed.), *United Germany and the New Europe*, Cheltenham, 1993, pp. 11–30.

Oppenheimer, Franz, *The State* (1907), New York, 1975.

——*System der Soziologie*, Jena, 1922–6.

Papcke, Sven, 'Dienst am Sieg. Die Sozialwissenschaften im Ersten Weltkrieg', in Papcke, *Vernunft und Chaos*, Frankfurt am Main, 1985, pp. 125–42.

—— 'Weltferne Wissenschaft. Die deutsche Soziologie der Zwischenkriegszeit vor dem Problem des Faschismus/Nationalsozialismus', in Papcke (ed.), *Ordnung und Theorie*, Darmstadt, 1986, pp. 186–222.

Parker, Geoffrey, *The Military Revolution. Military Innovation and the Rise of the West, 1500–1800*, Cambridge, 1988.

Plenge, Johann, *1789 und 1914. Die symbolischen Jahre in der Geschichte des politischen Geistes*, Berlin, 1916.

Pollack, Detlef, 'Religion und gesellschaftlicher Wandel. Zur Rolle der evangelischen Kirche im Prozeß des gesellschaftlichen Umbruchs in der DDR', in Hans Joas and Martin Kohli (eds), *Der Zusammenbruch der DDR. Soziologische Analysen*, Frankfurt am Main, 1993, pp. 246–66.

Porter, Bruce, *War and the Rise of the State. The Military Foundations of Modern Politics*, New York, 1994.

Prager, Jeffrey, 'Moral Integration and Political Inclusion. A Comparison of Durkheim's and Weber's Theories of Democracy', in *Social Forces* 59 (1981), pp. 918–50.

Raumer, Kurt von (ed.), *Ewiger Friede, Friedensrufe und Friedenspläne seit der Renaissance*, Freiburg/Munich, 1953.

Reinhard, Wolfgang, 'Staat und Heer in England im Zeitalter der Revolutionen', in Johannes Kunisch (ed.), *Staatsverfassung und Heeresverfassung in der europäischen Geschichte der frühen Neuzeit*, Berlin, 1986, pp. 173–212.

Reiss, Albert J., Jr and Jeffrey A. Roth (eds), *Understanding and Preventing Violence*, Washington, DC, 1993.

Reißig, Rolf, 'Das Scheitern der DDR und des realexistierenden Systems. Einige Ursachen und Folgen', in Hans Joas and Martin Kohli (eds), *Der Zusammenbruch der DDR. Soziologische Analysen*, Frankfurt am Main, 1993, pp. 49–69.

Roberts, David D., 'Croce and Beyond. Italian Intellectuals and the First World War', in *International History Review* 3 (1981), pp. 201–35.

Roth, Günter, 'Max Weber's Ethics and the Peace Movement Today', in *Theory and Society* 13 (1984), pp. 491–511.

Roxborough, Ian, 'The Persistence of War as a Sociological Problem', in *International Sociology* 14 (1999), pp. 491–500.

Royce, Josiah, *The Hope for the Great Community*, New York, 1916.

Rózewicz, Tadeusz, 'Neue philosophische Schule', in Rózewicz, *In der schönsten Stadt der Welt*, Berlin 1971, pp. 47–68.

Rüstow, Alexander, *Ortsbestimmung der Gegenwart*, 3 vols, Zurich, 1950ff.

Sabrow, Martin, 'Hinterrücks zusammengebrochen', in *Frankfurter Allgemeine Zeitung*, 20.11.1998, p. 46.

Sack, Fritz, 'Staat, Gesellschaft und politische Gewalt. Zur "Pathologie" politischer Konflikte', in Sack and Heinz Steinert (eds), *Protest und Reaktion. Analysen zum Terrorismus*, vol. 4/2, Opladen, 1984, pp. 17–386.

Santayana, George, *Character and Opinion in the United States: with Reminiscences of William James and Josiah Royce and Academic Life in America*, London, 1920.

—— *Egotism in German Philosophy*, in Santayana, *Works*, vol. VI, New York, 1936, pp. 145–249.

Scheler, Max, 'Der Genius des Krieges und der deutsche Krieg' (1915), in Scheler, *Gesammelte Werke*, vol. 4, *Politisch-Pädagogische Schriften*, Bern, 1982, pp. 7–251.

—— 'Die Ursachen des Deutschenhasses. Eine nationalpädagogische Erörterung' (1917), in Scheler, *Gesammelte Werke*, vol. 4, *Politisch-Pädagogische Schriften*, Bern, 1982, pp. 283–366.

Schildt, Axel, 'Ein konservativer Prophet moderner nationaler Integration. Biographische Skizze des streitbaren Soziologen Johann Plenge (1874–1963)', in *Vierteljahreshefte für Zeitgeschichte* 35 (1987), pp. 523–70.

Schmidt, Gunnar, 'Die konstruierte Moderne. Thorstein Veblen und der Erste Weltkrieg', in *Leviathan* 28 (2000), pp. 39–68.

Schmitt, Carl, Review (1926) of Friedrich Meinecke, *Die Idee der Staatsräson in der neueren Geschichte*, Munich/Berlin, 1924; reprinted in Schmitt, *Positionen und Begriffe im Kampf mit Weimar–Genf–Versailles*, Berlin, 1940 (2nd edn, 1988), pp. 45–52.

—— *The Concept of the Political* (1932), New Brunswick, NJ, 1976.

—— *Die Wendung zum diskriminierenden Kriegsbegriff* (1938), Berlin, 1988.

Schnädelbach, Herbert, *Philosophy in Germany, 1831–1933*, Cambridge, 1984.

Schulze, Winfried, 'Otto Hintzes Kritik und Rezeption der Soziologie', in Otto Büsch and Michael Erbe (eds), *Otto Hintze und die moderne Geschichtswissenschaft*, Berlin, 1983, pp. 134–49.

Schumpeter, Joseph, *Imperialism and Social Classes*, New York, 1951.

Schwabe, Klaus, 'Zur politischen Haltung der deutschen Professoren im 1. Weltkrieg', in *Historische Zeitschrift* 193 (1961), pp. 601–34.

—— *Wissenschaft und Kriegsmoral. Die deutschen Hochschullehrer und die politischen Grundfragen des Ersten Weltkriegs*, Göttingen, 1965.

Scott, Wilbur J., 'Competing Paradigms in the Assessment of Latent Disorders. The Case of Agent Orange', in *Social Problems* 35 (1988), pp. 145–61.

Senghaas, Dieter, 'Jenseits des Nebels der Zukunft: Europas ordnungspolitische Option', in Senghaas, *Europa 2000. Ein Friedensplan*, Frankfurt am Main, 1990, pp. 57–77.

—— 'Peace Theory and the Restructuring of Europe', in *Alternatives* 16 (1991), pp. 353–66.

—— *Friedensprojekt Europa*, Frankfurt am Main, 1992.

—— 'Frieden als Zivilisierungsprojekt', in Senghaas (ed.), *Den Frieden denken. Si vis pacem, para pacem*, Frankfurt am Main, 1995, pp. 196–223.

—— and Eva Senghaas, 'Si vis pacem, para pacem', in *Leviathan* 20 (1992), pp. 230–47.

Shafer, D. Michael, 'The Vietnam Combat Experience: The Human Legacy', in Schafer (ed.), *The Legacy. The Vietnam War in the American Imagination*, Boston, 1990, pp. 80–103.

—— 'The Vietnam-Era Draft: Who Went, Who Didn't and Why It Matters', in Shafer (ed.), *The Legacy. The Vietnam War in the American Imagination*, Boston, 1990, pp. 57–79.

Shatan, Chaim F., 'The Grief of Soldiers. Vietnam Combat Veterans' Self-Help Movement', in *American Journal of Ortho-Psychiatry* 43 (1973), pp. 640–53.

Shaw, Martin (ed.), *War, State and Society*, London 1984.

——'Ideen über Krieg und Militarisierung in der Gesellschaftstheorie des späten zwanzigsten Jahrhunderts', in Hans Joas and Helmut Steiner (eds), *Machtpolitischer Realismus und pazifistische Utopie. Krieg und Frieden in der Geschichte der Sozialwissenschaften*, Frankfurt am Main, 1989, pp. 283–308.

Simmel, Georg, *Soziologie* (1908), Berlin, 1968.

——'Bergson und der deutsche "Zynismus"', in *Internationale Monatsschrift für Kunst, Wissenschaft und Technik* 9 (1914), pp. 197–200.

——'Die Umwertung der Werte. Ein Wort an die Wohlhabenden', in *Frankfurter Zeitung*, 5.3.1915 (morning edition, p. 2).

——*Der Krieg und die geistigen Entscheidungen*, Munich, 1917.

Skocpol, Theda, *States and Social Revolutions. A Comparative Analysis of France, Russia and China*, Cambridge, 1979.

Slotkin, Richard, *Regeneration through Violence. The Mythology of the American Frontier, 1600–1860*, Middletown, Conn., 1973.

——*The Fatal Environment. The Myth of the Frontier in the Age of Industrialization, 1800–1890*, New York, 1985.

Small, Albion, 'Germany and American Opinion. Professor Albion Small to Professor Georg Simmel', in *Sociological Review* 7 (1914), pp. 106–11.

Smelser, Neil, *Theory of Collective Behaviour*, London, 1962.

Sofsky, Wolfgang, *The Order of Terror. The Concentration Camp* (1993), Princeton, 1997.

——'Die Meute. Zur Anthropologie der Menschenjagd', in *Neue Rundschau* 4 (1994), pp. 9–21.

Sombart, Werner, *Krieg und Kapitalismus*, Munich/Leipzig, 1913.

——*Händler und Helden. Patriotische Besinnungen*, Munich, 1915.

Sorel, Georges, *Reflections on Violence* (1914), Cambridge, 1999.

Sorokin, Pitirim, 'Sociological Interpretation of the "Struggle for Existence" and the Sociology of War', in Sorokin, *Contemporary Sociological Theories*, New York, 1928, pp. 309–56.

Speier, Hans, *Social Order and the Risks of War. Papers in Political Psychology*, Cambridge, Mass., 1969.

Spencer, Herbert, *The Principles of Sociology*, vol. 2, London, 1897.

Srubar, Ilja, 'War der reale Sozialismus modern? Versuch einer strukturellen Bestimmung', in *Kölner Zeitschrift für Soziologie und Sozialpsychologie* 43 (1991), pp. 415–32.

Stephan, Cora, *Das Handwerk des Krieges*, Berlin, 1998.

Sternhell, Zeev, *The Birth of Fascist Ideology. From Cultural Rebellion to Political Revolution*, Princeton, 1994.

Stromberg, Roland, *Redemption by War. The Intellectuals and 1914*, Lawrence, Kan., 1982.

Tenbruck, Friedrich, 'Émile Durkheim oder die Geburt der Gesellschaft aus dem Geist der Soziologie', in *Zeitschrift für Soziologie* 10 (1981), pp. 333–50.

——*Die unbewältigte Sozialwissenschaft*, Graz, 1984.

——'Gesellschaftsgeschichte oder Weltgeschichte?', in *Kölner Zeitschrift für Soziologie und Sozialpsychologie* 3 (1989), pp. 417–39.

Thome, Helmut, 'Gesellschaftliche Modernisierung und Kriminalität. Zum Stand der sozialhistorischen Kriminalitätsforschung', in *Zeitschrift für Soziologie* 21 (1992), pp. 212–28.

Tilly, Charles, 'Reflections on the History of European State Making', in Tilly (ed.), *The Formation of National States in Western Europe*, Princeton, 1975, pp. 3–83.

——*Coercion, Capital and European States 990–1990*, Oxford, 1990.

Tiryakian, Edward, 'Modernization: *Exhumetur in Pace* (Rethinking Macrosociology in the 1990s)', in *International Sociology* 6 (1991), pp. 165–80.

——'War: The Covered Side of Modernity', in *International Sociology* 14 (1999), pp. 473–90.

Tönnies, Ferdinand, 'Die Sozialpolitik nach dem Kriege', in Friedrich Thimme and Carl Legien (eds), *Die Arbeiterschaft im neuen Deutschland*, Leipzig, 1915, pp. 147–58.

——Der Wiederbeginn geistiger Gemeinschaftsarbeit zwischen den Völkern', in *Ethische Kultur* 23 (1915), pp. 105–6.

——'Gerechtigkeit in Kriegszeiten', in *Internationale Rundschau* 2 (1916), pp. 177–90.

——'Naturrecht und Völkerrecht', in *Die neue Rundschau* (1916), pp. 577–87.

——*Der englische Staat und der deutsche Staat*, Berlin, 1917.

——*Wege zu dauerndem Frieden?*, Leipzig, 1926.

Torrance, John, 'The Emergence of Sociology in Austria 1885–1935', in *Archives Européennes de Sociologie* 17 (1976), pp. 185–219.

Toulmin, Stephen, *Cosmopolis. The Hidden Agenda of Modernity*, New York, 1990.

Touraine, Alain, *The Voice and the Eye* (1978), Cambridge, 1981.

——*Return of the Actor. Social Theory in Postindustrial Society* (1984), Minneapolis, 1988.

Trotha, Trutz von, *Zur Soziologie der Gewalt* (*Kölner Zeitschrift für Soziologie und Sozialpsychologie*, Special Issue 37), 1997, pp. 9–56.

Turner, Ralph H., 'Race Riots Past and Present: A Cultural-Collective Behavior Approach', in *Symbolic Interaction* 17 (1994), pp. 309–24.

——and Lewis M. Killian, *Collective Behavior*, Englewood Cliffs, NJ, 1987.

Ulrich, Bernd, 'Nerven und Krieg. Skizzierung einer Beziehung', in Bedrich Löwenstein (ed.), *Geschichte und Psychologie. Annäherungsversuche*, Pfaffen-weiler, 1992, pp. 163–92.

Unger, Roberto Mangabeira, *Politics*, 3 vols, Cambridge, 1987.

Varcoe, Ian, 'Identity and the Limits of Comparison', in *Theory, Culture and Society* 15 (1998), pp. 57–72.

Veblen, Thorstein, *Imperial Germany and the Industrial Revolution* (1915), New Brunswick, NJ, 1990.

——*The Nature of Peace and the Terms of Its Perpetuation*, New York, 1917.

Vogt, Wolfgang R., 'Militär und Risikogesellschaft. Tendenzen "struktureller Unvereinbarkeit" zwischen bewaffneter Friedenssicherung und indu-striellem Zivilisationsprozeß', in *Sicherheit und Frieden* 4 (1989), pp. 198–205.

Waldmann, Peter, 'Gewaltsamer Separatismus. Am Beispiel der Basken, Franko-Kanadier und Nordiren', in *Kölner Zeitschrift für Soziologie und Sozialpsychologie* 37 (1985), pp. 203–29.

Walker, Keith, *A Piece of My Heart. 26 Women in Vietnam*, Novato, Calif., 1985.

Wallerstein, Immanuel, 'Modernization: *Requiescat in Pace*', in Wallerstein, *The Capitalist World-Economy*, New York, 1979, pp. 132–7.

——'1968, Revolution in the World-System. Thesis and Queries', in *Theory and Society* 18 (1989), pp. 431–49.

Walzer, Michael, 'Liberalism and the Art of Separation', in *Political Theory* 12 (1984), pp. 315–30.

Weber, Max, *General Economic History* (1923), New York, 1927.

——*Political Writings*, ed. Peter Lassman and Ronald Speirs, Cambridge, 1994.

Wehler, Hans-Ulrich, *Modernisierungstheorie und Geschichte*, Göttingen, 1975.

——*Deutsche Gesellschaftsgeschichte*, vol. 1, Munich, 1987.

Weinert, Rainer, 'Massenorganisationen in mono-organisationalen Gesellschaften. Über den strukturellen Restaurationszwang des Freien Deutschen Gewerkschaftsbundes im Zuge des Zusammenbruchs der DDR', in Hans Joas and Martin Kohli (eds), *Der Zusammenbruch der DDR. Soziologische Analysen*, Frankfurt am Main, 1993, pp. 125–50.

Welzer, Harald, ' "Verweilen beim Grauen". Bücher über den Holocaust', in *Merkur* 48 (1994), pp. 67–72.

Westbrook, Robert, *John Dewey and American Democracy*, Ithaca, NY, 1991.

Wette, Wolfram, 'Kein Kind der Demokratie', in *Die Zeit*, 19.2.1993, p. 5.

Wielgohs, Jan and Marianne Schulz, 'Von der "friedlichen Revolution" in die politische Normalität. Entwicklungsetappen der ostdeutschen Bürgerbewegung', in Hans Joas and Martin Kohli (eds), *Der Zusammenbruch der DDR. Soziologische Analysen*, Frankfurt am Main, 1993, pp. 222–45.

Wiese, Leopold von, *Politische Briefe über den Weltkrieg. Zwölf Skizzen*, Munich/Leipzig, 1914.

Willems, Helmut, 'Development, Patterns and Causes of Violence against Foreigners in Germany', in Thorbjörn Björgo (ed.), *Terrorism and Political Violence* 7 (1985), pp. 162–81.

——'Fremdenfeindliche Gewalt. Entwicklung, Strukturen, Interaktionsprozesse', in *Gruppendynamik* 23 (1992), pp. 433–48.

Winter, J.M., 'The Economic and Social History of War', in Winter (ed.), *War and Economic Development. Essays in Memory of David Joslin*, Cambridge, 1975, pp. 1–10.

Yack, Bernard, *The Fetishism of Modernities. Epochal Self-Consciousness in Contemporary Social and Political Thought*, Notre Dame, Ind., 1997.

Zapf, Wolfgang, 'Modernisierung und Modernisierungstheorien', in Zapf (ed.), *Die Modernisierung moderner Gesellschaften. Verhandlungen des 25. Deutschen Soziologentags* (1990), Frankfurt am Main, 1991, pp. 23–39.

——'Die DDR 1989/1990 – Zusammenbruch einer Sozialstruktur?', in Hans Joas and Martin Kohli (eds), *Der Zusammenbruch der DDR. Soziologische Analysen*, Frankfurt am Main, 1993, pp. 29–48.

Zweig, Arnold, *Young Woman of 1914* (1931), New York, 1932.

Name Index

Subject Index